Inclusive Texts in Elementary Classrooms

Developing Literacies, Identities, and Understandings

Amy J. Heineke and Aimee Papola-Ellis

TEACHERS COLLEGE PRESS

TEACHERS COLLEGE | COLUMBIA UNIVERSITY
NEW YORK AND LONDON

Published by Teachers College Press,® 1234 Amsterdam Avenue, New York, NY 10027

Copyright © 2022 by Teachers College, Columbia University

Front cover design and illustration by Holly Grundon / BHG Graphics.

Selection from Dreamers. Text and illustrations copyright © 2018 by Yuyi Morales.

Reprinted by permission of Holiday House Publishing, Inc. All Rights Reserved.

"Soñando Juntos / Dreaming Together" from Poems to Dream Together/Poemas para soñar juntos. Poems copyright © 2005 by Francisco X. Alarcón. Permission arranged with LEE & LOW BOOKS Inc., New York, NY 10016. All rights reserved. Learn more at leeandlow.com/books/poems-to-dream-together-poemas-para-sonar-juntos.

The excerpts from The Year of the Dog are copyright © 2007 by Grace Lin.

Reprinted with the permission of Hachette Book Group, Inc.

Library of Congress Cataloging-in-Publication Data

Names: Heineke, Amy J., author. | Papola-Ellis, Aimee, author.
Title: Inclusive texts in elementary classrooms : developing literacies, identities, and understandings / Amy J. Heineke and Aimee Papola-Ellis.
Description: New York , NY : Teachers College Press, [2022] | Includes bibliographical references and index. | Summary: "Put children's diverse experiences at the center of the curriculum with texts that promote their identity development, literacy engagement and comprehension, and learning across the content areas. This practical text includes guidance for setting learning goals that align with relevant standards and curricular directives, as well as classroom examples, teaching strategies, and reflective questions"—Provided by publisher.
Identifiers: LCCN 2021062651 (print) | LCCN 2021062652 (ebook) | ISBN 9780807766477 (hardcover) | ISBN 9780807766460 (paperback) | ISBN 9780807780787 (ebook)
Subjects: LCSH: Language arts (Elementary)—United States. | Culturally sustaining pedagogy—United States. | Literacy—Social aspects—United States.
Classification: LCC LB1576 .H3318 2022 (print) | LCC LB1576 (ebook) | DDC 372.60973—dc23/eng/20220211
LC record available at https://lccn.loc.gov/2021062651
LC ebook record available at https://lccn.loc.gov/2021062652

ISBN 978-0-8077-6646-0 (paper)
ISBN 978-0-8077-6647-7 (hardcover)
ISBN 978-0-8077-8078-7 (ebook)

Printed on acid-free paper
Manufactured in the United States of America

Contents

Acknowledgments

The journey to write this book began many years ago during our time as teachers. Whether on the south side of Phoenix, the North Slope villages of Alaska, rural farming communities of California, or foothills of the Colorado Rockies, students sparked our interest and commitment to using inclusive texts in schools. Little moments in time stand out, such as watching Mexican-immigrant students' eyes light up when seeing their families and stories through books like *Family Pictures/Cuadros de familia* (Garza, 1990) or watching Iñupiat children express how they never saw stories written about them until books like *Whale Snow* (Edwardson, 2004). With this in mind, we want to begin by thanking our former students, who are long grown and hopefully avid readers of the word and world, for continuing to drive and inspire our work.

Of course, we did not stumble onto inclusive texts and figure out their special niche in our pedagogy on our own. We both benefited from the expertise and mentorship of professors in our graduate programs. Carmen Martínez-Roldán, formerly at Arizona State University during Amy's graduate work and now at Teachers College at Columbia, shared her brilliance in Latinx children's literature and provided thoughtful guidance in researching the use of inclusive texts with both students and teachers. Julie Pennington expertly introduced Aimee to the world of critical literacy during her program at University of Nevada Reno, supporting her in applying this research to work with children and educators. Despite the years that have passed since these collaborations, the influence of these two scholars spans the pages of this book.

But our learning did not stop upon finishing graduate school and leaving the classroom. In fact, our work took on new meaning upon moving to Chicago and initiating this work with teachers in schools and students at our university. We have worked with incredible educators in the last decade, including those who are profiled in this text and others who have pushed our thinking in other ways. We want to thank the practitioners who have shared their innovative work with us over the years, including (but not limited to) Allison Acevedo, Kyla Bailenson, Anne Bond, Luke Carman, Sheila Cashman, Anna Cruz, Jenny Delessio-Parson, Victoria Dobies, Susan Feiler, Courtney Goodman, Charlotte Guntly, Megan Haapala, Bridget

Heneghan, Lisa Kennedy, Karen LaRue, Lindsay LeRoy, Mitch Mox, Felisha Parsons, Renee Phillippose, Bethany Tomlinson, Javier Torres, Lynn Tucker, Erica Tully, and Camille Unger.

We are also grateful for support from Teachers College Press and Loyola University Chicago. Emily Spangler and the editorial team at Teachers College Press provided incredible support and feedback throughout the process, and peer reviewers gave targeted and constructive ways to improve the final text. We are grateful to our institution for providing internal funding to support our research and writing of this book. Those funds allowed us to enlist our friend Chris Gattorna at Chris G. Ink to design engaging graphics to bring our text to life across these pages. We also owe a debt of gratitude to the helpful librarians at Loyola University Chicago, as well as our local public libraries, who supported us in finding, exploring, and getting our hands on the many amazing texts shared in this book.

Our work in this field has been elevated, alleviated, and pushed forward by others we have never met. Children's book publishing has changed drastically over the years due to the diligent writing and advocacy work of authors, educators, and scholars. We are so grateful to Sara K. Ahmed, Fenice Boyd, Sonja Cherry-Paul, Tricia Ebarvia, Lorena Germán, Cynthia Leitich Smith, Carmen Medina, Gholdy Muhammad, Ellen Oh, Sarah Park Dahlen, Kimberly Parker, Debbie Reese, Rudine Sims Bishop, and Julia Torres. Their work in writing amazing literature, advocating for inclusive publishing practices, and disrupting the canon in classrooms has transformed the field, resulting in more amazing texts to use in classrooms than when we began this journey two decades ago.

Finally, we thank our family, friends, and colleagues who sustained this work in a multitude of ways. We wrote this book during the COVID-19 pandemic, with our wonderful children—Shea and Oliver—home alongside us to support nearly every word. Our partners—Josh and Darby—provided some semblance of sanity with their consistent support and encouragement. We also benefited from an incredible group of friends and colleagues in Sarah Cohen, Adam Kennedy, and Lara Smetana, who provided daily amusement and frequent feedback to guide our thinking and drafting. Finally, five graduate students in the School of Education at Loyola University Chicago—Joe Elliott, Wenjin Guo, Mark Maranto, Augustina Mbata, and Elissa West-Frasier—sustained our efforts to produce the best book possible for practitioners.

Introduction

Books often evoke poignant memories from our childhood and schooling. Both of us loved to read as kids, devouring books inside and outside of school. We laughed at the quirky ways of *Amelia Bedelia* (Parish, 1963), connected with daily struggles and triumphs of Ramona (Cleary, 1955), endeavored the rugged wilderness in *Hatchet* (Paulsen, 1986), cherished our dogs during *Where the Red Fern Grows* (Rawls, 1961), and grappled with faith and coming of age alongside Margaret (Blume, 1970). We never had any shortage of books that reflected us as White, cisgender, heterosexual children without disabilities. Growing up in smaller cities in the Midwest and East Coast, books took us to fictional places like Narnia (Lewis, 1950) and Middle-earth (Tolkien, 1954), but not down the road to cities like Chicago or Philadelphia. We unquestioningly soaked in storylines about Indians in cupboards (Banks, 1980) and White settlers conquering the untamed people of the West (Wilder, 1932, 1935). Not until years later, when becoming education professors specializing in language and literacy, did we realize the racist, classist, and sexist depictions that characterized many of the texts that we cherished as children.

Despite the passing of multiple decades since reading these stories as elementary students, these titles still appear on must-read lists for children. Even as criticisms grow in circles of authors and educators, these texts still get suggested and prioritized for use in schools through influential policies like the Common Core Standards (Boyd, Causey, & Galda, 2015). The *canon*—the texts that continue to be used year after year, decade after decade, without interrogation—offers one of many examples of the deeply embedded racism that plagues our educational system. Even as the population changes, with White students now the minority in U.S. public schools, the curriculum continues to maintain the status quo, with texts that reflect White, English-dominant, cisgender, heterosexual, non-disabled characters, perspectives, and contributions (National Center for Education Statistics [NCES], 2019a). This means that most children in U.S. schools—students of color, immigrant-origin youth, LGBTQ children, students with disabilities, and others—might not readily see themselves in the texts that they read or have the same poignant experiences with texts that we remember as children.

1

We believe that texts in classrooms should reflect the beautiful pluralism of our communities and society. Texts should bring joy to readers, by seeing themselves on the pages of books, connecting to characters while reflecting on their identities and experiences, exploring and discussing big ideas in their communities, empathizing and building relationships with others, and thinking about ways to make the world a better place. Texts should not *other* children, situating their identities and experiences as different or less valuable than those prioritized in curricula and potentially silencing voices and stories in the classroom. Fortunately, we are not alone in these beliefs, with movements like *We Need Diverse Books*, *Disrupt Texts*, and *Own Voices* spurring awareness and action among both the companies that publish books and the educators who use them. Change is occurring as more and more people recognize the antiquated and exclusionary materials that continue to dominate 21st-century classrooms.

Educators play an integral role in this change, because they select the texts to which learners have access in classrooms and schools. We are not talking about creating a multicultural book bin but, rather, enriching holistic curricula through purposeful text selection and usage. With this book, we seek to provide practitioners with actionable ways to infuse libraries and curricula with authentic portrayals of multiple identities and experiences that characterize our pluralist society. We want teachers to enter classrooms with intentionality on elevating traditionally marginalized voices and identities, knowing how to enrich the curriculum by including diversity of voices and being confident in their reasons for doing so. Of course, simply adding texts with diverse characters does not transform educational spaces and up-end decades of racism. But we believe that selecting and using texts is one actionable way for teachers to disrupt the status quo; critically question how and why we use certain materials, curricula, and programs in schools; and seek ways to provide equitable and relevant instruction for the children in front of us.

Now many of the words in these initial paragraphs have recently been stigmatized in wider discussions among parents, educators, and policymakers in the United States. Words like *critical*, *race*, *culture*, *equity*, and *inclusion* have become dirty in some circles, with critics arguing that discussions on race and racism should not occur in schools. Many educators are concerned, recognizing the impossible feat of removing race from topics like the enslavement of African Americans, the Civil Rights movement, the forced assimilation in Indian boarding schools, and Japanese Americans' internment during World War II. In addition to history, racism happens every day before children's eyes, from slurs and hate crimes against Asian Americans during the COVID-19 pandemic, to the murder of George Floyd by police officers, to the containment of children in cages by U.S. Border Patrol agents. Children need space to grapple with racism in the face of painful historical and current events, to process what they see every day in the world around them, and to hopefully change our collective path forward. This same assertion stands with homophobia, ableism, sexism, classism, linguicism, and other ills of society. In the words of the Dalai Lama, we cannot change the past, but we can reshape the future.

We understand that some readers might require more convincing. The canon remains intact in schools due to strong ideological foundations embedded in the very fabric of our schools. We have found that teachers working in culturally and linguistically diverse locales are quicker to embrace this work, and their commitment to diversifying text collections grows as they see children's responses in classrooms. Teachers who work in seemingly homogenous settings often demonstrate hesitation. In one of our university courses, a White teacher from a predominantly White school asked, "What if all my students are White? Do I need to really be thinking about texts showing other backgrounds?" The response is an emphatic *yes*. Every child is unique—with multifaceted identities spanning race, ethnicity, class, cultural background, language, religion, gender identity, orientation, ability, and beyond. They have varied experiences, such as having two moms or living with grandparents or experiencing homelessness. Even in seemingly homogenous settings, children need a variety of texts to see the multiple facets of themselves, as well as learn about the lives of others (Sims Bishop, 1990).

To facilitate this work with *all* children across *all* contexts, we have devised a four-part framework, emergent from our work with teachers in schools over the past decade. This book outlines steps to select and use inclusive texts to nurture children's literacies, identities, and understandings in daily classroom practice. Drawing from the work of Rudine Sims Bishop (1990, 1997, 2003), we define *inclusive texts* as those that serve as mirrors and windows to readers while disrupting the dominant narratives that often pervade popular children's literature. Inclusive texts capture identities and experiences spanning race, ethnicity, class, culture, language, religion, gender, orientation, ability, family structure, and other facets. To support practitioners in incorporating inclusive texts to drive curriculum and nurture children's learning, we suggest four steps: (1) getting to know students' storied lives, (2) probing established goals and curricula, (3) selecting high-quality and authentic texts, and (4) integrating texts to support learning goals. The chapters of this text seek to develop and deepen understandings and practices to facilitate this important work in classrooms.

ORGANIZATION OF THIS BOOK

Chapter 1 introduces our Inclusive Texts (IT) framework, seeking to provide readers with the foundational theories and research that bolster this work. In this chapter, we deepen our exploration of the literary canon and put forth our four-facet framework as an approach to disrupt the canon and elevate traditionally marginalized voices, stories, and perspectives in classroom instruction. We situate our framework at the intersection of culturally sustaining pedagogy (Alim & Paris, 2018) and critical literacy (Luke & Freebody, 1997) to provide teachers with defined steps to select and use texts aligned to students' rich identities and seeking to promote social and critical consciousness of our world.

Chapter 2 dives into the IT framework by exploring the first component: starting with students. We first consider the rich and nuanced diversity among students with a three-pronged conceptualization of children's multifaceted identities, experiences in homes and communities, and dimensions as learners in schools. We then probe how inclusive texts should be *relevant* to learners' identities, experiences, and perspectives and *authentic* in their portrayal of the storied lives of individuals, families, and communities (Sims Bishop, 1997, 2003). Readers leave this chapter with various approaches to gather data to get to know students as unique and holistic individuals, as well as resources to begin to amass inclusive texts for their specific settings.

Chapter 3 continues with the second component of the IT framework: considering learning goals. Here, we support readers in maintaining culturally sustaining and critical literacy lenses in the realities of today's schools where texts used in classrooms often emerge from external standards and curricula. Within this context, we explore teachers' agency to select and supplement inclusive texts around various standards and within literacy and content-area curricula to promote students' deeper learning and complex identity work. Readers exit this chapter having critically evaluated texts in their classrooms to strategically draft learning goals to guide text selection and use with their unique students.

Chapter 4 targets the third facet of the IT framework: selecting texts that serve as *mirrors* reflecting their own identities and *windows* to learn about the experiences and perspectives of others (Sims Bishop, 1990). We probe how to select texts in response to students and goals, including texts that provoke connections to various facets of their identities and experiences and those that develop understandings and sociocultural consciousness for the communities and the world around them. Tapping into the idea that all texts serve as mirrors and windows depending on the student, we explore how to leverage text sets and collections to facilitate building classroom community, learn about family and cultural traditions, and develop empathy and social-emotional well-being. Readers walk away from this chapter with integral understandings and practices to reflect students' identities and perspectives in text selection.

Chapter 5 shifts to the fourth and final facet of the IT framework by exploring the purposeful integration of inclusive texts into language and literacy instruction. We discuss how inclusive texts bolster multiple aspects of students' interactions with texts, including motivation, engagement, comprehension, discussion, and writing. The chapter specifically targets each component of reading and writing workshops, demonstrating the value of inclusive texts across the curriculum beyond common-use read-alouds and independent reading. We integrate a focus on *biliteracy*, tapping into inclusive texts in multiple languages to support multilingual learners. Readers leave this chapter with actionable ways to enhance their literacy block.

Chapter 6 expands beyond literacy instruction to explore the integration of inclusive texts into disciplinary instruction, including math, science, social studies, and special areas. We dive into each content area to consider how various genres, texts, and strategies deepen students' disciplinary understandings by tapping into learners' multifaceted identities and experiences and adding perspectives, contributions, and stories often excluded from traditional curricula. The chapter takes a pertinent lens on instructional design, supporting teachers in thinking through how and where to integrate texts at the unit and lesson levels. Readers finish the chapter with instructional ideas for using inclusive texts across the content areas.

Chapter 7 extends beyond the classroom walls to consider the importance of inclusive texts at the macro level of schools, which involves an array of stakeholders in schools, districts, families, and communities. We lay out how instructional leaders can prioritize these efforts across buildings by amassing inclusive texts and resources, encouraging critical analyses and supplementation of curricula, and providing sustained professional development. The chapter also brings in the pertinent lens on families and communities, exploring how texts enhance family engagement and belonging in the school and surrounding community. Readers round out the text with actionable next steps to advocate for children to have consistent access and meaningful engagement with inclusive texts across classrooms and schools.

KEY FEATURES OF THIS BOOK

As you read and reflect on the chapters in this book, our aim is that you learn about new texts, consider how to use those texts with your students, and think critically about your own classroom resources and instruction. We believe that as educators, we make choices every day to either maintain or disrupt the status quo when it comes to texts and materials we use in our teaching. These active, intentional decisions that we make directly influence students' learning experiences in schools (Cochran-Smith & Fries, 2005). In this way, this text centers on practice, with the hope that what you learn on these pages directly and immediately supports your curricular decision-making and transfers into your daily work with children.

Throughout this book, we feature high-quality inclusive texts that you might consider adding to your classroom collection. These text examples seek to be inclusive of an array of classroom settings, providing options for you to explore and consider for your unique learners. But given the myriad of titles available to teachers, we could never capture all texts, authors, and illustrators. For this reason, we frame our discussion of texts around larger themes for readers to use categories to explore other texts for their settings. For example, you can find examples of texts that correspond to different facets of social-emotional development (e.g., microaggressions) and various genres for content-area learning (e.g., biographies).

Remember that the IT framework centers on application and integration in classroom practice. In other words, it is not just about *having* high-quality texts in classrooms, but *using* them to develop children's literacies, identities, and understandings. To promote the strategic use of inclusive texts in classroom instruction, we provide tools, strategies, and resources to facilitate readers' application into practice. Across the text, tables highlight instructional strategies, lesson plan templates, and resource lists that seek to enhance and alleviate your work in moving these amazing texts into your classrooms. You can also visit our website (inclusivetexts.weebly.com) for more detailed text lists. We hope that you use these flexible ideas as starting places to facilitate the learning of your unique learners.

Perhaps most importantly, this text features practitioners using inclusive texts in classrooms with children. Twenty fantastic teachers in the Chicago area have opened their classroom doors for you to learn from their ongoing work to incorporate inclusive texts with learners spanning from kindergarten to middle school. Throughout the book, we draw from these focal teachers' classrooms to exemplify implementation of the IT framework to show how their unique students and goals shape the selection and integration of texts in daily instruction. Through these classroom examples, we illustrate how to strategically weave high-quality texts into lesson- or unit-level instructional design. These examples should inspire ideas for application in your own classrooms and schools.

Building from these texts, tools, and examples, we close each chapter with a *Framework in Action* section, where readers envision the potential of inclusive texts in their own classroom. This section seeks to provide direct connections, next steps, and considerations for students, goals, texts, and instruction. We also offer discussion questions and prompts to deepen educators' thinking, reflections, and applications to unique teaching contexts. Whether you are reading independently, as a part of university coursework, or tied to professional development in your school or district, these features seek to support you in developing integral understandings and practices to bring high-quality inclusive texts into your setting.

CHAPTER 1

Framing the Work

Responsive and Critical Lenses on Classrooms

Books became our language.
Books became our home.
Books became our lives.
We learned to read,
to speak,
to write,
and to make our voices heard.

—From *Dreamers* by Yuyi Morales (2018, pp. 23–25)

Imagine, as a child, walking into your classroom on the first day of school. You are feeling nervous, excited, and curious. You look around the room at the posters on the walls, at the faces on book covers staring back at you. You hear the teacher talk about what you will learn this year, the people and events to explore, and the topics considered essential for you to know. How you feel in those first moments depends a lot on how much you feel seen, heard, and represented in the walls, texts, and curriculum. Do you feel like you, your identities, and your experiences are included in this classroom? Or do you feel *othered* to what seems to be tacitly accepted as the norm among other students?

Now more than ever, we believe that educators need to critically examine the texts and curricular materials they use in classrooms to ensure representation and inclusivity for all students. We need to be sure that children who walk into classrooms see themselves in the books they read, the texts we share, and the curriculum we teach (Christ, Chiu, Rider, Kitson, Hanser, McConnell, Dipzinski, & Mayernik, 2018). We want students to use texts to make sense of their experiences in the community and the world around them. If students do not see the rich nuance and diversity of lives, identities, and experiences represented in what they read and explore in schools, then they likely end up with narrow, singular stories about the communities and world in which they live (Adichie, 2009). Research has shown that *not* having these texts does disservice and harm to students who never get to see themselves represented in school curricula (Boyd et al., 2015). In short, the texts that we use in classrooms matter and warrant deeper exploration and attention.

Further, achievement data indicates that this White-washed approach to curriculum and instruction does not work for most students in U.S. classrooms (Carter & Welner, 2013; Center for Education Policy Analysis, 2019). Some educators express feeling pressured to select texts that fit the demanding skills and strategies expected of students' literacy learning, citing demands to teach to the standards or ensure that students perform well on standardized literacy assessments (Papola-Ellis, 2014). Nonetheless, research demonstrates that students more deeply engage in reading and develop literacy skills with texts that have relevance to their lives. For example, when texts represent the identities and experiences of students, readers construct meaning by connecting to background knowledge (Freeman & Freeman, 2004). Additionally, readers make fewer miscues and have higher comprehension when stories connect to their rich backgrounds in homes and communities (Ebe, 2010).

Just as Yuyi Morales captures in her book *Dreamers* (2018) in the opening quote, the books we share with children are much more than just stories on a page. They have the power to be the place where our students live, learn, and dream. But these transformational spaces do not happen by chance. The choices we make about the texts we include in classrooms need to be intentional to offer the spaces for students to find their home in the pages of a book. These texts should occupy a central role in the classroom curricula to mediate literacies, identities, and understandings in meaningful, authentic, and extensive ways.

CONTESTING THE CANON IN CLASSROOMS

Classrooms across the United States are more diverse than ever before, welcoming students from many racial, cultural, and linguistic backgrounds (NCES, 2019a). Globalization and immigration have sparked massive transformations in our nation's schools. Whereas White students comprised 80% of the U.S. student population in 1970, they now inhabit the minority (NCES, 2019a; Strauss, 2014). In 2014, students of color surpassed White students in kindergarten-through-grade-12 (K–12) public school enrollment, now representing the majority. But racial and ethnic demographics only begin to demonstrate the rich diversity of classrooms. Immigrant-origin children, including first-generation immigrants born outside and second-generation immigrants born inside the United States, make up 25% of the population younger than 18 (Suárez-Orozco, Abo-Zena, & Marks, 2015). With learners from countries across the globe and Indigenous children from tribes across the country, students speak over 350 languages when they enter U.S. educational settings (NCES, 2019a).

Despite the rich diversity of society, the U.S. education system remains homogeneous. White teachers dominate the profession, comprising 80% of the nation's teaching force (NCES, 2019b). Additionally, classroom curricula, texts, and instructional materials still readily portray the so-called mainstream—White, English-dominant, non-disabled, and middle- and upper-class (Huyck & Dahlen, 2019). The overall collective of children's books published in the United States has perpetuated a single story centered on Whiteness, monolingualism, and heterosexuality, with characters without disabilities who espouse stereotypical gender roles and identities within the traditional family structure of mother, father, and children (Borsheim-Black, Macaluso, & Petrone, 2014). These voices, stories, and perspectives have dominated the publishing industry and school-based practice for decades, subsequently minimizing and even erasing portrayals of children and families from diverse racial, cultural, linguistic, and socioeconomic backgrounds (Sims Bishop, 1990). This phenomenon is referred to as the *canon*.

The literary canon includes texts that represent particular time periods and subject areas, persisting through time and heralded as models in literature (Lapp, Fisher, & Frey, 2013; Perry & Stallworth, 2013). Typically, these texts have been around for decades and are framed as *must-reads* for all students, showing up on required reading lists or deemed as prerequisites for college success (Cope & Kalantzis, 1997). These so-called classics typically center White male authors and illustrators, as well as White characters, over all others. Take for example texts like *The Catcher in the Rye* (Salinger, 1951), *Lord of the Flies* (Golding, 1954), and *The Great Gatsby* (Fitzgerald, 1925). These texts tend to perpetuate dominant ideologies, written by White male authors who maintain the status quo with characters who are White, upper-class, English-speaking, cisgender, heterosexual, and without disabilities (Borsheim-Black et al., 2014). Canonical texts that do incorporate characters of color prioritize White perspectives, resulting in stereotypical characters like Jim in *The Adventures of Huckleberry Finn* (Twain, 1885) or plots like *To Kill a Mockingbird* (Lee, 1960) that detail the heroic White man saving the Black man.

In addition to these common texts in U.S. high schools, the canon pervades in elementary settings. Elementary teachers are likely familiar with books that presumably need to be included in early grades, such as those by Dr. Seuss, Eric Carle, and Bill Martin Jr. While some of these texts can be excellent choices, others are problematic but included per nostalgia from personal, family, or teaching experiences or because popular publishers and websites list them as must-reads for all children. The work of Dr. Seuss, for example, is riddled with cultural stereotypes and racist origins of characters such as the *Cat in the Hat* (Nel, 2014). In 2021, Dr. Seuss Enterprises pulled several Seuss texts from future publications because of racist stereotypical illustrations, such as Asians depicted with yellow pigment, slanted eyes, and ponytails while eating rice with chopsticks in conical hats. While educators and organizations have started to push back amid these revelations, such as the National Education Association changing its yearly Read Across America celebration to decenter Seuss's works and instead focus on diverse literature, Dr. Seuss texts continue to sit on shelves in classrooms across the world. Once a text or author is considered canonical, shifting mindsets is challenging.

The persistence of the canon also finds its way into curricular policies that shape instruction and related materials in schools. One prominent example is the exemplar texts listed in Appendix B of the Common Core Standards. These texts appear as suggestions for grade bands, serving as guidelines to help teachers choose texts of grade-appropriate complexity and quality (National Governors Association Center for Best Practices & Council of Chief State School Officers [NGA & CCSSO], 2010a). Upon critical probing of listed texts, you see the strong grasp of the canon. Certain titles are marred by racism and stereotypes, such as the negative portrayals of Indigenous people in *Little House in the Big Woods* (Wilder, 1932) and Mary's anti-Blackness in *The Secret Garden* (Burnett, 1911/1985). Considering that millions of teachers in the United States use these standards as guideposts for curriculum and instruction, we assert the need to prioritize this work to thoughtfully diversify our text collections in response to students in classrooms and communities. The texts that we use in classrooms matter, and occupy a role in shifting the educational experiences and outcomes of students of color, as well as other traditionally marginalized student groups in U.S. schools and society.

CONCEPTUAL FOUNDATIONS TO SHIFT TEXT SELECTION AND USE

As we look to narrow the predominance of the canon in classrooms, we tap into existing approaches that push back against dominant ideologies and curricular norms. Two conceptual frameworks ground this work. The first, *culturally sustaining pedagogy*, emphasizes the strengths, languages, and cultural practices of students in classrooms, particularly children who have been historically situated as deficient from their White, English-dominant peers (Alim & Paris, 2018; Ladson-Billings, 2014). The second, *critical literacy*, seeks to disrupt the status quo in traditional schooling and promote social action, with learners delving into multiple perspectives and understanding complex issues in society beyond the predominant White voices and stories often prioritized in classroom curricula (Harste, Breau, Leland, Lewison, Ociepka, & Vasquez, 2000; Morrell, 2009). In this section, we share the key tenets of these frameworks that shape this work.

Enacting Culturally Sustaining Pedagogies

Situated within an educational system that was designed by and for White stakeholders, culturally sustaining pedagogy serves as an integral theoretical and pedagogical approach to transform the purpose and nature of schooling for students of color (Paris, 2012). Recognizing that contemporary schooling continues the longstanding tradition of marginalizing and situating students of color as deficient from White students, culturally sustaining pedagogy seeks to foster "linguistic, literate, and cultural pluralism as a part of schooling for positive social transformation" (Alim & Paris, 2018, p. 1). By redefining the goals of schooling and moving away from historical practices that emphasize cultural and linguistic assimilation as forms of academic achievement, educators engage in practices that embrace children as holistic individuals with strengths that are sustained and harnessed rather than erased and ignored in classrooms (Alim & Paris, 2018; Moll, Amanti, Neff, & González, 1992).

This focus on sustaining children's backgrounds in classrooms stems from related approaches often referred to in school-change efforts, including *culturally relevant pedagogy* (Ladson-Billings, 1995) and *culturally responsive teaching* (Gay, 2018). Both acknowledge students' cultural heritages and seek to build bridges between home and school experiences, with the prior focusing on the larger pedagogy of classrooms and schools and the latter prioritizing teachers' practice within those settings. Gloria Ladson-Billings's framework of culturally relevant pedagogy involves nurturing students' intellectual growth, weaving nuanced cultural practices into daily practice, and developing sociopolitical consciousness that promotes problem-solving in the community and world. Geneva Gay's work on culturally responsive teaching centers on the teachers who facilitate this work, seeking those who acknowledge and validate children's cultural heritage and enact instruction to embrace cultural ways of knowing and out-of-school experiences. Culturally sustaining pedagogies, introduced by Django Paris (2012), builds from these frameworks to emphasize the need to not only recognize and tap into students' cultures as resources but to sustain those rich and multifaceted identities.

These three terms (i.e., culturally relevant pedagogy, culturally responsive teaching, and culturally sustaining pedagogies) share a common focus on *culture*, which is often misconstrued in implementation (Ladson-Billings, 2018). Culture refers to "a dynamic system of social values, cognitive codes, behavioral standards, worldviews, and beliefs used to give order and meaning to our own lives as well as the lives of others" (Gay, 2018, p. 8). In short, culture is everything that shapes who we are and how we see the world. In this way, practitioners seeking to value students' cultures cannot stop with a display of world flags on the wall and a multicultural book section in the library. Instead, we must shift the nature of schooling away from the firm grasps of dominant ideologies that center on Whiteness, therefore benefiting White students and others who assimilate to the so-called mainstream. This begins by getting to know students, recognizing that culture is not the static ascription of family origins but a dynamic array of actions, communications patterns, values, perspectives, and beliefs. When we know children's nuanced cultural practices and embrace them as strengths, we not only leverage them to reach learning goals but seek to sustain them in children, families, and communities (Alim & Paris, 2018).

Classroom texts and materials play integral roles in facilitating culturally sustaining pedagogies in elementary classrooms. The texts that teachers bring into their curriculum should provide children with mirrors into their identities and experiences, as well as windows into others' lived experiences and larger issues in society (Sims Bishop, 1990). Through strategic selection of texts, teachers acknowledge, include, and elevate stories of marginalized races, ethnicities, cultures, and languages (Boyd et al., 2015). But further, teachers use these texts in ways that sustain cultural practices and embrace multifaceted identities, as well as interrogate external power structures and internal perspectives and ideologies (Alim & Paris, 2018). We explore these tenets of culturally sustaining pedagogy as applied to this work below.

Sustaining Cultural Knowledge and Practices. Asset-based pedagogies recognize that children have rich and valuable knowledge and experiences in their homes and communities. Often used to call educators' attention to these assets, the term *funds of knowledge* refers to "historically accumulated and culturally developed bodies of knowledge and skills essential for household or individual functioning and well-being" (Moll et al., 1992, p. 133). In this way, children are recognized as bringing resources to school that springboard learning. But culturally sustaining pedagogy does not stop at using funds of knowledge to scaffold access to the mainstream curriculum; it also seeks to maintain and situate those strengths as integral to participation in our multiethnic and multilingual society (Alim & Paris, 2018). The texts that teachers select and use in classrooms sustain children's identities through exploration and preservation of cultural practices (e.g., *Jingle Dancer*; Leitich Smith, 2000), family traditions (e.g., *Dim Sum for Everyone*; Lin, 2001), and home languages (e.g., *Leila in Saffron*; Guidroz, 2019). By shifting curricula to center on texts like these rather than canonical texts, we allow children's rich backgrounds and identities to drive instruction.

Embracing Complex and Dynamic Identities. Students' funds of knowledge and cultural backgrounds are integral, but often yield simplifications that deter from the intent of culturally sustaining pedagogies. Students espouse complex identities that change over time as they engage in new experiences. These emergent identities may differ from traditional conceptions or expectations that stem from static cultural labels, which necessitates focus on the individual rather than the larger culture. In his research, Paris has found that students "fashioned new linguistically and culturally dexterous ways of being Latinx or Fijian that relied upon longstanding cultural practices and emerging ones" (Alim & Paris, 2018, p. 9). We see these complex identities in children's literature, such as the identity of the protagonist in the middle-grade novel *Amina's Voice* (Khan, 2017). Amina is an 11-year-old Pakistani-American and Muslim girl who loves to sing Motown and spend time with her Korean-American best friend. When her uncle comes from Pakistan, she and her brother recognize how their emergent identities do not always mesh with traditional cultural expectations. Identity is a frequent theme in texts with protagonists of color, reflecting the realities of children maneuvering divergent cultures in homes and schools.

It is not just students who bring complex and dynamic identities to the classroom. To facilitate culturally sustaining pedagogies, teachers need to deconstruct their own cultural identities, particularly White teachers who see themselves as culture-less (Ladson-Billings, 2018). Since culture is often misconstrued as a static label associated with ethnicity (e.g., Latinx) or country of origin (e.g., Mexican), White individuals subsequently assume that they do not have a culture. By digging into the all-encompassing nature of culture, White teachers and students begin to discover their identities and the multiple influences on those identities from families, communities, and other life experiences. Texts provide examples of these self-explorations. In the middle-grade novel *Becoming Naomi León* (Muñoz Ryan, 2005), the biracial protagonist lives in a trailer park with her White great-grandmother in the rural United States. When her alcoholic mother returns to seek custody, the two flee to Mexico in search of her father, which prompts Naomi to explore her Oaxacan heritage. As the saying goes, we all come from somewhere. When White teachers recognize their own multifaceted identities, they begin to embrace the complex and dynamic identities of the children that they serve.

Critiquing Dominant Power Structures. Learners' identities take center stage in the implementation of culturally sustaining pedagogies, with one critical component demanding attention. *Critical consciousness,* also referred to as *sociopolitical consciousness,* is an integral yet often neglected pillar of this approach (Alim & Paris, 2018; Ladson-Billings, 1995, 2018). Ladson-Billings (2018) defines this consciousness as "the ability to take learning beyond the confines of the classroom using school knowledge and skills to identify, analyze, and solve real-world problems" (p. 75). The focus on real-world problem solving must have relevance, as students should not be asked to solve problems that the teacher cares about (e.g., saving the rain forest) but, rather, issues influencing their lives (e.g., family separations). For example, if students had interest in voter suppression, the teacher might begin with a book like *Lifting as We Climb: Black Women's Battle for the Ballot Box* (Dionne, 2020) to prompt discussion about voting rights and advocacy efforts to register voters or lobby politicians in their community.

But culturally sustaining pedagogy is not as simple as bringing a book with a Black protagonist into the classroom (Ladson-Billings, 2014). That book is just a drop in the bucket of the larger curriculum "centered on White, middle-class, monolingual/monocultural norms and notions of educational achievement" (Alim & Paris, 2018, p. 12). To resist the canon and seek pluralist outcomes in our multilingual and multicultural world, teachers must recognize the pitfalls of traditional curricula and assert the importance of culturally sustaining pedagogy across the school day. In the current context of the United States, where stakeholders have politicized discussions of race and racism in classrooms, this facet becomes simultaneously more challenging and important. Children of color—the majority of students in U.S. schools—need transformative teachers with the courage to dismantle the status quo that has harmed and discriminated against communities of color for centuries (Alim & Paris, 2018; Gay, 2018). Teachers play an integral role in recognizing the detriments of current approaches to curriculum and instruction in classrooms, and in taking action to transform the experiences of students of color and subsequently fight against racism and oppression in schools. Classroom texts can play an integral role in these efforts.

Probing and Problematizing Perspectives. In addition to asset-based conceptions of children's identities and critique of dominant power structures, culturally sustaining pedagogy encourages looking inward to probe regressive practices rooted in dominant ideologies (Alim & Paris, 2018). Whereas asset-based pedagogies situate students with positive lenses, the latest work in the field asserts that students may espouse problematic perspectives that need to be confronted, and pedagogy can unknowingly perpetuate these perspectives. Alim and Paris (2018) provide an example from hip-hop education, describing the masculinity embodied in rap battles and how these improvised oral exchanges may exclude learners who do not identify as cisgender, heterosexual men without disabilities. Teachers can prompt students to problematize perspectives like homophobia, misogyny, xenophobia, and ableism. Children can engage with picture books like *The Boy and the Bindi* (Shraya, 2016), where a South Asian boy explores his gender identity through the bindi traditionally worn by Hindu women, or *Emmanuel's Dream: The True Story of Emmanuel Ofosu Yeboah* (Thompson, 2015), where the protagonist disrupts expectations based on his physical disability. Through strategically selected texts, children probe tacitly accepted norms within communities and cultures and subsequently develop critical literacy, which we describe below.

Promoting Critical Literacy with Children

Shifting away from the canon requires disrupting the status quo of curricular practices in schools. *Critical literacy* prompts us to problematize what is considered valuable or acceptable knowledge in classrooms, while bringing traditionally marginalized voices to the center of the curriculum (Harste et al., 2000; Luke & Freebody, 1997). Reading with a critical literacy lens involves making meaning from text with a critical eye toward historical, social, and political contexts and elements to probe issues of power, representation, and normativity and learn about historically marginalized groups (Comber & Simpson, 2001; Morrell, 2009; Shannon, 1990; Stevens & Bean, 2007). When embraced in teaching, this stance promotes interrogation of multiple viewpoints on topics, questioning practices of privilege and oppression, and including sociopolitical issues within the curricula (McLaughlin & DeVoogd, 2019). Applying a critical literacy lens to text selection promotes inclusivity of the identities, experiences, and perspectives prioritized in instruction to develop critical thinkers and justice-oriented changemakers.

To embrace critical literacy, practitioners need to explore the concept of no text being neutral (Vasquez, Janks, & Comber, 2019). Authors and illustrators create texts through a series of intentional decisions influenced by their multifaceted identities and myriad life experiences (Janks, 2018). Their storied lives inevitably come into texts, whether through the portrayals of characters, word choices to discuss topics, or perspectives to frame the story. Since all texts have an agenda, critically literate readers must have the tools to recognize how authors position them through the text in order to make informed decisions about their thoughts, feelings, and reactions (Lewison, Flint, & Van Sluys, 2002). In the classroom, this ranges from recognizing who is telling a story and how the story might change if told by someone else, to analyzing social media for inaccurate news and manipulative language in current events.

Critical literacy scholars have encouraged this lens to be developed with both educators and students (Lewison et al., 2002). To critically engage with texts, as well as larger events and occurrences in the world, readers must uncover how dominant voices and ideologies have come to be perceived as the norm. For teachers, we want to look carefully at whose voices are represented, minimized, and erased in curricular materials, as well as examine how texts position readers and connect to power (Lewison et al., 2002). We also need to create spaces for students to use critical literacy skills in producing texts, where they use their identities to create texts that disrupt the status quo and connect to aspects of their lives (Luke, 2013). Of course, obstacles emerge in these efforts, particularly if teachers do not have preparation and comfort in disrupting the status quo alongside students (Gutierrez & Rogoff, 2003; Hall & Piazza, 2008; McLaughlin & DeVoogd, 2019). In our exploration of critical literacy tenets below, we consider how teachers enact critical literacy mindsets by selecting texts for instruction, as well as use those texts to develop criticality among students.

Disrupting the Status Quo. Critical literacy prompts readers to view commonplace events, referred to as the *status quo*, through new lenses (Lewison et al., 2002). When considering texts for instruction, critically literate educators seek to disrupt the status quo of texts, decentering the dominant ideologies and recentering other voices and perspectives with equal importance. This might involve pushing back on canonical texts or prepackaged curricula to prioritize inclusive, relevant, and appropriate resources for the unique children in the classroom. A critical literacy mindset leads educators to consider inclusive and wide representation across the texts they pull into classroom instruction. For example, teachers may disrupt the status quo by reading texts about a princess who saves herself (e.g., the graphic novel series *Princeless*; Whitley, 2014) or choosing to center the voices of Indigenous people in texts near Thanksgiving instead of traditional Thanksgiving stories (e.g., *Fry Bread*; Maillard, 2019).

Positioning students as critically literate readers encourages noticing and wondering about representation in texts while uncovering issues of power (Lewison et al., 2002). When reading critically, one pays attention to marginalized voices and thinks about how to bring those voices to the front of the curriculum (Harste et al., 2000). Teachers support students in determining which narratives are privileged and silenced, as well as analyzing the portrayals of different individuals and identities. Teachers might have students evaluate a set of popular texts, looking at who is represented on the pages and what identities are missing, or pull in advertisements to probe how toy and clothing catalogs reflect race, culture, gender, and ability. While doing so, students recognize how companies prioritize or erase identities, as well as consider how these resulting stereotypes might reinforce the status quo.

Interrogating Multiple Viewpoints. Because dominant ideologies pervade curricula, voices are either highlighted or silenced (Luke & Freebody, 1997). Critical literacy involves readers' recognition of diverse personal, political, and cultural perspectives on issues, opening the door to conversations surrounding this diversity of ideas (Hall & Piazza, 2008). Teachers play an integral role in bringing multiple viewpoints into the curriculum. By reading a range of texts from different perspectives, readers develop deeper insight by understanding the same topic from multiple perspectives and probing how one text holds different meanings based on the reader's background and experience (Ciardiello, 2004; Papola, 2013). For example, in a civil rights unit, teachers might provide multiple viewpoints by bringing in LGBTQ perspectives and histories (e.g., *Stonewall: A Building, an Uprising, a Revolution*; Sanders, 2019) or books about lesser-known Black individuals (e.g., *The Youngest Marcher: The Story of Audrey Faye Hendricks, A Young Civil Rights Activist*; Levinson, 2017) in addition to traditional figures often studied in these units.

For children developing critical literacy, we want them to interrogate texts through multiple viewpoints, considering their own and other perspectives simultaneously (Lewison et al., 2002). Consider building a collection of texts that portray life in a city. You might pull together texts that show both challenges and advantages of city life (e.g., *Maybe Something Beautiful: How Art Transformed a Neighborhood,* Campoy & Howell, 2016; *Last Stop on Market Street,* de la Peña, 2015; *Something Beautiful,* Wyeth, 2002) to have students talk about different portrayals of cities in texts and consider what authors and illustrators use to share their perspectives. For instance, in the beginning parts of *Something Beautiful,* illustrations and words make the city seem dangerous and scary. Conversely, in *Last Stop on Market Street,* the grandmother helps us see beautiful things in the city. In this way, students see multiple perspectives on city living in order to probe how text creators position readers to see the focal topic.

Focusing on Sociopolitical Issues. Critical literacy recognizes that teaching is not neutral, as schools and schooling involve elaborate connections among sociopolitical systems, power, and language (Comber, 2016; Lewison et al., 2002). This extends to texts, which are written in the context of larger social issues in our society. Teachers can select texts that uncover sociopolitical issues from multiple perspectives, such as racism, war, immigration, and poverty, using them to push readers beyond personal responses and connections to deeply examine how systems of power shape people in different ways (Jewett, 2007). Consider the picture book *Those Shoes* (Boelts, 2009), which focuses on the concepts of needs and wants as the main character, Jeremy, wants the new trendy pair of sneakers. Jeremy and his grandmother do not have room for *wants,* as his grandmother says, and readers see the value of a dollar in Jeremy's family. Students explore how privilege and social class often determine how we perceive needs and wants, discussing Jeremy's problem-solving of visiting thrift stores to search for the shoes and experiencing empathy with his decision to gift the shoes to his friend. With multiple layers for critical conversation, students can delve into the sociopolitical concept of poverty after reading this text together.

Taking Action to Promote Justice. Similar to culturally sustaining pedagogy, critical literacy aims to promote action and justice in schools and society, specifically by disrupting the status quo while taking multiple perspectives on sociopolitical issues. Critical literacy definitions have evolved over the years, with many researchers now viewing it not as just a way to read texts and the world (Freire & Macedo, 1987), but as a way of living, learning, and teaching (Vasquez, 2015; Vasquez et al., 2019). Part of our job as educators is to support students in gaining the skills they need to engage with all kinds of texts in critical and meaningful ways, being able to interrogate language and consider how their identities position them as readers and thinkers in our world (Janks, 2018). In this way, we select texts that probe important issues in the community and then incorporate those texts into classroom instruction in a way that promotes children's action. For example, after reading a text about someone experiencing the impact of poverty or hunger (e.g., *Maddi's Fridge;* Brandt, 2014), students might investigate ways for the class to support the local food pantry. Through this text, we share ways that inclusive texts support students on this journey.

THE INCLUSIVE TEXTS FRAMEWORK

Drawing from culturally sustaining pedagogy and critical literacy, we have created the Inclusive Texts (IT) framework to guide the use of texts in classrooms. We use the term *inclusive texts* to encapsulate those texts that reflect and include the multifaceted identities of children in schools and societies, with intersecting lenses on race, ethnicity, culture, language, ability, class, gender, family, and community. Drawing from the work of Rudine Sims Bishop (1990), we conceptualize texts as providing *mirrors* for children to see themselves and *windows* to look into and learn about the lives of others. This framework has emerged from our work with teachers over the past decade. Grounded in scholarship spanning curriculum and instruction, language and literacy, and children's literature, the framework centers on incorporating texts that elevate the diverse voices and experiences of students in classrooms and communities.

Other terms have been used to describe texts that portray traditionally marginalized individuals, including *culturally relevant, diverse,* or *multicultural texts.* While these terms have a common goal of diversifying the topic and background of the characters, differences emerge. The historical term *multicultural texts* captures the attempt to represent voices missing from the canon to develop tolerance or positive beliefs regarding cultural groups other than one's own (Strickland, 2001). These texts often provide surface-level accounts of cultural difference and still center on Whiteness as the norm, creating a way of thinking about texts that is a dichotomy of *regular* and *multicultural* (Glazier & Seo, 2005). *Culturally relevant literature* and *diverse texts* seek to counter the traditional pitfalls of the original terminology, with both seeking to elevate texts by and about individuals whose experiences have been often silenced or omitted in literary collections. The former term emphasizes the need for *relevant* accounts that connect texts and readers, whereas the latter seeks to provide portrayals of people, places, and themes that reflect our societal *diversity* in race, ethnicity, culture, and language (Boyd et al., 2015).

With the term *inclusive texts,* we embrace both relevancy and diversity of portrayals spanning backgrounds, identities, experiences, and perspectives. In the larger field, *inclusion* refers to classrooms where all students receive high-quality, grade-level instruction with scaffolds to support learning and access (Bui, Quirk, Almazan, & Valenti, 2010). This movement has challenged the traditional educational practices of tracking students based on language or ability into separate self-contained classrooms for watered-down instruction. Seeking to disrupt another institutionalized practice that has historically benefited White, English-dominant students without disabilities, scholars of children's literature have applied this lens to challenge the canon and bring diverse voices and perspectives into the curriculum. To provide high-quality mirrors and windows for all children to explore in classrooms, *inclusive texts* signify authentic literary portrayals of culture (Rowan, 2001), disability (Pennell, Wollak, & Koppenhaver, 2017), orientation (Page, 2017), gender identity (Rockefeller, 2009), and family structure (Tschida & Buchanan, 2017).

We contend that inclusive texts should be a central feature of instruction, thus allowing students' identities, experiences, and perspectives to drive practice. Our four-part framework guides readers in (a) getting to know the unique identities, experiences, and competencies of students; (b) probing established goals, standards, and curricula; (c) selecting high-quality and authentic texts reflective of students and goals; and (d) integrating texts in meaningful ways across the school day (see Figure 1.1). Flexible to allow for application within any curriculum or approach to instructional design, these research-based steps support practitioners in thoughtfully engaging in text selection and usage. When approached in this way, inclusive texts have the potential to bolster students' identity development, social-emotional well-being, empathy, language and literacy development, and overall learning and understanding.

Getting to Know Students' Storied Lives

The IT framework begins with the recognition that students sitting in classrooms are complex human beings with evolving perceptions of themselves and the world around them. Their daily experiences in homes, communities, and schools influence these perceptions of self, others, and broader society (Herrera, 2016). Even within the same classroom, students have widely unique backgrounds and circumstances, ranging from family structures, to cultural backgrounds, home languages, socioeconomic status, religions, and abilities. Children also begin to develop a sense of who they are in relation to gender, orientation, and expression (Kosciw, Clark, Truong, & Zongrone, 2019). These multifaceted identities and related lived experiences shape learning and literacy development in schools, as learners come to the classroom with cultural ways of knowing, dynamic competencies in

Figure 1.1. Inclusive Texts Framework

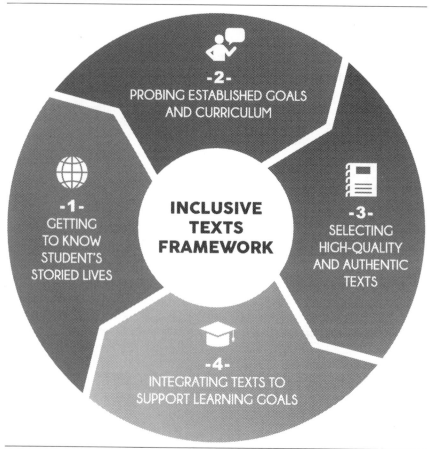

language and literacy, and various academic experiences and notions of self-efficacy (Collier & Thomas, 2007; Moll et al., 1992). With this initial step of the IT framework, we aim to get to know students, embracing children's multifaceted identities and diverse lived experiences as assets that we seek to sustain in classroom instruction.

Probing Established Goals and Curricula

The second step of the IT framework seeks to situate inclusive texts in the standards and curricula that often drive classroom practice. This step strives to challenge the common approach of having inclusive texts on the shelves of classroom libraries for occasional use in read-alouds or independent readings (Ladson-Billings, 2014). To serve as a medium for culturally sustaining pedagogies and critical literacies, inclusive texts need to occupy a central role in the curriculum. This necessitates interrogating existing standards and curricula to consider the inclusion and exclusion of voices, stories, and perspectives. By critically analyzing standards (e.g., Common Core) and curricula (e.g., Lucy Calkins's Units of Study), teachers make deliberate decisions about where inclusive texts fit into instruction and disrupt institutionalized practices that guide practice (Borsheim-Black et al., 2014). This situates the teacher as the expert who uses standards and curricula as ingredients to the recipe that they define based on their knowledge of learners in the classroom (Muhammad, 2020; Wiggins & McTighe, 2011). With this second step of the framework, we aim to develop awareness of where and how inclusive texts should be integrated into the curriculum to facilitate students' learning and development.

Selecting High-Quality and Authentic Texts

The third step of the IT framework involves selecting texts based on students' identities, experiences, and perspectives, as well as learning objectives for focal lessons or units. Here, we want the first two steps on students and goals to guide text selection. Holistic understandings of children (Framework Facet 1) provide an analytic lens to probe existing resources (Framework Facet 2), which prompts thoughtful selection of texts that mediate unique learners' progress toward defined goals (Framework Facet 3). When learners drive text selection, teachers look for texts that provide readers with relevant and authentic portrayals of children, families, communities, and experiences (Short & Fox, 2003; Sims Bishop, 1997, 2003). We seek to elevate authors and illustrators who are insiders to focal identity groups, recognizing the need to disrupt the canon and provide nuanced and accurate depictions of characters, settings, and plots (Bista, 2012). Dependent on goals, teachers select texts to nurture identity development (Al-Hazza & Bucher, 2008), social-emotional learning (Verden, 2012), classroom community (López-Robertson & Haney, 2017), reading comprehension (Pilonieta & Hancock, 2012), writing (Méndez-Newman, 2012), and critical literacy (Souto-Manning, 2009).

Integrating Texts to Support Learning Goals

The fourth step of the IT framework involves purposeful integration into classroom instruction. In our plight to move inclusive texts out of the classroom library and into the spotlight of literacy and content-area curricula, we recognize the need for approaches to design and implement instruction with inclusive texts. This framework facet recognizes that teachers *and* texts facilitate learning, necessitating educators' thoughtful actions, approaches, and strategies to use texts in classrooms with children (May, 2011). Within units, teachers might weave inclusive texts into instruction with consistent procedures, such as literature discussions (DeNicolo & Franquiz, 2006; Kim, Wee, & Lee, 2016) or written reflections (Feger, 2006; Méndez-Newman, 2012). In lessons, teachers might design activities to facilitate students' connections with texts and progress toward learning goals, such as personal storytelling (Martínez-Álvarez & Ghiso, 2017; St. Amour, 2003) or social action projects (Newstreet, Sarker, & Shearer, 2018; Souto-Manning, 2009). With this final facet of the IT framework, we integrate inclusive texts into classroom instruction through lesson- and unit-level curricular design, as well as with instructional procedures and strategies to facilitate students in using the texts to reach learning goals.

KEY CONCEPTS AND TERMS

Several terms and concepts emerge across this text. Below, we outline how we define them in the context of our work.

- *BIPOC* signifies Black, Indigenous, Persons of Color. We use this in place of *students of color* for the remainder of the text to avoid one-size-fits-all terminology for a diverse array of individuals and to center the experiences of Black and Indigenous children.
- *Critical literacy* is a lens through which to challenge texts and society regarding power, privilege, and representation. Its use in the classroom promotes multiple perspectives and dialogue about sociopolitical issues (Knobel, 2007).
- *Culturally sustaining pedagogies* seek to recognize, build upon, and sustain BIPOC children's cultural identities and language practices in classroom curriculum and instruction (Alim & Paris, 2018; Ladson-Billings, 2014).
- *Funds of knowledge* aim to capture the collection of knowledge students bring with them from home, communities, culture, and experiences (Moll et al., 1992). In this text, we often refer to these as children's *experiences* in homes, communities, and schools.
- *Identity* refers to who we are as individuals, including the myriad factors that shape how we see ourselves and the world. Identities are intersectional, with facets like race, culture, language, family, gender identity, sexual orientation, and (dis)abilities influencing our experiences and worldviews (Crenshaw, 1991; Gay, 2018).
- *Inclusive texts* are texts and instructional materials that reflect the multifaceted identities and experiences of children and disrupt dominant narratives across race, culture, class, language, gender, and ability.

- *LGBTQ* refers to all individuals and topics that fall under the general identity labels of lesbian, gay, bisexual, transgender, queer, questioning, intersex, asexual, and ally.
- *Multilingual learners* refer to children with rich language competencies from homes and communities. We use this term to emphasize the linguistic competencies of children who have been labeled as *English learners* in schools.
- *#ownvoices* began as a hashtag movement on Twitter in 2015 by young adult author Corinne Duyvis to recommend books written by authors who identified in the same identity group as characters. We prioritize #ownvoices authors throughout this text.
- Throughout the text, we use *primary* to refer to pre-kindergarten through 2nd grade (students aged 4–7) and *middle grades* to denote 3rd grade through middle school (students aged 8–12). Since many texts can be used across grade levels, we encourage readers to flexibly make connections between the examples and their classrooms.

THE FRAMEWORK IN ACTION: CONSIDERING THE POTENTIAL IN PRACTICE

This book aims to shift readers' perspectives and actions about whose voices and stories belong in classrooms. As teachers, we aspire to do what is best for our students. Begin by imagining a classroom where every child feels seen, heard, and included. In this classroom, children feel validated, that their multiple and complex identities not only matter but are considered valuable additions to the classroom community. In this way, students walk into the classroom every day with a strong sense of personal identity and collective belonging within these walls, as the teacher shares, reads, and highlights books that center different identities. Students have meaningful dialogue with one another, showing respect for differences and seeking ways they connect through similarities.

These inclusive texts do not only fill the bookshelves but also occupy central roles in literacy and content-area instruction. Various voices, stories, and perspectives emerge from texts and resources across the school day, from videos to books to poems to story problems. Literacy instruction engages students with texts that reflect their identities and experiences, as well as those that promote critical literacy and social action in the world. Children engage in discussions and reflective writing in multiple languages as they connect with texts, themselves, and the world. Content-area instruction centers on critical thinking, empathy, and global-mindedness, and strategically selected texts provide multiple perspectives on topics in math, social studies, science, and special areas. In this way, children's stories, identities, and experiences become the curriculum to deepen their literacies, identities, and understandings of the world.

Now envision the school where this classroom exists. Administrators provide and teachers embrace the autonomy to make decisions that center their students. In this way, standards and curriculum serve as rough road maps, with ultimate decision-making resting with teachers who know their students' rich strengths, interests, and competencies. Administrators procure amazing and wide-ranging resources for use in classrooms, as well as prioritize funding and time for professional development that supports teacher learning around high-quality texts, inclusive classroom practices, and centering students' identities. Teachers focus on designing curriculum for the unique students in their classroom, using inclusive texts when appropriate to nurture students' identities and understandings and support progress toward pluralist goals for learning, multilingualism, and critical consciousness.

Perhaps this seems to be an idealized version of schooling, but all teachers have the potential to enact various features that fit their unique contexts. Reflect upon your classroom to consider areas of potential. What do you already do in your classroom with inclusive texts? Where are additional entry points? Maybe you begin by extending your text collection to be inclusive of different identities or by supplementing existing curriculum to include multiple perspectives on focal topics. As you consider your context, be honest about the hurdles you may encounter, such as funds to purchase materials, agency to make curricular decisions, or potential pushback from various stakeholders. Whatever might be ahead on your path, maintain a clear vision of goals to achieve and obstacles to overcome. Our hope is that this book supports you on your journey to make inclusive texts a reality in your classroom.

QUESTIONS AND ACTIVITIES FOR PROFESSIONAL DEVELOPMENT

1. When you hear the term *inclusive texts*, what comes to mind? Do you picture specific students or topics? Do you think of your own classroom and texts? What do you wonder about the term and its role in your classroom? Consider writing an informal definition of *inclusive texts* before you go further in your reading. Revisit this definition and add or revise as your understanding and conceptualization change.
2. What is your prior knowledge of *culturally sustaining pedagogy* and *critical literacy*? Did you see yourself in the texts and materials used in your schooling? Were you taught to be a critical reader as a student or through your professional preparation?

3. Make a list of several books you would consider the *canon* in your grade level. Why do these titles make it to your list? Who wrote these books, and who is represented in these books? Do you agree that they should be considered as *must-reads* for your students?

4. What are your goals for reading and engaging with this text? What kinds of shifts would you like to make in your practice? What factors might support or deter you from reaching your goals? Consider these potential supports and obstacles as you work through this text. Look for ways to minimize obstacles and build upon supports.

CHAPTER 2

Starting With Students
Relevant and Authentic Texts

Melody and I went to the library and asked for a Chinese book. We looked at
the book *The Seven Chinese Brothers.*
"See," Melody said, "Chinese people."
"Those aren't real Chinese people, though," I said. "Your brother doesn't have
a ponytail."
"It's not supposed to be real," Melody said. "Who can swallow the ocean like
they do in the book?"
"But I wanted a real Chinese person book," I complained. "One with people
like us—Chinese Americans."
"You're just being picky," Melody said. "Go write your own, then."
"Okay," I said . . . "I will."

—From *The Year of the Dog* by Grace Lin (2007, pp. 71–72)

In many classrooms and schools around the world, students do not see
themselves in the texts available in libraries or prioritized in the curriculum.
The canon, which pervades even as the world changes and inclusive titles
increase, has a deep hold on the educational institution. The prevalence
of texts featuring White, English-speaking, cisgender, and non-disabled authors and characters is a detriment to our work as educators, as we seek
to sustain children's identities and tap into their lived experiences as rich
resources for reading and learning. Children like Grace and Melody should
not struggle to find texts that portray "people like us," only to find essentialized and stereotyped versions of their identities in one solitary text in the
school's library. We want all children to see authentic portrayals of themselves and others in texts to facilitate reading, learning, and understanding, which necessitates starting with students and knowing who they are as
unique, complex, and multifaceted individuals.

In this way, the Inclusive Texts (IT) framework starts with students.
In this chapter, we explore how to center text selection and usage around
the children in your classroom, seeking to provide relevant and authentic
portrayals that reflect identities, enhance engagement, promote language

and literacy development, and deepen understandings and learning. Building from the conceptual literature described in the previous chapter, we conceptualize effective instruction as centering on children's multi-faceted identities, rich experiences, and storied lives (e.g., Alim & Paris, 2018; Ladson-Billings, 1995, 2014; Moll et al., 1992). We then use these integral understandings about children to select and use texts that authentically provide both windows and mirrors for readers (Sims Bishop, 1990). To build expertise around this first framework facet, we organize this chapter into three sections: (a) getting to know children's storied lives, (b) analyzing texts for relevance and authenticity, and (c) seeking out high-quality resources.

EXPLORING THE STORIED LIVES OF CHILDREN

Every educator reading this text knows firsthand that classrooms are incredibly complex. Each little human comes with distinct circumstances, competencies, interests, strengths, preferences, and needs. In an attempt to quell the complexity, labels serve to codify students, such as by racial and ethnic background (e.g., Asian), or ability, as determined by standardized tests (e.g., English learner). Despite piquing general awareness and providing quick snapshots of students' backgrounds and abilities, institutional labels tell teachers little about the children themselves, particularly their multifaceted identities and storied lives that enhance learning and instruction in classrooms. Labels also have the potential to promote deficit-based thinking about children, rather than emphasize the rich strengths that each child brings to the classroom. In this section, we explore the nuances of students' identities and experiences from an asset-based lens and provide tools and approaches to get to know individual students.

Every child is a unique and complex individual with a multitude of experiences inside and outside of school. Recognizing the multifaceted and dynamic nature of children's identities and experiences is integral to selecting texts with relevance and authenticity to their lives. We conceptualize children as having intersectional identities (Crenshaw, 1991), which influence and are influenced by varied experiences in homes, communities, and schools (Herrera, 2016; see Figure 2.1). Children espouse complex identities, with different facets shaped by social constructs such as race, gender, and disability (McDermott & Varenne, 1995). Identities change over time as children engage, develop, and learn through experiences in various contexts across the life trajectory. Children's nuanced identities and experiences influence their learning and participation in school (Collier & Thomas, 2007), making them central to understand before selecting texts to mediate learning in classroom instruction.

Figure 2.1. Considering Identities and Experiences

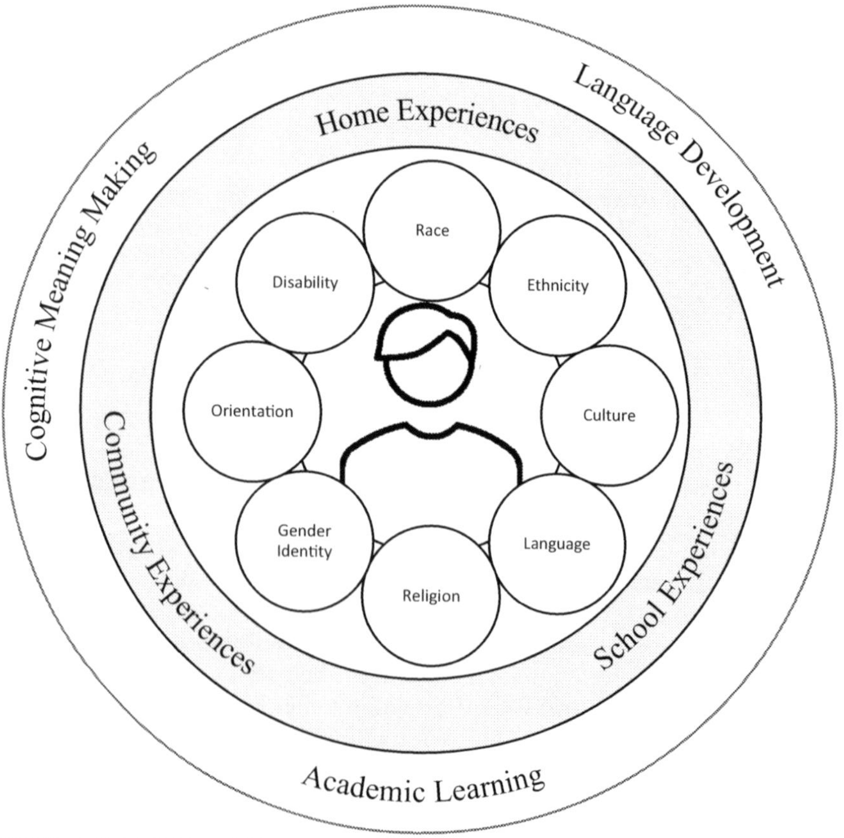

Focus on Identity

Identity is influenced by numerous factors, including who we say we are, who others say we are, and who we want to be. In the classroom, identity work fosters children's confidence and self-esteem, and also impacts how they make sense of their experiences and interactions with texts (McCarthey & Moje, 2002; Muhammad, 2020). But identity is not a straightforward concept, as identities fluidly change over time, with various facets of individual identities intersecting to influence our lived experiences in unique ways. Kimberlé Crenshaw (1991) describes the *intersectionality* of identities, emphasizing how race, gender, and class converge to distinctively shape one's actions and interactions in the world. This concept supports exploration beyond socially constructed categories to embrace intragroup differences, such as understanding the nuanced experiences of a Black female student who cares for her siblings (Bell, 2016). An intersectional lens allows us to probe overlapping systems of privilege and oppression based on identity facets, particularly in an education system designed by and for White, English-dominant, middle- to upper-class stakeholders without disabilities (Bell, 2016; Crenshaw, 1991). Here, we look at the elements of race, ethnicity, family, gender, orientation, and (dis)ability but recognize the many other ways in which individuals define their identities.

Race and Ethnicity. The U.S. Census prompts respondents to self-identify into racial categories that reflect socially defined groups in the country, including White, Black and African American, American Indian, Asian, and Native Hawaiian or Pacific Islander. Ethnicity refers to familial origins, recognizing the racial diversity within regions. For example, the commonly used terms of Hispanic, Latino, or Latinx encompass individuals from Mexico, Central America, South America, and the Caribbean who span racial categories. While race and ethnicity are social constructs, both have impacts on children's identities and experiences within our world (Rountree, 2008; Stevenson, 2014). Family origins often inform students' cultural backgrounds, traditions, and practices, as well as the languages that family members use with one another. The relationship between religion and culture might also shape individuals' identities, as captured in the picture book *Yo Soy Muslim* (Gonzales, 2017), which celebrates the beautiful intersections between culture, ethnicity, language, and religion. Written in verse as a father's letter to his daughter, the text recognizes the identities we own ("I speak Spanish, Arabic, and dreams," p. 15) as well as ones that are put upon us ("There are questions this world will ask. What are you? and Where are you from?," p. 10). The text reminds us of the complex and multifaceted nature of racial, cultural, and linguistic identities, which do not fit into prescribed boxes that may be given to families when they enroll their children in schools.

Family. In addition to cultural, linguistic, and religious identity facets that emerge from one's family origins, family structure and members play an integral role in identity development. Family members are often those who are closest to us both physically and emotionally, which prompts great influence in shaping our identities, daily experiences, and perceptions of the world (Rogoff, 2003). Influential family members vary by child, given the diverse array of family structures that span beyond the traditional conception of the so-called nuclear family of mother, father, and biological children in middle-class homes (Ryan & Hermann-Wilmarth, 2018). Children may live with grandparents (e.g., *Just Like Jackie*; Stoddard, 2018), extended families (e.g., *Merci Suárez Changes Gears*; Medina, 2020), adoptive families (e.g., *I Can Make This Promise*; Day, 2020), blended families (e.g., *Love Like Sky*; Youngblood, 2019), same-sex parents (e.g., *Umi and Uma: The Story of Two Mommies and a Baby*; Davis-Williams & Davis-Williams, 2018), or single parents (e.g., *Hurricane Season*; Melleby, 2019). These are not meant to be conceptualized as categories, as every family is beautiful and unique, such as the child adopted into a family with two moms and children from different racial and ethnic backgrounds in Patricia Polacco's (2009) *In Our Mothers' House*. By knowing and embracing each child's unique family, teachers bring their stories into the classroom.

Gender. The concept of gender in relation to identity spans a range of definitions from gender identity (i.e., identifying as a boy, a girl, or nonbinary) and gender expression (i.e., breaking or conforming to stereotypes that connect to clothing, interests, hairstyles), as well as transgender individuals. This is an aspect of identity with growing importance to address in schools, as approximately 150,000 youth over the age of 13 identify as transgender (Herman, Flores, Brown, Wilson, & Conron, 2017), with likely more in elementary grades who are not captured in these data. In relation to texts, considering gender includes disrupting the status quo regarding gender roles, such as Princess Adrienne from *Princeless* (Whitley, 2014), who hates fancy dresses and does not want to be rescued, or transgender individuals like George, who comes out as *Melissa* (Gino, 2022). In *When Aidan Became a Brother* (Lukoff, 2019), the author helps readers understand this aspect of identity through simple explanations, such as, "When Aidan was born, everyone thought he was a girl . . . But Aidan didn't feel like any kind of girl. He was really another kind of boy" (p. 2). Gender is a prominent part of Aidan's identity because of his own lived experiences, but his identity is multifaceted, with various interests and favorite activities, his impending identity as *brother*, and his role as *son* within a loving and accepting family. This text challenges conformity and shows gender through a wider lens in connection to identity (Hayik, 2016; Marshall, 2004).

Orientation. While overlap exists between gender and orientation on the LGBTQ spectrum, we separate them here to ensure clarity in the distinctions. *Orientation* refers to the gender or genders to which a person is sexually attracted, including heterosexuality (attracted to different gender), homosexuality (attracted to same gender), and bisexuality (attracted to both genders). While no conclusive data exist on numbers of LGBTQ students, 300,000 children in U.S. schools have one or more parents who identify as LGBTQ (Ryan & Hermann-Wilmarth, 2018). But we almost certainly have children in our classrooms who already identify as LGBTQ or may come out later in life. Take, for example, Caroline, the 12-year-old protagonist in *Hurricane Child* (Callender, 2018), who is bullied by her peers at school on the U.S. Virgin Islands. Caroline develops a crush on her new friend, Kalinda, and together they venture into a hurricane to find her missing mother while she negotiates her identity, orientation, and feelings toward herself and those around her. Like Caroline, more than half of children who identify as LGBTQ report harassment, bullying, or feeling unsafe in schools as they grapple with orientation, acceptance, and identity, prompting the need for educators to engage in discussions at early ages to support students and create positive conversations around orientation (Kosciw et al., 2019).

Ability. Ability and disability provide another layer of identity, linking to membership to a certain community depending on the disability and impacting various aspects of an individual's life (Dunn & Burcaw, 2013). Schools classify millions of children as needing special education due to physical or learning disabilities, which include visual, hearing, motor, and cognitive impairments (NCES, 2021). Other children have chronic illnesses, such as diabetes, fibromyalgia, or anxiety, that require supports in classrooms. Yet in 2019, only 3.4% of children's books reviewed by the Cooperative Children's Book Center (2020) featured characters with disabilities. Disability intersects with other identity facets, such as LGBTQ or BIPOC individuals with a disability. In the text *Featherless/Desplumado* (Herrera, 2004), Tomás has spina bifida and navigates questions about his wheelchair from kids at school, which results in him being left out of a soccer game. To inspire him, his father brings home a featherless bird with a scrunchy leg who is born a little differently from others, just like Tomás. Encouraged by the new pet and an invitation to play from a new friend, Tomás learns to score a soccer goal with his head instead of his feet, leading him to declare that there's "more than one way to fly" (p. 30). Children with disabilities and chronic illnesses need their stories included in classrooms.

Focus on Experiences

Children's identities shape their experiences in homes, communities, and schools, which subsequently results in rich sources of background knowledge that students bring to reading and learning. Herrera (2016) defines these facets of background knowledge as funds of knowledge from homes, prior knowledge from communities, and academic knowledge from school.

Funds of Knowledge from Home. Children spend a significant amount of each day in their homes, where they interact with families and loved ones during meals, activities, holidays, and traditions. These rich experiences yield an array of *funds of knowledge,* a widely used term that refers to the knowledge and skills that children have accumulated over time in their homes through individual activities and family interactions (Moll et al., 1992). Children's funds of knowledge include their roles in the household, such as cleaning or taking care of siblings, family members' expertise from hobbies and employment, and holistic family traditions and activities (see Table 2.1). Take, for example, the character in *A Different Pond* (Phi, 2017),

Table 2.1. Examples of Background Knowledge and Experiences

Source	Examples
Funds of Knowledge From Home	• Family dynamics (e.g., interactions with siblings, home responsibilities) • Family employment (e.g., farming, teaching, technology, construction) • Household management (e.g., child care, cooking, item repair) • Language & literacy (e.g., storytelling, singing songs, reading) • Traditions (e.g., holidays, religious events, food, dress) • Values & beliefs (e.g., religion, moral ethics, medicinal healing)
Prior Knowledge From the Community	• Community surroundings (e.g., businesses, transit, farmland) • Community language use (e.g., language brokering, translanguaging) • Informal learning opportunities (e.g., museum visits, libraries) • Language learning locales (e.g., Saturday school, religious classes) • Peer interactions (e.g., sports teams, music classes, gatherings) • Support systems (e.g., church, community center, cultural organization)
Academic Knowledge From School	• Collaboration skills (e.g., small-group work, peer interaction) • Disciplinary language (e.g., terminology in various languages) • Disciplinary understandings (e.g., place value, water cycle) • Learning tools (e.g., computers, tablets, tech platforms, texts) • Literacy practices (e.g., reading & writing in various languages) • School dynamics (e.g., formal procedures, expectations, rules)

whose parents immigrated from Vietnam following the war. In this award-winning picture book, readers see the many funds of knowledge of the young boy who goes fishing with his father early each morning and helps his mother in preparing the fish they catch for the family's dinner. The father, who works two jobs to support his family, tells his son stories about fishing with his brother and fighting in the war in Vietnam while they spend time together each morning.

Prior Knowledge from Communities. In addition to interactions in homes, children experience daily life in their communities, where they engage with others at churches, restaurants, stores, events, and gatherings. *Prior knowledge* extends beyond the home to consider the understandings that children accrue from living in and being a part of these larger communities (Herrera, 2016). Community-based prior knowledge emerges from children's exposure to different repertoires of cultural and linguistic practices in the surrounding environment, as well as social interactions with a variety of individuals and groups. In the picture book *My Papi Has a Motorcycle* (Quintero, 2019), readers experience the nuances of protagonist Daisy's California community from the back of her father's motorcycle. We see the stores, homes, and places that they frequent, the various people with whom they interact, and the murals that depict the rich immigrant history of the community. We hear the revving of the motorcycle and the music that plays as workers build homes replacing the citrus groves in this changing community. These experiences shape Daisy's daily life and yield rich knowledge regarding relationships, history, and change.

Academic Knowledge From Schools. School is another locale that situates experiences and identities. Understanding learners' trajectories of schooling is helpful in order to understand the knowledge that they bring to classrooms, as well as how they engage and see themselves as learners. *Academic knowledge* denotes what students bring from previous experiences in formal educational settings, which includes schools in different communities and countries (Herrera, 2016). Often starting from early ages, children have engaged in various educational experiences, resulting in literacy and content knowledge in addition to familiarity with school-based procedures, expectations, and pedagogies. In *Nelson Beats the Odds* (Sidney, 2015), readers learn about the schooling of Nelson, who gets diagnosed with ADHD and a learning disability. The comic-book-like format details Nelson's various experiences in school, including both positive and negative interactions with teachers, placement in special education classes, struggles to stay engaged with classwork, and persistence to graduate and attend college. This window into Nelson's schooling demonstrates how school experiences shape identities.

Focus on Learning

Central to understanding the diversity and complexity among students, children's multifaceted identities and experiences influence how they learn in classrooms, which involves cognitive, linguistic, and academic dimensions (Collier & Thomas, 2007).

Cognitive Processing. Culture shapes how children think and learn (Gay, 2018). When considering the *cognitive dimension* of learning and development, we recognize that students read, process, and make meaning using various lenses and schema (Collier & Thomas, 2007; Herrera, 2016). When selecting texts, teachers can consider how children might connect to topics, genres, and storylines. For example, some students might prefer folktales, graphic novels, poetry, or nonfiction based on cultural and familial traditions, as well as common forms of artistic and literary expression in their homes. Many texts tap into oral storytelling traditions, such as *Shanyaak'utlaax/Salmon Boy* (Marks, Chester, Katzeek, Dauenhauer,

& Dauenhauer, 2017). Based on oral history told across generations, this Tlingit and English bilingual picture book shares the story of what happens to a Kiks.ádi boy who disrespects salmon. For students with related cultural background knowledge and oral storytelling traditions, this text might facilitate reading and meaning-making in different ways than texts disconnected from their identities and experiences.

Language Development. Students' languages also facilitate reading, understanding, and learning in classrooms. Influenced by both their identities (e.g., ethnic and cultural background) and experiences (e.g., home and community language use), language is the key medium that allows children to access and engage with texts. The *linguistic dimension* of learning and development considers students' preferences and competencies in multiple languages (Collier & Thomas, 2007), both of which inform text selection. Teachers can consider students' preferred languages for the text narrative (e.g., English-only, Spanish-only, bilingual or translingual in Spanish and English). Multilingual inclusive texts are available in a growing number of immigrant and Indigenous languages, such as Hmong (*Ka's Garden*; McHugh & Lo, 2010) and Lakota (*Shota and the Star Quilt*; Bateson-Hill, 1998). Language competencies also factor into how teachers select and use texts. For example, teachers might select graphic novels or novels in verse with students still developing English proficiency due to the natural scaffolds provided by the genre. They might use the text alongside cognates, sentence structures, and text features to support students' language development while reading.

Academic Learning. Children's identities and experiences also influence their academic learning in classrooms, particularly their unique interests and self-efficacy in various content areas, including literacy, mathematics, science, social studies, and fine arts (Collier & Thomas, 2007). Individual students may have preferred topics for texts, such as the arts, athletics, or technology, which connect to their interests and funds of knowledge (Moll et al., 1992). In addition to selecting texts that align with prior experiences, teachers select texts to build learners' self-efficacy in the disciplines. For example, strategically selected memoirs and biographies of BIPOC scientists and mathematicians (e.g., *Buzzing with Questions: The Inquisitive Mind of Charles Henry Turner*; Harrington, 2019) allow children to see themselves in various professions and potentially shift their perceptions of who occupies those careers.

Capturing and Responding to Students' Storied Lives

Recognizing students' multifaceted identities and experiences from an asset-based lens lays the groundwork for teachers to gather related data that reveals the resources that each child brings to the classroom. While teachers often begin with formal data provided by the school to get an overarching sense of their class and students (e.g., age, race, ethnicity, language, ability), these institutional ascriptions often simplify the complexity that we seek to understand about individual children and situate learners as being deficient to White, English-dominant, non-disabled students without those labels. We encourage teachers to use their preferred approaches to getting to know the unique nuances of students, as well as consider new ways to gather anecdotal data both early and throughout the school year. Table 2.2 lists ways to gather data from students, families, and communities with the goal of getting to know the multifaceted identities and experiences children have in homes, communities, and schools.

Let's travel to Anne's classroom in suburban Chicago, where she teaches middle-grade language arts. The school's population is 36% White, 33% Asian, 12% Latinx, 11% multiracial, and 8% Black, with a quarter of students considered multilingual learners and a third designated as low-income. Before children roam the halls of this 1st-through-5th-grade school, Anne reviews her class list and cumulative files to get a sense of her incoming class. In addition to demographic information like race, ethnicity, and age, she looks for institutional designations such as individualized education plans (IEPs), English or bilingual language supports, and reading proficiency levels as designated by previous standardized tests. Once the school year begins, she digs deeper into getting to know students, sending home questionnaires for students and families to get to know children's reading preferences and families' funds of knowledge. Anne also uses whole-class discussions to glean information, such as learning that students speak nine different languages and that 80% of students are either first- or second-generation immigrants. These data prompt initial analyses of her classroom library and language-arts curriculum to ensure that students can access and connect with an array of texts.

Anne continues to prioritize getting to know students throughout the school year, which serves to deepen her rapport with students, understand individual children's identities and experiences, and facilitate student-centered literacy instruction using inclusive texts. She weaves procedures into language-arts units, including reading conferences, dialogue journals, and student self-assessments, which allow her to individually connect with and learn from students. Her instruction centers on essential questions, which prompt students to reply at the beginning and throughout units. As students grapple with big questions related to the focal unit, such as those focused on discovering identity (e.g., What shapes identity?) and exploring immigration (e.g., What is the immigrant experience?), she learns more about children's nuanced identities and experiences. Anne uses her evolving information about students to select texts to mediate her teaching, including reading texts aloud for the whole class, using others in small-group settings

Table 2.2. Data Collection Strategies

Data Source	Directions
Cumulative Files	Review formal data in students' cumulative files as a starting place to gather demographic information, home language, immigration details, previous schooling, literacy abilities, and other potentially helpful details.
Dialogue Journals	Engage students in dialogue via writing, where they write and you respond. Craft writing prompts that allow you to learn more about children's identities, experiences inside and outside of school, and learning preferences.
Discussions	Whether during morning meeting, read-aloud, or another time during the school day, listen to students' responses. Focal texts and topics can encourage discussion on topics that you wish to know more about (e.g., home, family).
Family Conferences	Whether informally before or after school or formally during parent-teacher conferences, maintain communication to build rapport and learn about family backgrounds, experiences, and various resources for learning.
Home Visits	Visit family homes to discover children's funds of knowledge firsthand. Use an asset-based lens to glean all that students bring to learning from their home environment, including the relationships with their family members.
Neighborhood Walk	Walk or drive around your school's neighborhood to observe the surroundings with an asset-based lens. Use the perspective of your students to understand the prior knowledge they are bringing from community experiences.
Self-Assessments	Have students use surveys, writing prompts, and other self-assessment tools to reflect on what they see as important to shaping their identities, sources of background knowledge, and preferences with regard to reading and learning.
Student Conferences	Whether informally during lunchtime or formally during class time, sit down with students to get to know them as individuals, readers, and learners. Build rapport and relationships to promote open sharing over time.

for discussion, or suggesting specific titles during reading conferences. Her goal is to provide texts as mirrors into children's nuanced lives and experiences and windows to push students' thinking and understanding about the world around them.

Consider the various students in your own classroom, including their multifaceted identities and experiences inside and outside of school. Certain variables might be easily discerned from formal data provided by your school or district, such as a student's race, ethnicity, and age, often listed on class rosters. Dig deeper into available students' records in an attempt to learn more nuanced aspects of students' identities, such as ethnic and cultural background, country of origin, circumstances of immigration, home languages and language varieties, religion, sexual orientation, gender identification, family structure, and parent employment. These formal data may prompt the need for more learning. For example, you might read from a student's file that their family immigrated from Cambodia and speak Khmer at home, but that information contributes little if you are unfamiliar with that country and language. Find reliable sources to seek out more information to contextualize the information that you discern about students.

Whereas formal data provide a starting place to learn about students, the most valuable information about students comes directly from the source. Static and generalizing by nature, the labels and ascriptions codified in formal school documentation fail to capture students' varied backgrounds, experiences, interests, perspectives, and competencies. Fortunately, teachers spend time during the school day with their students, where they can collect anecdotal data to get to know students more deeply. Simply engaging students in conversations is a great starting place, whether informally during transition times or formally during classroom discussions. Dialogue journals and other written outlets provide students with more intimacy to share perspectives and experiences. From these data, consider learners' funds of knowledge from home (e.g., traditions), prior knowledge from community (e.g., other support systems), and academic knowledge from school (e.g., prior school experiences; Herrera, 2016).

Knowing students is the integral first step, as well as the recurrent step that must be continually taken over time. Students' identities and experiences are complex and dynamic, and our ever-changing understandings of learners become the backdrop from which we critically consider classroom teaching, curricula, and materials. In the next section, we consider how to analyze and select texts based on relevance and authenticity to students in your classroom.

Analyzing Texts for Relevance and Authenticity

Knowledge of children's multifaceted identities and experiences is the starting place for selecting inclusive texts to mediate learning and instruction. Teachers use what they know about children in classrooms as a lens for analyzing texts to ensure relevance to readers' lives, as well as authenticity in the representation of individuals, families, and communities. When starting with students to critically consider texts, we consider (a) relevance of texts to students, (b) authenticity of portrayals, (c) relation of authors to storylines, and (d) potential stereotypes to avoid and disrupt. The subsections below correspond with these factors for consideration.

Considering Relevance to Students

Rudine Sims Bishop (1990, 1997) has paved the path for today's growing use of inclusive texts in classrooms. Her work calls attention to three types of *multicultural texts* to demonstrate divergent ways to include culture in literature (see Table 2.3). Culturally *neutral* texts feature characters of color who could be traded out for White characters without changing the storyline. Culturally *generic* texts include BIPOC characters with surface-level features to indicate particular backgrounds, but they lack deeper details portraying their lives. Culturally *specific* texts provide nuanced narratives that capture characters' multifaceted identities and experiences. In the IT framework, we prioritize the selection and use of texts with specificity and attention to the rich and nuanced lives of children spanning identities and experiences.

Cultural *relevance* refers to how students connect with a text, whether that be physically, culturally, or emotionally (Johnson, Koss, & Martinez, 2018). When considering the relevance of texts for students, any of the above types of texts could spark connections for readers. Neutral and generic texts might allow students to see themselves through the physical representation

Table 2.3. Culture in Children's Literature

Term	Definition	Example
Culturally Neutral	The text features BIPOC characters but the storyline is neutral to race, ethnicity, and culture such that the character could be traded out for a White character and the storyline would not change.	Caldecott-winning *The Snowy Day* (Keats, 1962) depicts protagonist Peter as Black, though his snow-day adventures could be those of any child.
Culturally Generic	The text includes BIPOC characters, but the presentation includes only generic references to race, ethnicity, or culture, such as an ethnic surname or surface-level cultural details (e.g., food, dress).	*One Green Apple* (Bunting, 2006) tells the story of a Farrah, who recently started school in a new country. Other than wearing a head scarf, her experiences could be that of any newcomer.
Culturally Specific	The text provides nuanced portrayals of BIPOC characters with direct connections and intersections of race, ethnicity, culture, language, religion, family, and community within the storyline.	*Cuando amamos cantamos/When We Love Someone We Sing to Them* (Martínez, 2018) taps into the cultural tradition of the Mexican *serenata*. This bilingual book rhythmically details the protagonist seeking his father's help to serenade a boy he likes.

of characters, such as illustrations depicting characters with cultural forms of dress or narrative, noting similar names, foods, or traditions. For some readers, this physical representation is exciting and engaging, particularly if other texts in the classroom portray White characters. But with nondescript inclusion of BIPOC characters, children may not connect and use their rich identities and experiences to facilitate reading and learning. Further, texts that only present surface-level details essentialize cultures and communities—leading readers to make assumptions that individuals belonging to a certain group are monolithic in food, dress, and traditions.

Culturally specific texts typically allow for multiple, complex, and dynamic connections between readers and texts. Because of the specificity that delves into the lived experiences of individuals, these texts capture intersectional identities (e.g., race, culture, language, religion) as shaped by various experiences in homes, communities, and schools. Rather than relying solely on physical representation, readers connect with various nuances of characters, settings, storylines, and topics. Relevancy spans genres, with authors' specificity promoting varied connections whether writing fiction, nonfiction, folklore, or poetry. Consider a fictional text like *Cuando amamos cantamos/When We Love Someone We Sing to Them* (Martínez, 2018), where readers see the intersectional identity of a Mexican-American boy who reveals his love for another boy and seeks his father's help to serenade him. In a nonfiction text like *Counting on Katherine: How Katherine Johnson Saved Apollo 13* (Becker, 2018), readers see the protagonist develop into a mathematician through experiences in her home, community, and school. When authors portray intersectional identities and multifaceted experiences in texts, they provide multiple connections points for readers to engage with texts (Sims Bishop, 1990).

Ensuring Authenticity of Portrayals

Whereas relevance considers the connections between reader and text, authenticity emphasizes if and how the text captures the essence of an individual or community (Sims Bishop, 2003). Authentic texts accurately portray real life to foster personal and intercultural understandings about target identities and experiences (Short & Fox, 2003). Analyzing texts for authenticity is an integral step in this facet of the IT framework, as we seek to provide children with authentic textual portrayals to mediate their reading and learning. Table 2.4 lists questions for practitioners to use while critically considering a text for classroom use, including lenses on cultural, linguistic, and experiential authenticity.

Cultural authenticity probes the accurate and purposeful use of cultural details in a given text. At its most basic level, authenticity relies on accuracy. Authors must present topics, characters, settings, and storylines in ways that truly capture the lived realities and experiences of individuals, families, and

Table 2.4. Analyzing Texts for Relevance and Authenticity

Category	Questions to Consider
Text Details	• In what year was the book published? How does that influence the text? • Is the author an insider or an outsider to the text's focal identities and experiences?
Relevance to Students	• In what ways does the text connect to students' multifaceted identities? • How does the text reflect home, community, and school experiences? • Does the text tap into my students' multilingualism and learning preferences?
Cultural Authenticity	• Does the text (i.e., narrative, illustrations) feature rich, nuanced, and accurate cultural details? Are these details used to deepen and enhance the narrative? • Does the text essentialize or promote stereotypes of particular groups? • What are the presumed standards of success for BIPOC characters? • How are different people situated in the text (e.g., problem, problem solver)?
Linguistic Authenticity	• Do characters use authentic dialogue (i.e., how people interact in daily life)? • How are other languages woven into the text? Does the author immediately translate, italicize, or provide a glossary? How does this influence authenticity? • In bilingual books, which language is prioritized? Does a particular language consistently come first on the page? Is the translation accurate? • Are there words or phrases that signal racism, sexism, or ablism?
Experiential Authenticity	• Do characters reflect intersectional identities without perpetuating stereotypes? • Does the text capture the nuances of childhood and daily experiences? • Does the text portray various experiences and emotions (e.g., struggle, joy)? • How are relationships between characters rendered (e.g., family, friends)? • Are settings portrayed without essentialization (e.g., homes, communities)?

communities. This precision must extend across the text's nuanced narrative and illustrations, which authors and illustrators have purposefully crafted to deepen the storyline. Consider the above example of *Cuando amamos cantamos/When We Love Someone We Sing to Them* (Martínez, 2018), which centers on the cultural and familial tradition of the Mexican *serenata*. Rather than inserting a random mention of the *serenata* for cultural flavor while maintaining a generically American plot, the author weaves the storyline around this rich cultural practice. Additionally, readers see the caring yet complex father-son relationship as the protagonist reveals his orientation and seeks his father's help to serenade the boy he loves. In this way, the authenticity of the text relies on precise, purposeful use of rich cultural details that deepen the story without essentializing the target cultural group.

Linguistic authenticity focuses on if and how language in texts reflects how people use language in real life. Think about how your students interact with families and friends, including in different languages and language varieties (Barrera & Quiroa, 2003). For example, children use languages interchangeably, such as the bicultural protagonist in *I Love Saturdays y domingos* (Ada, 2004), who spends Saturdays with her English-speaking grandparents and Sundays with her *abuelos hispanohablantes*. *Translingual texts* like this one capture dynamic language use to deepen overall authenticity (Flores, 2019). Nonetheless, many authors use literal translations, where characters speak in one language and immediately translate into another. While allowing access to monolingual readers, this approach does not accurately reflect how bilingual individuals interact in real life and thus deters from the text's authenticity. In addition to accuracy, practitioners should consider the purpose and potential outcome of language use. For example, authors might sprinkle in another language for cultural flavor and subsequently promote harmful stereotypes. Take *Skippy Jon Jones* (Schachner, 2003), for example, where a cat pretending to be a chihuahua adds *-ito* to the end of words to sound like a Spanish-speaker. Although this text does not aim to capture the experiences of an individual or a group, this type of language use might be viewed as disparaging and problematic.

Experiential authenticity considers the nuanced representation of intersectional identities and related experiences in homes, communities, and schools. Since cultural authenticity often prompts critical probing of narratives and illustrations based on race, ethnicity, and culture, we find that this lens on experiential authenticity provokes additional analysis on other identity facets (e.g., gender identity, disability, religion) and experiences (e.g., family relationships, immigration stories, peer interactions). The key focus here is on nuance; details should capture the essence of childhood and realities of daily life, which includes rich and varied experiences, relationships, and emotions. Think back to the example of *When Aidan Became a Brother* (Lukoff, 2019), which focuses on a transgender protagonist whose family grows and evolves around his gender identity. In addition to the focus on

Aidan's identity and experiences as a transgender child, we see him playing with friends, picking flowers, shopping with his mother, painting with his father, and preparing for the birth of his sibling. This nuance facilitates readers' connections and understandings that emerge from the text, emphasizing characters as human beings who experience life in ways that are both similar to and different from the reader.

Authenticity concerns span genres, requiring analysis of text and illustrations in all books. Fictional texts are often the focus of discussions on authenticity, as authors pair their imaginations with prior experiences to shape characters and storylines (Cai, 2003). But across genres, authors' and illustrators' creative choices can yield inaccuracies or essentializations. Let's take two texts about water. *Water Is Water* (Paul, 2015), an informational text about the water cycle, portrays children engaging with water in different forms, such as drinking beverages, looking at clouds, jumping in puddles, and playing with snow. This culturally neutral book portrays BIPOC characters in the illustrations yet captures the nuances of childhood in relation to the text's theme. In another book, *Water's Children: Celebrating the Resource That Unites Us All* (Delaunois, 2017), poems probe how children around the world use water in daily life. But in this text, the culture-by-culture format with related illustrations essentializes cultures, such as the Brazilian child paddling a canoe in a loincloth or the Japanese child wearing a conical hat while working the rice field. By analyzing texts across genres, teachers prioritize authentic portrayals for use in classrooms.

Prioritizing Authors With Insider Experiences

Any analysis of authenticity must be tied to the person who writes the text. As inclusive texts have grown in number in recent decades, scholars, authors, publishers, and practitioners have engaged in the ongoing discussion of who has the *right to write* about a particular group or experience (e.g., Bista, 2012; Cai, 2003; Ching, 2005). This debate focuses on the *positionality* of authors, delineating between authors who are *insiders* and *outsiders* (Cai, 2003). Insiders share in the focal identities portrayed in the text, which subsequently yields personal insight and authentic nuances stemming from their own experiences and sentiments. Outsiders write about identities and experiences other than their own, which requires careful research, reflection, collaboration, and feedback to authentically capture the lived experiences of characters with significantly different backgrounds and perspectives (Lasky, 2003; Moreillon, 2003). Authors' backgrounds influence authenticity, requiring outsiders to ensure that texts are both accurate and nuanced to deepen the storyline without essentialization.

To explore how authors influence authenticity, let's compare two texts with similar themes and target groups—one written by an insider and one by an outsider. Table 2.5 walks through an analysis of two texts: *The*

Table 2.5. Comparing Insider and Outsider Texts

	Insider Text	Outsider Text
Text Details	*The Christmas Gift* (Jiménez, 2000)	*When Christmas Feels Like Home* (Griffith, 2013)
Author Background	Mexican-American male who immigrated to California as a child	White female; former elementary teacher from North Carolina
Cultural Authenticity	In this memoir of his experiences growing up in a family of migrant workers, Jiménez recalls one rainy Christmas season when his family moved in search of work. Cultural nuances enrich the story, such as Catholic traditions and discourse (e.g., *Que Dios los bendiga*). Thoughtful details depict poverty while maintaining focus on the family's love for one another. In an authentic ending that does not reflect U.S. standards of success, Panchito does not get the red ball he wanted for Christmas.	Protagonist Eduardo and his family move to the United States, assumedly from Mexico, though this is never stated. We learn of his affinity for *fútbol* and Christmas throughout the text as he settles into his new house on Sleepy Tree Lane. Despite recently coming from Mexico, his family celebrates Halloween, rather than *Día de los Muertos*. He also has his school friends over to his home to eat turkey with his family on Thanksgiving.
Linguistic Authenticity	In this bilingual picture book, the English narrative is presented first, followed by the Spanish. In the English narrative, Spanish words are included and italicized to reflect authentic dialogue between characters (e.g., *Feliz navidad, vieja*.)	Spanish phases are italicized and directly translated in the dialogue in English (e.g., When? *Cuándo?*). Although Eduardo only speaks Spanish, his dialogue is presented in English, as well as in English with direct Spanish translations.
Experiential Authenticity	In the author's note, Jiménez recalls his poignant memories of this Christmas season, which come through in the text in the vivid details in which he describes his experiences (e.g., the nuances of the pregnant couple's clothes).	To begin the story, Eduardo and his family load into his uncle's van from his village and drive to their new home in the United States. On one page, they are in Mexico and the next in the United States, with no details on crossing the border.

Christmas Gift (Jiménez, 2000) and *When Christmas Feels Like Home* (Griffith, 2013). Both picture books focus on Mexican immigrant families in the United States with the similar theme of celebrating Christmas. Whereas Jiménez writes from his experiences growing up in a family of migrant workers, Griffith writes as a White woman born and raised in the United States. Their distinct backgrounds shape the authenticity of the narrative. Whereas Jiménez captures rich cultural and linguistic details that reflect daily life and discourse, Griffith's story presents unlikely occurrences, such as the family celebrating Halloween rather than *Día de los Muertos* and the Spanish-dominant protagonist speaking in English with intermittent translations of words (e.g., When? *Cuándo?*). Tapping into his poignant memories of this Christmas during his childhood, Jiménez describes vivid details that portray the deep love and tradition of family amidst the poverty that they face as migrant workers. Conversely, Griffith's text glosses over experiential nuances, with the family hopping in the van in Mexico on one page and delving into essentialized American life on the next.

This comparative example is one of many reinforcing that authors influence the cultural, linguistic, and experiential authenticity of texts. To provide authentic representations and disrupt the canon by elevating historically marginalized voices, we recommend prioritizing texts written by insiders. This is not always straightforward and might require research into an author's background. For example, Julia Alvarez is an author from the Dominican Republic who has written fabulous books from her insider perspective (e.g., *Before We Were Free*; Alvarez, 2004; *How Tía Lola Came to (Visit) Stay*; Alvarez, 2002). But another book centers on a Mexican protagonist who is undocumented (*Return to Sender;* Alvarez, 2009), subsequently situating her as an outsider. Now this book is a personal favorite, as well as the recipient of the Pura Belpré Award, which recognizes high-quality Latinx literature. Although Alvarez writes from the outside, she uses her background as a Latina, immigrant, and author to research and capture an experience unlike her own. While we suggest prioritizing insiders, this does not mean excluding all outsiders—but rather scrutinizing the text and process that authors use to craft the text. Students can support these analyses using their own insider lenses to probe authenticity.

Countering Stereotypes Through Text Selection

Selecting texts that authentically reflect and represent intersectional identities and experiences is integral in the IT framework, which includes prioritizing authors who write from insider perspectives. But one final lens is pertinent to consider when using students as the starting place for resource selection: how texts disrupt stereotypes. Think about common stereotypes and assumptions that pervade society in relation to different identity facets. Societal discourse frames racial and ethnic groups in particular ways, often negatively skewed and wrought with essentialization across members of that group. Gender norms and expectations guide what many deem appropriate for how children act, dress, and display emotions. Disabilities are often framed as detriments, situating people with disabilities as helpless or unable to contribute. Culturally generic texts, which only include broad generalizations about identity facets (e.g., ethnicity, gender identity), tend to exacerbate stereotypes. Conversely, when explicitly and authentically delving into individuals' nuanced identities and experiences, texts counter these essentializations and misperceptions.

Teachers can disrupt stereotypes through text selection. When teachers select individual texts for lessons, it is important to attend to cultural, linguistic, and experiential authenticity as described above. But even the most authentic texts can result in essentializations and stereotypes if presented as the only reality. For example, if readers have not engaged with texts portraying Latinx characters, then *The Christmas Gift* (Jiménez, 2000) could situate Panchito and his family as representative of tens of millions of people often lumped into the demographic category of Hispanic or Latino. In her Ted Talk, Chimamanda Ngozi Adichie (2009) refers to this phenomenon as the "danger of a single story" (p. 1). If we only share one story related to an identity facet (e.g., ethnicity) or experience (e.g., adoptive family), we risk promulgating stereotypes. For this reason, we recommend incorporating an array of relevant and authentic texts across units. As exemplified across this book, this strategic inclusion spans literacy, content-area, and special-area instruction.

Extensive text collections in classroom and school libraries enable teachers to widely and strategically incorporate inclusive texts into the curriculum. To push past the single story for any given identity or experience, we want to build out text options for students to read and enjoy—both tied to classroom instruction and independent reading for pleasure. As collections grow, practitioners keep interrogating how text offerings portray target groups and subsequently hold the potential to sustain stereotypes or assumptions. For example, we have found that even the best-stocked classroom libraries tend to emphasize struggle, such as Black characters toiling for civil rights, immigrant families crossing borders, and LGBTQ youth maneuvering acceptance. But the focus on struggle deters readers from seeing joy in families and communities, as well as kids just being kids. By extending and consistently probing titles in classrooms, teachers nurture children's understandings about multifaceted identities and experiences.

SEEKING OUT HIGH-QUALITY TEXTS AND RESOURCES

When seeking to compile high-quality inclusive texts with relevance and authenticity to children's experiences, it is helpful to start with organizations committed to bringing diverse voices into classrooms. For example, the Cooperative Children's Book Center (CCBC) compiles statistics on the publication of children's and young adult books by and about BIPOC authors and illustrators. In the 1980s, the CCBC found that only 18 of 2,500 books that year were written by African-American authors, prompting a closer look at books written and illustrated by Black authors each year. A decade later, documentation grew to include Asian/Pacific, Asian/Pacific American, First/Native Nations, and Latinx authors and illustrators. They documented books *by* BIPOC individuals, as well as books *about* those groups, to distinguish books created by White authors or illustrators. Since this documentation began over 3 decades ago, the existence of texts written by and for BIPOC has not changed dramatically. In 2018, half of children's texts published focused on White characters and another 27% about animals or nonhuman characters, with just 24% of the texts featuring characters of color (Huyck & Dahlen, 2019).

Social media plays a key role in efforts to shift the texts we use and disrupt the use of the canon and classics. We Need Diverse Books, a nonprofit organization devoted to changing children's book publishing to reflect the lives of all children, maintains a strong social media presence and website with resources for educators. Hashtags on platforms like Twitter focus on diversity in children's and young adult literature. #DisruptTexts is a grassroots effort by teachers to challenge the canon, diversify the language-arts curriculum, and disrupt the status quo for text selection. They share blogs and current events related to texts, as well as host chats on professional texts that focus on antiracist education and diverse texts. #OwnVoices is an effort by authors to spread awareness about the importance of texts written by those of the same identity about which they write. With an extensive history of authors from dominant identities (e.g., White, cisgender, non-disabled) writing the stories of traditionally marginalized voices, this movement aims to promote authenticity via authors as insiders to cultures and experiences.

In addition to educators and authors committed to increasing representation in texts, many publishing companies now prioritize books that portray diverse characters. For example, Lee & Low Books seeks out texts with diverse characters and notes a preference for authors and illustrators whose backgrounds align with their texts. Several book publishing companies in Canada, such as Groundwood Books and High Water Press, focus on highlighting the stories of Indigenous/First Nations individuals and communities. Some of the larger publishing companies have also started movements within their companies to address diversity in a variety of ways. Most recently, HarperCollins announced a 2021 launch of a Native-focused imprint called *Heartdrum*, which offers a range of stories by Indigenous creators. Simon & Schuster established *Salaam Reads* to introduce readers of all backgrounds to the experiences of Muslim children, as well as an opportunity for Muslim readers to see themselves represented positively in children's literature. Penguin Books launched the imprint *Kokila*, whose aim was to "center stories from the margins" to give diverse voices a platform.

Table 2.6 provides the web addresses and Twitter handles for various awards, publishers, and organizations that prioritize high-quality inclusive texts. After getting to know children's multifaceted identities and experiences, websites might facilitate initial searches for relevant and authentic texts,

Table 2.6. Recommended Resources to Find High-Quality Inclusive Texts

Source	Details & Weblinks
Awards	• Américas: http://www.uwm.edu/Dept/Clacs/outreach_americas.html • Asian Pacific American: http://www.apalaweb.org/awards/literature-awards/ • Coretta Scott King: https://www.ala.org/rt/emiert/cskbookawards • John Steptoe: https://www.ala.org/rt/emiert/cskbookawards/johnsteptoe • Púra Belpré: https://www.ala.org/alsc/awardsgrants/bookmedia/belpre • Tomás Rivera: https://www.education.txstate.edu/ci/riverabookaward/ • Schneider Family: http://www.ala.org/awardsgrants/schneider-family-book-award • Stonewall: http://www.ala.org/rt/glbtrt/award/stonewall/honored
Publishers	• Arte Público Press: https://artepublicopress.com (@artepublico) • Birchbark Books: https://birchbarkbooks.com (@birchbarkbooks) • HighWater Press: https://www.portageandmainpress.com/highwater-press/ (@PortageMainPres) • Lee & Low Publishers: https://www.leeandlow.com (@LEEandLOW) • Oyate: http://www.oyate.org
Organizations	• Cooperative Children's Book Center: https://ccbc.education.wisc.edu • Disrupt Texts: https://disrupttexts.org (@DisruptTexts) • Latinxs in Kid Lit: https://latinosinkidlit.com (@LatinosInKidLit) • Teaching for Change: http://www.tfcbooks.org (@teachingchange) • We Need Diverse Books: http://weneeddiversebooks.org (@diversebooks) • American Indians in Children's Literature https://americanindiansinchildrensliterature.blogspot.com

whereas social media can provide updates of new titles, authors, and ideas. We also hope that this text provides a plethora of ideas for inclusive texts, as well as examples of ways to center these texts in the curriculum to elevate students' identities and springboard learning by tapping into background knowledge. Nonetheless, there is no way to include all texts, nor can we represent all children in all classrooms. Throughout this text, we draw from our work in classrooms to detail how exemplar teachers select and use inclusive texts that start with their students. We recognize that no two classrooms are the same, and the examples may not directly align with your students. But all examples connect and show the IT framework in action, which starts with students and facilitates application in any context. We recommend returning to this chapter to ground the application of inclusive texts in response to your students.

THE FRAMEWORK IN ACTION: STARTING WITH STUDENTS

As we talk about prioritizing your unique learners, we recognize that starting with students is not a new concept. This student-centered approach drives the practice of many teachers who aim to nurture children as readers and inquirers. Nonetheless, the educational institution deters from this practice by relying on standardized tests normed with White, English-dominant, middle-class students without disabilities and ascribing static labels that seek to simplify the heterogeneity of classrooms. Assumptions, biases, and deficit-based perceptions about BIPOC children emerge from these institutional structures, which unknowingly influence teachers' mindsets, expectations, and decisions about instruction. We need to explore the complexity of identities and experiences to connect learners to texts that reflect, challenge, and engage.

Think for a moment about the labels used in your school community. Educators often hear terms like *struggling reader*, *reluctant learner*, *limited English proficient,* or *behavior issue*. These deficit-based labels might unknowingly limit perceptions of students, their funds of knowledge, and the range of their abilities and strengths. Additionally, misperceptions might emerge from labels that mask diversity among children. For example, the demographic label of *Hispanic*, or the related term of *Latinx*, homogenizes students spanning countries of origin (e.g., Mexico, Puerto Rico, Argentina) and languages (e.g., Spanish, English, Indigenous languages), in addition to other identities like family structures, circumstances and generation of immigration, gender identity, and beyond. To combat deficit-based and simplified labels, we want to deconstruct them to get to know students' identities and experiences through more nuanced data collection beyond formal testing measures. Standardized tests or language proficiency scores do not tell us a child's cultural background knowledge, rich language practices, affinities for certain topics, preferences and needs as readers, or so much more.

In addition to disrupting labels and biases about students, educators need to disrupt the canon to seek out relevant and authentic texts for students. The seemingly straightforward activity of text selection has deeper ideological underpinnings that need to be recognized and negotiated. We are all influenced by the canon, tending toward books we read as children or those inherited on the shelves of classroom libraries. Even if others frame texts as *must-reads*, we must remind ourselves that there are no must-read texts, and many of these texts are steeped in racism, sexism, heteronormativity, and other longstanding ideologies that maintain the status quo (Borsheim-Black et al., 2014; Huyck & Dahlen, 2019). When we get to know our students, we use their identities and experiences to drive our text selection, opening doors to new titles, authors, and illustrators that may diverge from those historically used in classrooms.

As you begin to think about using inclusive texts in classrooms, start by deconstructing perceptions of your students and the resources that they bring to the classrooms, as well as how that influences the texts and materials that you use in daily instruction. Continue to be mindful of any potential assumptions or biases as you engage in the activities described in the chapter. Begin to collect rich data through conversations, dialogue journals, and community walks, all while challenging yourself to focus on children's identities and experiences as resources for reading and learning. Explore new titles for your classroom collection on award, organization, and publisher websites, while allowing yourself to tackle any emergent thoughts regarding what can or should be read in the elementary classroom.

Remember that our mindsets as practitioners often stem from the educational institution. The system prioritizes standardized testing data, gives children static and homogenizing labels, and centers instructional decision-making around those test-informed labels. Because teachers work within that system every day, these structures may unknowingly influence assumptions about students or biases about text usage. We all make assumptions and hold biases, so use this book and related conversations to thoughtfully confront these on the path to implement inclusive texts in meaningful and authentic ways for the students in your classroom. In the upcoming chapter, we continue to explore how to maintain focus on children during text selection while also embracing your agency to make curricular decisions.

QUESTIONS AND ACTIVITIES FOR PROFESSIONAL DEVELOPMENT

1. Inclusive text selection and usage should emerge from the multifaceted identities and experiences of students. Take some time to reflect: Who are my students? What are my students' stories and

lived experiences? What identity facets emerge as poignant to reflect in text selection? These initial reflections may prompt the need for additional data collection, looking at both formal data (e.g., home language survey) and anecdotal data (e.g., conversations with students). Discuss findings with your teaching team to ground and frame the selection and use of texts.

2. Primary and middle-grade classrooms often have classroom libraries for students to access texts for reading at home and school. Your classroom library is an excellent place to begin analysis of the relevance and authenticity of texts readily available to your students. Consider the following questions as you explore: Does your collection authentically reflect students' identities and experiences? What percentage of texts feature BIPOC characters, as well as LGBTQ students or children with disabilities? Do texts tend to fall into the category of culturally neutral, generic, or specific? Do you see trends in the identities and backgrounds of authors and illustrators? Share your findings with your teaching team.

3. Define your goals for procuring inclusive texts for your classroom. You might begin with the gaps in your current collection in relation to your students. Do you need more books reflecting particular identities or experiences? Do you need particular genres of inclusive texts to use more broadly across the curriculum? Based on these goals, start your wish list of texts and add as you read the remainder of this text. Begin the list by exploring websites listed in Table 2.6, such as publishers (e.g., Lee & Low), awards (e.g., Pura Belpré), and organizations (e.g., We Need Diverse Books). Note titles that correspond to your goals. Upon completion, be sure to forward this list to your administrator or librarian to potentially secure these texts for your classroom collection.

CHAPTER 3

Connecting Texts With Learning Goals

Standards and Curricula

The fields in the valleys were now filled with office towers. The whole mountain was covered with houses. The main road became a highway. There were only a few trees and not one flower.

The children had nowhere to play.

—From *The Streets Are Free* (Kurusa, 1995, p. 10)

In the previous chapter, we asserted the need to consider students' identities and experiences to initiate selection of inclusive texts in classroom instruction. After digging into learning about students' funds of knowledge, lived experiences, and multiple identities, we shift to probing the learning goals that drive daily work with students, particularly the standards, curricula, and objectives that shape instructional planning. Like the sprawling Venezuelan city depicted in the opening quote, classrooms have become increasingly overloaded with mandates that usurp instructional time. The goal is to find spaces for children to flourish.

Decision-making around instruction in public schools has long been influenced by policies, standards, and dominant ideologies (Edmondson, 2004; Papola-Ellis, 2014). Often teachers' autonomy comes into question when other stakeholders make top-down decisions about instruction, such as mandating generalized standards or heavily scripted curricula. In many U.S. schools, state policymakers have predetermined which standards teachers must use to design instruction, and district administrators have selected and procured related curricula for literacy and content-area instruction. But standardization defaults to the status quo, with goals and resources shaped around the so-called mainstream student: White and English-dominant without disabilities. In this way, standards and standardized curricula do not factor in the unique identities and experiences of students (Demko, 2010). Standards also do not consistently approach instruction with a critical lens to develop holistic, empathetic, and socially conscious children (Milner, 2013). For these reasons, an imperative step in the Inclusive Texts

(IT) framework is critically analyzing standards and curricula to define your own learning goals that ultimately shape your text selection and implementation in the classroom with students.

In this chapter, we flesh out considerations to interrogate the standards, curricula, and learning goals that shape your instruction (Gay, 2018; Harste et al., 2000; Luke & Freebody, 1997; Muhammad, 2020). This involves first examining assumptions, stereotypes, and problematic issues that may be present in external documents and then accounting for those shortcomings by defining your own objectives for lessons and units (Burke & Collier, 2017). When doing so, you may discover the perpetuation of dominant narratives within texts, resources, and approaches to instruction, with many of your students' identities and experiences being underrepresented or completely erased (Milner, 2013). This second IT framework component provokes (a) asking who is privileged by curricula, (b) examining standards and materials for bias, (c) exploring the presentation of sociopolitical issues and diverse identities, and (d) considering ways to disrupt the oft evident status quo (Lewison et al., 2002).

As we probe standards and curricula, it is essential to remember that these critical analyses should occur at the classroom level. There is no one curriculum to serve as *the* curriculum for all students in all classrooms. As you read in the previous chapter, starting with students and communities means that instruction in every classroom looks different because of the rich and nuanced learners in those settings (Herrera, 2016; Moll et al., 1992). By analyzing school curricula, district policies, and state standards, you select and integrate inclusive texts grounded in the identities of your unique students and aligned to critically minded and strategically drafted learning goals. The purpose of this chapter is to support you in questioning policies, curricula, and standards to mindfully draft goals to guide your use of inclusive texts. Amid the urban sprawl of San José, Venezuela, described in the opening quote, a librarian supported a group of children in advocating local lawmakers to turn a vacant lot into a park so they had space to play. In sum, it only takes one committed educator to listen, respond, elevate, and prioritize children despite structural and institutional challenges, subsequently changing their daily experiences and overall well-being.

ANALYZING STANDARDS AND CURRICULA

In this section, we analyze the most prevalent standards in the context of the United States: the Common Core Standards. In U.S. classrooms spanning K–12 settings, these standards guide both literacy and math instruction, where teachers typically use them to shape the trajectory of instruction. While some readers may not teach in contexts that utilize the Common Core, the same lens can be taken to critically situate text selection and usage in classrooms with other sets of standards. We also examine science and social studies standards, as well as curricula and resources that often shape teachers' instructional decision-making.

Standards

Since 2009, the Common Core has become the largest influencer on what is taught in language and literacy blocks across schools in at least 40 states (NGA & CCSSO, 2010b). With these standards, state and national stakeholders have attempted to define the skills and knowledge that students should master at each grade level in English language arts (ELA) and mathematics. Despite their reach and importance in today's classrooms, it is integral to remember that these standards, as well as other standards, are *not* the curriculum. Borrowing an analogy from Grant Wiggins and Jay McTighe (2011), standards are the ingredient lists for a meal, but teachers determine the recipe. The ingredients of the Common Core center on 10 *anchor standards* that spiral across grade levels, with elaborations within each grade level to guide instructional design. Additionally, Common Core authors include several appendixes and supplemental resources, which aim to offer additional guidance to teachers and administrators.

The anchor standards for reading focus on the skills and strategies deemed necessary to become a proficient and competent reader. While seemingly dictating specific types of reading skills, teachers can, and should, critically interpret standards. For example, the third anchor reading standard states, "Analyze how and why individuals, events, or ideas develop and interact over the course of a text" (NGA & CCSSO, 2010b, p. 10). Whereas this standard guides the instructional focus, teachers get to select focal texts that make the most sense for students. By using texts centering on a range of identities, students analyze *how* those identities shape the way characters interact or how events unfold in a story. Consider how this interpretation of a standard could be used to support students with deep, meaningful interactions with a book like *Blended* (Draper, 2018), where the protagonist is navigating intersectional identities of being biracial and the child of divorce, as well as experiencing racial violence in her community. Instead of focusing only on how a character evolves over time, students consider how the intersection of the character's identities causes interactions and evolution across events throughout the storyline.

Teachers can also interpret standards in ways that enhance students' critical thinking and social consciousness. For example, one integral component of critical literacy lies in analyzing texts to determine the author's agenda (Luke & Freebody, 1997). While this critical lens might not be articulated in the Common Core, teachers' interpretations of existing standards can emphasize this with learners. For example, a 5th-grade literature standard states, "Describe how a narrator's or speaker's point of view influences how events are described" (NGA & CCSSO, 2010b, p. 12). A traditional way to approach this standard is with fractured fairy tales told from perspectives of different characters, such as *The True Story of the Three Little Pigs* prioritizing the wolf's viewpoint (Scieszka, 1989). But teachers could instead use texts that provoke in-depth understandings of a focal social issue, such as police violence and racial injustice, like in *Something Happened in Our Town* (Celano, 2019). In line with the standard, middle-grade students could analyze word choice in news headlines about the same topic to determine how the author positions readers to think or feel. This then applies to topic-specific picture books and novels, as readers consider factors like the background and identities of authors and illustrators and how those impact the way events and characters are framed within texts.

Supplemental Resources to Literacy Standards. In addition to the standards themselves, teachers can look critically at accompanying supplemental resources. Among these is the *Publisher's Criteria*, which aims to guide publishing companies and curriculum creators in aligning resources and materials with the standards (Coleman & Pimentel, 2012). Despite the document's authors stating that their intention was not to dictate instructional practice, this singular interpretation of the standards has led many school districts to take similar approaches. The document outlines criteria to select texts, including text complexity and genre, specifically calling for more informational texts. At only one point in the document do authors connect to students, briefly mentioning the use of "classic myths and stories, including works representing diverse cultures" (Coleman & Pimentel, 2012, p. 6). Not only does the use of the term "classics" clearly emphasize the canon, but the sole mention of "diverse cultures" in the document demonstrates that children's multifaceted identities and experiences are not the main criteria suggested for selecting texts for literacy instruction. Educators and curricular decision-makers must recognize the shortcomings of these criteria and ensure that students' identities are kept high on the priority list when selecting resources for instruction.

Another commonly referenced resource to the standards lies in the recommended text exemplar list in Appendix B of the Common Core (NGA & CCSSO, 2010a). In this supplemental resource, the authors provide a list of suggested texts for districts to procure and teachers to use in daily instruction. This document asserts that listed texts "exemplify the level of complexity and quality that the Standards require all students in a given grade band to engage with." It further states that "they are suggestive of the breadth of texts that students should encounter in the text types required by the Standards" (NGA & CCSSO, 2010a, p. 2). Upon release of the standards, many schools and districts rushed to purchase large quantities of these highlighted texts, as state leaders, school boards, and other stakeholders pushed local educators and administrators to immediately align practice with the Common Core. As a result, many teachers continue to use these texts to mediate instruction, understandably tapping into resources available to them.

While not required readings, districts might encourage use of these texts because of their presence within Common Core documentation.

The continued reliance on this static and outdated text list is problematic, as many texts within the list of exemplars do not reflect the rich cultural and linguistic diversity of students in today's classrooms (Boyd, 2012). Various scholars have problematized the list, calling attention to the imperative for local educators to select their own texts to mediate instruction. Gomez-Najarro (2020) has explored the Common Core exemplar texts for 2nd and 3rd grades; of the 20 listed fictional texts, 10 had animals as protagonists, 17 had male protagonists, and only three had BIPOC protagonists. Boyd, Causey, and Galda (2015) have engaged in similar analysis of exemplar texts for 4th and 5th grades, finding some representation of BIPOC authors and characters, but most authors and characters representing White and other dominant identities. In this way, we see why criticality emerges as pertinent to consider who is included and who is missing, specifically with a lens on the children in your classroom. Teachers should not rely heavily on these recommended exemplars when seeking texts for instruction, but rather start with students to determine how to tap into and portray rich identities and experiences.

In addition to not reflecting the diversity of U.S. classrooms, the recommended text list demonstrates strong rooting in the literary canon, driving what is considered valued reading in classrooms (Boyd, 2012). Many texts are so-called classics, including outdated titles that lack relevance to today's students (Moss, 2013). Several of these classical texts are also considered problematic in the field of children's literature, such as *Little House in the Big Woods* (Wilder, 1932). This text is the first in the *Little House* series, a series that is now recognized as featuring overt and unchallenged racism against Black and Indigenous people. A selection from *The Secret Garden* (Burnett, 1911/1985) is recommended for middle grades, despite the larger text containing explicitly harmful discourse to Black children. Additionally, White authors and protagonists typify many texts on the list. Unquestioningly using these texts can cause harm to students by perpetuating stereotypes, erasing identities, and using racist and sexist language without the provided space to disrupt and dismantle together with teachers.

Science Standards. Analyzing content standards also yields spaces to integrate inclusive texts to enhance learning. The Next Generation Science Standards (NGSS) focus on three dimensions of science learning: (a) the practices of scientists and engineers inquiring and engaging in work in the natural world; (b) disciplinary core ideas in physical science, life science, earth and space science, and engineering; and (c) cross-cutting concepts that connect the four disciplines to develop coherent views of the world around them (NGSS Lead States, 2013). By probing the standards, you might see logical places to bring in trade books to enrich children's exploration. For example, picture-book biographies provide excellent windows into practices in the field and can simultaneously disrupt children's potentially limited perceptions of scientists. For example, books like *The Girl With a Mind for Math: The Story of Raye Montague* (Mosca, 2018) and *The Girl Who Thought in Pictures: The Story of Dr. Temple Grandin* (Mosca, 2017) illustrate the practices of female and BIPOC scientists with disabilities. By reading and discussing texts in response to the students in the classroom, children see the real-world practices of scientists as aligned to the standards while also seeing mirrors of possibilities into future careers and actions.

Bringing diverse voices and perspectives into science instruction aligns with the NGSS approach, which bolsters teachers' case for inclusive texts in the curriculum. In Appendix D of the NGSS Standards, titled *All Standards, All Students* (NGSS Lead States, 2013), authors discuss the application of standards with underrepresented populations. This document references privileged groups (e.g., White, English-dominant, middle- to upper-class) traditionally having higher expectations from teachers in the sciences than nondominant groups (e.g., BIPOC students). NGSS sets the expectation that all students have equitable scientific learning opportunities and recommends instructional strategies to support traditionally marginalized groups, such as using learners' funds of knowledge (Moll et al., 1992). By analyzing these supplemental documents in addition to the standards, teachers often find spaces and rationales for engaging in this important work.

NGSS also promotes inquiry and action by applying scientific ideas to sociopolitical issues, equity, and inclusion of a range of identities. Aligned to the NGSS disciplinary core idea on ecosystem dynamics, functioning, and resilience (NGSS LS2.C), 3rd-through 5th-graders explore interdependent relationships and ecosystems, specifically the environmental impact on organisms. The biographical picture book *The Boy Who Grew a Forest: The True Story of Jadav Payeng* (Gholz, 2019) provides children with a real-world example. The text follows a young boy who notices environmental impacts on animals in his local community in India. In the story, Jadav plants trees to help reverse the negative environmental effects and creates a watering system resulting in richer soil, eventually seeing the population of animals increase. Before, during, and after the interactive read-aloud, children can make and refine claims about the merits of Jadav's solutions to this environmental problem (NGSS 3-LS4-4). In this way, the text supports students in thinking about climate justice issues from a global perspective and provides space for them to apply the standards with a sociopolitical lens.

Social Studies Standards. Educators use the College, Career, and Civic Life (3C) Social Studies standards with greater frequency in schools. National leaders in social studies education created these standards in 2013 to align to Common Core and enhance classroom instruction. The four dimensions of the standards seek for children to (a) develop questions and plan inquiries, (b) apply disciplinary concepts and tools, (c) evaluate sources and use evidence, and (d) communicate conclusions and take informed action (National Council for the Social Studies [NCSS], 2013). This inquiry- and action-focused approach aligns with our efforts to promote sociocultural and critical consciousness resulting in action in communities and society (Ladson-Billings, 1995; Lucas & Villegas, 2013). When teachers approach social studies instruction with these standards, inclusive texts play a central role in critically probing social issues, identities, and diverse perspectives.

Inclusive texts also prompt critical lenses on topics spanning the four disciplines of social studies: civics, economics, geography, and history (NCSS, 2013). In civics, trade books offer multiple perspectives on what constitutes good citizenship beyond basic textbook definitions (e.g., *What Can a Citizen Do?*; Eggers, 2018). In economics, the text *A Bike Like Sergio's* (Boelts, 2018) supports ideas around financial decision-making, using the protagonist's dilemma around spending one hundred dollars. In geography, teachers can support critical literacy with maps by discussing Indigenous land acknowledgments alongside the trade book *We Are Still Here! Native American Truths Everyone Should Know* (Sorell, 2021). In history, inclusive texts mediate learning on topics that textbooks often neglect, such as the Japanese American internment camps during World War II. The picture book *Fish for Jimmy* (Yamasaki, 2019) offers a child's perspective on these camps, which prompts children's critical exploration of American history through an inclusive text.

Even if your school does not use the Common Core, Next Generation, or 3C Standards, this critical lens applies to any set of standards. Teachers should look within standards for ways to center students' voices and identities in their instruction. Remember that the standards are *not* the curriculum. While they provide the ingredients (e.g., knowledge and skills students acquire in your grade level), only you as the expert teacher get to define the recipe to achieve the final meal (Wiggins & McTighe, 2011). You know your students, and after critical interrogation of the standards, you define learning goals and design instruction that builds from the rich identities and experiences that your unique students bring to the classroom. In the next section, we probe how curricula might influence your decisions for text selection and usage in the IT framework.

Curricula

After looking at standards, the next place to turn a critical lens is curricula. While many teachers have autonomy to design instruction using their choice of texts and materials, others have decisions regarding curriculum made for them by school or district administrators. For example, some teachers must teach from prepackaged curricula, such as Harcourt Trophies for reading, Lucy Calkins's Units of Study in writing, McGraw Hill for social studies, or Eureka Math for mathematics. While these curricula provide teachers with resources and guidance for classroom implementation, they do not serve as hard-and-fast scripts that teachers must follow to the letter. All teachers have agency and make decisions within their curricula to serve the best interests of students (Pardo, Highfield, & Florio-Ruane, 2011).

Despite strides over the decades to enhance inclusive representation, canned curricula cannot be responsive by their very nature, since every classroom is full of richly unique children. In other words, the authors of the curriculum guides that you use in your classroom do not know *your* students. They are likely experts in their respective fields of literacy, math, social studies, or science education, with sound knowledge of the related standards and age-appropriateness of certain tasks and texts. But only you are the local expert who knows the most important piece of the puzzle—the rich identities, experiences, and learning dimensions of the children who sit in front of you every day (Collier & Thomas, 2007; Crenshaw, 1991; Herrera, 2016; Moll et al., 1992). To provide instruction that sustains and promotes the learning of your students, embrace and use that expertise to supplement texts and materials that reflect your students.

Canned curricula also typically lack a lens on critical literacy. Programs aim to develop students' knowledge and skills in line with standards but may not push students to think critically about the world around them. Programs in the area of reading, commonly referred to as *basal readers*, often focus heavily on reading skills without promoting and tapping into the identities and experiences reflected within the stories (Demko, 2010). In this way, students use basals by reading the provided stories and then engaging in prepackaged activities, which may prompt them to use context clues to determine the meaning of vocabulary terms or break down words with base words, prefixes, and suffixes. When skills monopolize instruction, learners do not get the encouragement to go deeper—to disrupt the status quo, explore sociopolitical issues, take multiple perspectives, and recognize issues of power (Dresser, 2012; Stevens & Bean, 2007).

Whether you and your colleagues plan your own curriculum, such as through a process like Understanding by Design (UbD; Wiggins & McTighe, 2005), or you have predefined curricula, taking a critical lens on texts and materials is an integral step. For literacy curricula, take the time to analyze the stories, protagonists, and authors in texts and materials. Who do your students see on the pages of the reading series? What identities are considered valuable enough to be included in the stories? For disciplinary curricula, consider the lens through which the authors present the content. Is there a single story told in social studies, science, and mathematics? Or does the curriculum allow for multiple perspectives, a diversity of voices and figures, and spaces for critical conversations around social issues? These reflections provide a valuable starting place to determine where and how to incorporate inclusive texts in response to the unique learners in your classroom.

Table 3.1 provides prompts to guide curricular analysis. If you plan instruction with others on a grade-level or departmental team, we recommend

Table 3.1. Analysis Tool for Classroom Curricula

Prompts to Analyze Curriculum	Rating
Organized around facets of the Inclusive Texts framework	*5 = agree; 1 = disagree*
Framework Facet 1: *Getting to Know Children's Storied Lives*	
• Texts and resources are relevant to students' lives and allow for personal, cultural, and linguistic connections.	5 4 3 2 1
• Texts and resources authentically portray the nuances of children, families, and communities.	5 4 3 2 1
• Texts and resources serve as mirrors to the students in my classroom in multifaceted ways.	5 4 3 2 1
• Texts and resources serve as windows to expand and challenge my students' perspectives.	5 4 3 2 1
Framework Facet 2: *Probing Established Goals and Curricula*	
• I actively interpret the required standards in a way that best supports my students' learning.	5 4 3 2 1
• My curriculum presents multiple perspectives on the events and experiences, including those from BIPOC communities.	5 4 3 2 1
• My curriculum connects learning goals to sociopolitical issues that impact students' lives.	5 4 3 2 1
• I define learning objectives for my students that incorporate aspects of their identities and elements of critical literacy in connection to academic skills and strategies.	5 4 3 2 1
Framework Facet 3: *Selecting High-Quality and Authentic Texts*	
• Authors and illustrators are members of the identity groups about which they write.	5 4 3 2 1
• Stories feature different identities, including cultures, languages, abilities, citizenship status, gender, orientation, socioeconomic status, family structures, and religions.	5 4 3 2 1
• Characters and storylines demonstrate rich nuance, avoiding stereotypes and ambiguity across cultures and identities.	5 4 3 2 1
• BIPOC, LGBTQ individuals, and individuals with disabilities are main characters, not just side characters.	5 4 3 2 1
• Problems faced by BIPOC, females, or individuals with disabilities are not resolved through problem solving or rescuing by White, male individuals without disabilities.	5 4 3 2 1
Framework Facet 4: *Integrating Texts to Support Learning Goals*	
• Inclusive texts are a consistent feature across the curriculum, beyond read-alouds and independent reading.	5 4 3 2 1
• Inclusive texts serve as seed ideas for students to flexibly connect, make meaning, and tell their own stories.	5 4 3 2 1
• Inclusive texts pair with instructional strategies to facilitate learning and (bi)literacy development.	5 4 3 2 1
• Inclusive texts are featured in individual lessons, as well as incorporated across larger units of study.	5 4 3 2 1
• Across the curriculum, inclusive texts portray a wide array of identities and experiences through various genres.	5 4 3 2 1

collectively analyzing your curriculum, as more voices and perspectives—shaped by our own identities and experiences—enrich the findings and discussions. Whether embarking upon this analysis individually or collaboratively, select the best grain size to start, whether one component of the curriculum (e.g., one theme or unit in a reading basal) or the holistic curriculum spanning multiple units. Use the prompts, organized around the four facets of the IT framework, to guide your critical analysis and discussion. First, consider the reflections of your students in the curriculum, including their identities, experiences, perspectives, and languages. Second, explore how existing tools influence learning goals and materials. Third, critique texts for relevance and authenticity, ensuring inclusivity of a wide array of identities. Fourth, consider how texts mediate children's literacies, identities, and understandings. Ultimately, this critical analysis should indicate areas where your curriculum might benefit from the incorporation of inclusive texts.

Let's return to Anne's middle-grade classroom, which we introduced in the previous chapter. At her diverse suburban elementary school, administrators have purchased curricula for teachers, including the Journeys Reading Program from Houghton Mifflin. But Anne's principal, Courtney, has made it clear to her teachers that the program should be used as a resource for their own instructional planning. Courtney encourages teachers to design units that incorporate authentic texts, a charge that Anne embraces with open arms. She and her colleagues organize instruction into four eight-week units of study: Discovering Our Identities, Faces of Immigration, Equal Rights for All, and Unsung Heroes. These units center on texts that reflect the multifaceted identities and experiences, as well as promote critical literacy among learners.

Take, for example, her use of a children's biography picture book about Christopher Columbus. Students read online book reviews and challenged the biases present in those reviews. They pushed back on the author and publisher, questioning the single narrative and exclusion of Indigenous voices. Following this, Anne shared the book *Encounter* (Yolen, 1996), a picture book often used as a counternarrative attempting to center the perspective of a Taíno child. But this book has been criticized for language and inaccurate messages, such as the statement that all Taíno people have perished. Using their critical lens developed across the school year, students (a) challenged the language, (b) pondered the influence of a White author instead of an Indigenous author, and (c) questioned the research process used to create the text. Through her strategic decisions about curricular materials, students developed the critical lens to interrogate texts for bias, power, privilege, and inclusivity.

Not all teachers have such flexibility to design units of study while leaving expensive curricular materials on the shelf. Felisha is a middle-grade teacher who works within her reading curriculum to fill gaps in representation for her students. When her district purchased a new reading curriculum for all elementary classrooms, she recognized that texts and materials did not reflect her learners' identities and experiences. At a school with 42% Black, 31% Latinx, 14% White, 8% multiracial, and 4% Asian, with 15% multilingual learners and 54% students considered low-income, Felisha felt that her curriculum represented White children but lacked Black and immigrant voices. Being cognizant of voices included and excluded in curricular materials, Felisha made strategic decisions to supplement the curriculum with inclusive texts. In this way, she used the provided materials to teach the required curriculum but supplemented with other resources throughout the literacy block.

This critical analysis of materials also applies to classroom libraries. We like to use the *Culturally Responsive Curriculum Scorecard* (Bryan-Gooden, Hester, & Peoples, 2019) from the Metropolitan Center for Research on Equity and the Transformation of Schools at New York University. For example, one tool prompts teachers to tally characters and authors represented in classroom collections by gender identity (i.e., male, female, nonbinary) and demographic groups, including Asian/Pacific Islander, Black/African, Indigenous, Latinx, Multiracial, White, nonhuman characters, LGBTQ, and individuals with disabilities (p. 9). This tallying of books often results in poignant findings regarding whose voices and stories dominate the classroom library, as well as those lacking or excluded. For teachers who design their own curricula and draw from available texts and materials, this approach helps probe the inclusivity of resources.

Anna, a middle-grade, Spanish-English dual-language teacher, discovered that her library had a plethora of texts reflecting the identities of Latinx students. Working at a dual-language school and welcoming half of her students from Spanish-speaking homes, she felt strongly about the mirror texts for her children who identified largely as Mexican American and Puerto Rican. But in her analysis of materials, Anna noted the lack of books representing other cultural and racial groups, especially books capturing Black voices. She recognized the need to explicitly build a more inclusive collection to provide students with a rich array of voices and stories—both to read in the classroom library and to incorporate into her instructional design.

While looking for resources to supplement curricula, we urge caution when using popular online and social-media resources, including sites where people pin ideas or websites where teachers pay for access to lessons and materials. These sites do not have measures in place to ensure the quality or research-based nature of materials, and instructional ideas come from anyone with access. Quick searches for certain topics, such as Native Americans or civil rights, often bring up lessons and images that perpetuate stereotypes, share inaccurate or overgeneralized information, and omit essential voices and perspectives. The authors also do not know your students, which means that the activities likely do not respond to their identities, experiences, and perspectives. Like the analyses of other curricular materials described above, practitioners should exercise criticality if they browse these sites. We want teachers to embrace their agency to make instructional decisions in the best interests of students in their classrooms and communities, which requires their expertise in the selection and implementation of materials.

USING LEARNING GOALS TO FRAME TEXT SELECTION

Critically analyzing standards and curricula is an integral step to determining how inclusive texts can enrich instruction. Just as we want to prepare students as critical consumers of texts and information, we as educators want to approach the tools given to us with healthy skepticism and thoughtful inquiry to ensure use in appropriate ways with children. But remember that both standards and predefined curricula should serve as guideposts and suggestions, with the expert teacher making the informed decisions about best practice for each unique setting. Instructional planning should begin with practitioners defining learning goals for students and then determining the trajectory to support learners in reaching those goals (Wiggins & McTighe, 2005). Numerous factors shape how teachers define learning goals, including grade- and content-specific standards, language objectives by multilingual learners' proficiency levels, social and emotional learning foci, and other student-specific supports. These goals or objectives subsequently inform decisions about the texts teachers use for instruction.

Within the IT framework, we see defining learning goals as a critical step in instructional design aiming to elevate the traditionally marginalized voices and perspectives in literacy and disciplinary curricula. For us, it is not just about getting high-quality texts reflecting multifaceted identities and experiences in the hands of children for independent reading. We want to see inclusive texts as one of the centerpieces of instruction, where students have a multitude of mirrors and windows to learn about and through across the school day and year (Sims Bishop, 1990). To accomplish this in the standards- and objective-driven context of schools today, the use of inclusive texts must be aligned to the learning goals driving instruction. These learning objectives should include developing strong cultural identities, connecting with experiences of characters and communities in texts, and interrogating issues and power structures in the world around them (Alim & Paris, 2018; Ladson-Billings, 1995; Moje, 2007).

Think about the learning goals that you set for your students, whether yearlong goals, unit-level goals, or lesson-level objectives. Consider what shapes these goals, such as grade-level standards or the curriculum for a given content area. Now, returning to the first component of the IT framework, ponder how those goals could expand in response to your unique students. Ask yourself what understandings, knowledge, and skills are most meaningful and relevant to your students, not just what is required to learn per standards. Remember our discussion above about how standards often focus on discrete skills rather than the rich identities and critical lenses that we seek to develop in children. Embrace your agency as an expert practitioner to use standards as a guidepost, but draft related learning objectives to open the potential for instruction that sustains students' rich assets and develops critical literacy and social consciousness.

While reflecting on what shapes your learning goals, think about how texts might serve as a medium to reach those goals. High-quality, inclusive texts foster learning and allow for more expansive goals outside of what standards or curricula suggest. For instance, if a teacher relies solely on the textbook to teach social studies without considering multiple perspectives offered by trade books and multimedia resources, this leads to narrowed understandings (McLaughlin & DeVoogd, 2018; Stillman & Anderson, 2011). The texts that you choose for instruction enhance and create opportunities for learning goals that lead to increased understanding not just about the content, but about the world and experiences of others (Colwell, 2019). Building awareness of inclusive texts available to use in instruction piques additional ways to expand learning goals. In this way, learning goals and inclusive texts become mutually beneficial; enhanced learning goals beyond the standards open the potential to use of inclusive texts; and the knowledge of the vast array of incredible titles and authors shape enhancement of future learning goals.

Let's head back to Anne's middle-grade classroom for an example of how learning goals and inclusive texts work hand-in-hand. Table 3.2 shows an example of one of the four thematic units that Anne and her team design to integrate literacy, language development, and disciplinary learning centered on justice-oriented themes. In this unit, Anne lists the focal standards for the unit, including reading, writing, language-arts, and content-area standards, which shape curricular decisions regarding discussion topics (e.g., geographical influences on identity), text selections (e.g., personal narratives), and instructional tasks (e.g., comparing window and mirror texts). In addition to standards, Anne poses essential questions to frame the unit: *How do people see themselves? What shapes identity? Does identity change?* These open-ended, thought-provoking questions seek to deepen learners' understandings of identity as they grapple with big ideas across the unit (Wiggins & McTighe, 2005). Teachers then select a range of thematically aligned inclusive texts to provoke inquiry, interaction, and engagement across the unit of study.

Standards and Texts

As we described earlier in this chapter, careful and critical analysis of standards is an important step. This same critical lens applies when selecting texts to pair with those standards and learning goals. When using the

Table 3.2. Sample Unit of Study

Discovering Our Identities (8 weeks)		
Essential Questions	**Academic Language**	**Social Studies & Science**
How do people *see* themselves? What shapes identity? Does identity change?	Genre-specific text features and structures Terms: protagonist, antagonist, major/minor characters, plot, problem, theme, exposition, rising action, climax, falling action, resolution, traits, dialogue, identity, values	Earth's Place in the Universe (5-ESS1-1, 5-ESS1-2, 5-PS2-1) Unit 1—Geography and Indigenous People (SS.G.1.5, SS.H.3.5)
Reading Standards	**Writing Standards**	**Supporting ELA Standards**
RL 5.2—Theme/ Summary RL 5.5—Structure SL 5.1—Collaborative Discussions L 5.4—Vocabulary RL 5.3—Compare/ Contrast Characters, Settings	W 5.4—Clear and Coherent Writing W 5.3—Personal Narratives	RL.5.1 & RI.5.1— Quote, infer RL.5.9—Compare and contrast stories in the same genre RL.5.7—Analyze how visual and multimedia elements contribute to the meaning, tone, or beauty of a text
Texts for Read-Aloud & Shared Reading	**Texts for Book Clubs**	**Other Texts & Activities**
Garvey's Choice (Grimes, 2016) *I Am Every Good Thing* (Barnes, 2020) *Jacob's New Dress* (Hoffman, 2014) *Julián Is a Mermaid* (Love, 2018) *Marley Dias Interview* (video) *My Name Is Sangoel* (Williams & Mohammed, 2009) *Red: A Crayon's Story* (Hall, 2015) *Stella Brings the Family* (Schiffer, 2015) *When We Were Alone* (Robertson, 2016)	*Better Nate Than Ever* (Federle, 2018) *Booked* (Alexander, 2016) *Brown Girl Dreaming* (Woodson, 2016) *Fish in a Tree* (Hunt, 2017) *Out of My Mind* (Draper, 2012) *Smile* (Telgemeier, 2010) *Short* (Sloan, 2018) *Hello Universe* (Estrada Kelly, 2020a) *Lily and Dunkin* (Gephart, 2018) *Harbor Me* (Woodson, 2018) *Witch Boy* (Ostertag, 2018)	Think-Puzzle-Explore Color-Symbol-Image What Makes You Say That? Windows and Mirrors Unit Culmination & Celebration: Coat of Arms

Common Core for literacy instruction, think about the standards in connection to cognitive learning goals as well as goals related to critical literacy. By extending learning goals beyond basic skills required by the standards and moving toward deeper understandings and skills related to critical literacy, teachers create goals that (a) center multifaceted identities and experiences, (b) develop global-mindedness, (c) support socioemotional learning, and (d) chart learners' paths toward social justice and action. Table 3.3 provides examples of Common Core literacy standards with connections to possible learning goals and inclusive texts. This is meant to show how the standards offer opportunities for broader interpretation to learning goals that center on students, not just skills.

Content standards also provoke the drafting of learning goals that go beyond disciplinary knowledge and skills to provoke critical and expanded

Table 3.3. Examples of Connections Between Standards, Learning Goals, and Texts

Standard	Learning Goal	Critical Literacy Goal	Possible Texts
CCSS.ELA-LITERACY. CCRA.R.4 Interpret words and phrases as they are used in a text, including determining technical, connotative, and figurative meanings, and analyze how specific word choices shape meaning or tone.	Analyze text for meaning of figurative language.	Explain how the use of language positions the reader to think or feel a certain way.	*Black Is a Rainbow Color* (Joy, 2020)
CCSS.ELA-LITERACY. CCRA.R.9 Analyze how two or more texts address similar themes or topics in order to build knowledge or to compare the approaches the authors take.	Compare and contrast the themes of two texts.	Analyze how different perspectives on the same topic allow space for different identities and voices.	*The Cat Man of Aleppo* (Shamsi-Basha & Latham, 2020)
CCSS.ELA-LITERACY. CCRA.W.3 Write narratives to develop real or imagined experiences or events using effective technique, well-chosen details and well-structured event sequences.	Write a narrative with strong details and organization.	Write a narrative that highlights an event that is important to your own identity.	*I Dream of Popo* (Blackburne, 2021)

perspectives on society and the world. In science, one NGSS for 3rd through 5th grades call for students to "obtain and combine information to describe climates in different regions of the world" (NGSS 3-ESS2-2). Instead of relying on the information presented on the topic in the textbook, teachers could include trade books reflecting the climate and life in various parts of the world, such as *The Boy Who Harnessed the Wind* (Kamkwamba & Mealer, 2016), *Olinguito, From A to Z! Unveiling the Cloud Forest* (Delacre, 2016), and *One Plastic Bag: Isatou Ceesay and the Recycling Women of Gambia* (Paul, 2015). By doing so, instruction seeks not only to develop standards-related skills but to disrupt common stereotypes about different global regions, such as a singular image of the entire continent of Africa (Adichie, 2009).

Another example emerges when teaching about water supply and conservation. The NGSS for 3rd through 5th grade prompts students to "describe and graph the amounts of salt water and fresh water in various reservoirs to provide evidence about the distribution of water on Earth" (NGSS 5-ESS2-2). In addition to cognitive goals related to graphing or learning amounts of fresh water versus salt water, learning goals can extend to sociopolitical issues of water conservation. These goals would extend children's understandings beyond basic scientific facts and ideas, as well as open the potential for use of inclusive texts such as *The Water Princess* (Verde & Badiel, 2016), *All the Water in the World* (Lyon & Tillotson, 2011), and *We Are Water Protectors* (Lindstrom, 2020).

In social studies, teachers incorporate inclusive texts to broaden learning goals for students to interrogate multiple perspectives. For instance, primary and middle-grade standards both approach the topic of the purpose of rules and laws. In primary grades, children "explain the need for and purposes of rules in various settings inside and outside of school" (C3 Standards, D2.Civ.3.K-2). In middle grades, learners "examine the origins and purposes of rules, laws, and key U.S. constitutional provisions" (C3 Standards, D2.Civ.3.3–5). Teachers draft learning goals and subsequently select texts to broaden the conversation around the ways that identities, backgrounds, and communities shape how rules and laws affect individuals. This includes conversations about justice over compliance, with texts like *Sometimes People March* (Allen, 2020) or *No Voice Too Small: Fourteen Young Americans Making History* (Metcalf, 2020). In Chapter 6, we further explore the use of inclusive texts across the content areas.

Beyond the Standards

Looking outside of standards and required curricula to center students in the creation of learning goals presents challenges, given the traditional reliance on these tools. This challenging but invaluable work to extend beyond traditional academic standards and skill-based, White-washed curricula has been alleviated with Gholdy Muhammad's (2020) *historically responsive literacy framework*. Muhammad roots literacy learning in 19th-century Black literary societies, asserting that by beginning our instruction as Blackness-centered, we work toward equitable and empowering literacy instruction for all students. Muhammad outlines four layers: (a) identity development, (b) skill development, (c) intellectual development, and (d) criticality. This approach seeks to frame goals for literacy and content-area education in response to the current sociopolitical climate and diverse makeup of classrooms. This equity-based framework prompts teachers to look beyond and blend cognitive goals with critical literacy skills like understanding power in text and sense-making about students' own and others' identities.

Within this framework, Muhammad asks that instruction begin with students' identities for content to be relevant and engaging. In this way, goals for *identity development* enrich instruction from the beginning of unit or lesson design, ensuring focus on children's rich and storied lives and experiences. She includes the importance of *skill development*, which is often the basis of learning goals and interpretations of standards. But her layer of *intellectual development* pushes beyond basic skills to question the bigger picture of what we want learners to understand and how we want them to apply the new knowledge. *Criticality* supports recognizing power, privilege, and oppression, encouraging children as active consumers of text. Mirroring the tenets of culturally sustaining pedagogies (Alim & Paris, 2018) and critical literacy (Luke & Freebody, 1997) shared in Chapter 1, these multilayered objectives align with the goals of the IT framework in seeking to dynamically nurture children's literacies, identities, understandings, and criticality through strategically selected and incorporated texts.

We find that Muhammad's framework (2020) guides practitioners in extending learning goals beyond standards and curricula that often reinforce the White, English-dominant narrative in schools. Drafting multifaceted learning objectives beyond those centered on cognitive skills springboards the selection and use of a rich array of inclusive texts to nurture criticality, identities, skills, and intellectual development. Table 3.4 provides guiding questions and examples of these multilayered goals with the text *Under My Hijab* (Khan, 2019), which shows different women in a young girl's life who wear the hijab with their own style. By tapping into various resources and approaches, you can draft learning goals that respond to your students (IT Framework Facet 1) and set up the selection and use of high-quality inclusive texts (IT Framework Facets 3 and 4). In this way, children move beyond skills to develop personal connections to texts and think broadly about application to the wider world.

Table 3.4. Example of Multilayered Learning Goals

Focal Layer (Muhammad, 2020)	Questions & Prompts	Application to *Under My Hijab* (Khan, 2019)
Identity	• How does this text or topic connect to my students lived experiences and how they see themselves? This can connect to their cultural backgrounds, interests, future goals, or any aspect of how the students see themselves or others see them.	Students ask themselves how they express themselves with their hair or clothing.
Skills	• What skills do I want students to practice during this lesson? This is much like traditional goal-setting in many schools.	Students compare and contrast the different characters' hair and hijabs in the text.
Intellectualism	• What big ideas do you want students to understand about the topic? This pushes skills and into broader understandings, much like an essential question.	Students inquire into the tradition behind hijabs and why it is important in some cultures.
Criticality	• How does this help students recognize issues of power and privilege in texts and the world?	Students explore misconceptions surrounding hijabs or representation of Muslim characters in texts.

THE FRAMEWORK IN ACTION: ALIGNING TEXTS WITH GOALS

Whereas the IT framework centers on students, we also prioritize teachers' identities and agency in instructional decision-making. Teachers and other school-based practitioners, such as librarians, instructional coaches, and reading specialists, are experts in teaching, learning, and, most importantly, learners. These stakeholders (a) make decisions about the texts and resources needed to facilitate their students' learning, (b) disrupt traditional reliance on standards and curriculum to recognize them as solely guidance documents, and (c) use students' identities, experiences, and perspectives as the starting point of instructional design. We recognize that the top-down implementation of policies like the Common Core and other standards do not always situate the teacher as the active decision-maker as we do in this book; however, you ultimately set the goals and decide on the tools to help learners reach those goals. Embrace that agency and be confident in the expertise that you bring to those decisions.

We have found that confidence stems from expertise. Teachers are often more likely to exercise their agency and make decisions surrounding standards, curricula, and learning goals when they are deeply familiar with those documents and resources. You might begin by exploring the standards in more depth, taking a critical lens on who wrote them, with what process, for what purpose, and for which audience. You can take this same lens on any existing curricula, ensuring that you maintain the lens on your unique students. How do the children in your classroom see themselves in the curricular materials? In what ways does the curriculum support learners in developing identities, connecting to experiences, revealing perspectives, and deepening critical consciousness? The first step is to recognize these external documents as guideposts and resources for your informed decision-making, and the second step is to use your expertise to pinpoint the detriments of these existing tools to support your instructional design. This latter step also supports any advocacy and communication that you may need to do with instructional coaches or administrators who may question your straying from the curriculum. When you clearly define *why* you plan to supplement the curriculum, specifically in terms of student learning, others are likely to respect and endorse those changes.

In addition to shifting mindsets about who makes instructional decisions, we encourage personal reflection on what learning goals should drive classroom practice. Of course, your previous experiences, assumptions, and beliefs guide your teaching, potentially without you even realizing it. You may knowingly or unknowingly espouse a traditional view of schooling where children develop discrete literacy skills (e.g., phonics, sight words), complete math fast facts (i.e., timed drills of math operations), and memorize science terminology (e.g., parts of a flower). We encourage reflection and interrogation of what you see as the purpose of schooling, particularly in this 21st-century world marked by globalization, innovation, and collaboration, as well as racism, poverty, and violence. Instruction does not have to be limited to skills dictated by standards and curricula; instead, it can sustain children's identities and encourage dismantling inequities and accepting one another (Alim & Paris, 2018). Just as Anne expanded learning goals to incorporate critical literacy strategies or Felisha supplemented her curriculum with books reflecting children's identities, you can nurture inclusivity in your classroom.

After reflecting on your role in instructional decision-making and purpose of schooling, return to the tools, ideas, and examples presented in this chapter to begin to critique the standards, curricula, and learning goals used in your setting. You might use the evaluation tool to critically analyze your classroom curricula or explore the representation of different identities in your classroom library. While you might do this independently, consider bringing in your grade-level team or professional learning community to these activities. Having multiple perspectives and voices at the table bolsters the expertise shaping these decisions, as well as the justification for these curricular changes that may need to follow.

In upcoming chapters, we explore ways to align learning goals with high-quality, inclusive texts that serve as mirrors and windows to students. Inclusive texts can effectively mediate progress toward a multitude of goals, but not all achieve the same results, making mindful text selection based on lesson or unit goals key. For instance, one specific text might prompt identity exploration among some students, whereas another may promote broader discussions across students to build community. By maintaining goals in mind from the outset, teachers can select texts that both reflect students' identities and effectively support teaching and learning. The upcoming chapters look at the framework in action within your instruction, both in language and literacy and in the content areas.

QUESTIONS AND ACTIVITIES FOR PROFESSIONAL DEVELOPMENT

1. Look at the standards that guide your instruction. Select one that connects to text selection, and think about the way it is worded: Does the standard place value on a certain type of language or literacy experience? Does it narrow text options, or can you select the text? How does this standard allow for inclusivity within your text selection and literacy instruction?

2. With your teaching team, take a close look at required curricula for language arts and other disciplines. If you were a student learning from these materials, would you feel represented and included? Would you feel like you were learning about other perspectives and identities? Are different identities represented among authors or illustrators or within the contributors to the textbook? If not, how can you ensure a more inclusive curriculum? This might involve looking for supplemental materials or approaching administration to look at new curricula.

3. Look at an existing lesson or unit of study. What are the learning goals? Critically consider what shaped those learning goals (e.g., standards, scripted curriculum, students' abilities). Do your learning goals factor in students' identities, strengths, and background knowledge? What inclusive texts might support your unique students in reaching these learning goals?

CHAPTER 4

Developing Identity and Community
Texts as Mirrors and Windows

Be like a star. Shine your light. Shine your stories. For stories will lead us home.

—From *When Stars Are Scattered,* by Victoria Jamieson & Omar Mohamed (2020, p. 256)

The texts that we use in classrooms hold great potential for readers to connect in various ways to push forward learning, development, and understandings. As noted in previous chapters, inclusive texts are often considered from the lenses of *mirrors* where readers see themselves and *windows* where they look into the lives of others (Sims Bishop, 1990). We want children to see themselves in texts to validate their identities and experiences, serving to bolster reading comprehension and sense of belonging in the classroom (e.g., López-Robertson & Haney, 2017). But we also want readers to learn about identities and experiences that differ from their own, elevating all authentic stories and perspectives as valuable and important enough to be included in school curricula (Boyd et al., 2015; Larrick, 1965; Sims Bishop, 1990). In this way, we prioritize the strategic selection of both mirror and window texts.

But texts and the readers who interact with them are complex and multifaceted. Any given text might be a mirror for one reader and a window for another. Or perhaps a text serves as a mirror to one facet of a child's identity (e.g., ethnicity, home language) but a window into new experiences and perspectives (e.g., being adopted, migrating to another country). As conveyed in this chapter's opening quote from the graphic novel *When Stars Are Scattered,* we all have unique stories. Like stars, stories are for everyone—they help develop a sense of who we are and where we come from, as well as link our experiences to those of others to nurture belonging and understanding. But the vast array of stars in the universe is complex, as are the multitude of stories, identities, and experiences of children. Embracing this complexity of readers, texts, and classrooms is central to text selection, providing flexible avenues for children to connect and make meaning while reading and working toward goals.

Building from previous chapters on students and learning goals, this chapter focuses on the third facet of the Inclusive Texts (IT) framework on selecting texts. We share how texts serve as mirrors to validate children's identities, tap into background knowledge and experiences, build classroom community, and support social-emotional well-being. We then consider texts as windows to promote critical exploration of topics through multiple perspectives to develop sociocultural consciousness, increase empathy, grapple with sociopolitical issues, and expand global-mindedness. The chapter closes with ideas for selecting individual texts, as well as text sets and options in classroom instruction. We encourage you to visit this text's supplemental website (inclusivetexts.weebly.com) for book ideas to provide mirrors and windows for primary and middle-grade readers.

TEXTS AS MIRRORS

Rudine Sims Bishop (1990) describes a mirror as a text that "transforms human experience and reflects it back to us, and in that reflection, we can see our own lives and experiences as part of the larger human experience" (p. x). Texts can be relevant to the reader by reflecting some aspect of themselves—physical, cultural, or emotional (Johnson et al., 2018). *Physical* reflections prompt students to see themselves in the illustrations or narrative. *Cultural* reflections invite connections between readers' identities and experiences. *Emotional* reflections inspire readers to connect with characters and classmates as texts provoke similar emotional responses. Whether through pictures or words, students seeing themselves in texts is powerful, providing opportunities to (a) validate and develop identities, (b) tap into background knowledge, (c) build classroom community, and (d) support social-emotional well-being.

Validating and Developing Identities

Mirror texts prompt personal connections between readers and texts, serving as a means for children to see themselves and explore identities (Al-Hazza & Bucher, 2008; Medina & Martínez-Roldán, 2011). The mirror metaphor infers physical reflection, as we typically look into a mirror and see our exterior selves. This is indeed important for readers, particularly those who have been traditionally excluded from school-based curricula. But physical representation is limited to observable features of identities, such as race, gender, and some disabilities. By providing texts that allow for nuanced cultural and emotional connections, children explore multifaceted identity facets and related experiences, such as ethnicity, culture, language, orientation, class, immigration status, and beyond. When selecting texts, teachers can be mindful of the multiple facets of identities and experiences described in Chapter 2.

One of our favorite entry points for using inclusive texts as mirrors in classrooms lies in name-based texts for children to connect in multifaceted ways with identities and experiences. Names are central to our identities, shaped by our families, cultures, and languages while simultaneously shaping how we define and share ourselves with the world. In this way, name-based texts provide entry points to get to know students' familial, cultural, and linguistic backgrounds (Peterson, Gunn, Brice, & Alley, 2015). Using texts as seed ideas, students explore and share the origins and sentiments around their own names to develop identity and build community, rapport, and mutual respect in classrooms. Name-based explorations also provide valuable information for teachers to ensure the appropriate usage and pronunciation of students' names, another integral facet to initiating and sustaining a welcoming classroom environment where all students feel validated and respected.

Javier is a middle-grade, Spanish-English bilingual teacher with predominantly Latinx students. To begin the school year, he read aloud the bilingual picture book titled *René Has Two Last Names* (Colato-Laínez, 2009), which told the author's story of moving to the United States from El Salvador, where his teacher shortens his last name to his dismay. Through a family tree project, René educated his classmates and teacher on his culture and the importance of his names. Javier selected this text since many students in his classroom had more than one last name, tied to a tradition of recognizing both maternal and paternal surnames. He wanted students to connect and explore their names and identities and learn about one another's stories and families. For children who had two last names, they excitedly made connections and shared details about parents, *abuelos*, and *bisabuelos*. Those with one last name asked inquisitive questions, both in class and at home, resulting in meaningful identity exploration for all children.

Down the hall at the same school, Susan is a world language teacher with students from an array of language backgrounds. She selected texts to align with children's backgrounds and promote exploration of names and identities, including *The Name Jar* (Choi, 2001) and *My Name Is Bilal* (Mobin-Uddin, 2005). In both texts, protagonists discover the importance of cultural and familial identities in the face of assimilative practices in U.S. schools. After reading the texts aloud, learners wrote reflection pieces on their own names. One student from Bosnia shared the origin and meaning of her name and that she was proud to maintain its Bosnian proununciation, mirroring the realizations of both Unhei and Bilal from the picture books. Her students also connected with the texts around the issue of school-based bullying, specifically Unhei feeling pressure to choose an Americanized name, or Bilal and his sister being bullied for being Muslim. Children discussed combatting and responding to bullying, using relatable and authentic school experiences from both stories as mirrors for students from diverse cultural and linguistic backgrounds.

Tapping Into Background Knowledge

As discussed in previous chapters, students bring background knowledge to classrooms, including the funds of knowledge and skills that have been culturally and historically shaped and accumulated within families and larger communities (Moll et al., 1992; Moll & González, 1997). Copious research and theory assert the need to integrate funds of knowledge into classroom instruction to enhance learning and engagement across disciplines (e.g., Gay, 2018; Villegas & Lucas, 2007). By recognizing and bringing children's identities into learning, teachers ensure that children feel validated and engaged in educational settings (Alim & Paris, 2018; Ladson-Billings, 2014; Moll et al., 1992; Moll & González, 1997). Through strategic selection of inclusive texts, students can see themselves in books, as well as use texts as seed ideas for sharing their own traditions and experiences in homes and communities.

Sheila teaches in the primary grades of an elementary school with rich cultural and linguistic diversity. She was thrilled when she discovered the book *Golden Domes and Silver Lanterns: A Muslim Book of Colors* by Hena Khan (2012). Two-thirds of her students were Muslim from various Middle Eastern countries, so she was eager to read the book aloud, calling attention to the marvelous artwork centered on the colors of the father's rug for praying, the mother's hijab, grandpa's traditional hat, and grandma's Quran, as well as her family's mosque, favorite Ramadan treat, Eid gift, henna ink, and Arabic letters. Students espousing Muslim identities responded exactly as Sheila had hoped—they were wild about the book, needing a turn-and-talk at every page because they eagerly and excitedly made personal connections that they wanted to share. Children talked about family members, religious traditions, favorite holiday treats, and the Arabic language. As students shared and discovered connections with one another, the teacher learned about their rich funds of knowledge.

Despite being overjoyed to see these connections, Sheila recognized that not all students were equally engaged, particularly those who did not recognize the text's items, people, and places. Upon reflecting on the lesson and exploring other book options, she decided to read aloud a series of books focused on family and community traditions with food, including *Bilal Cooks Daal* (Saeed, 2019), *Bee-bim Bop!* (Park, 2005), *Lailah's Lunchbox: A Ramadan Story* (Faruqi, 2015), and *What Can You Do With a Paleta?* (Tafolla, 2009). Reflective of the heterogeneous cultural backgrounds of her students, these colorful and engaging picture books prompted connections to making and eating culturally specific foods with family and friends. Not only did students see themselves in at least one text, the food-focused text set also prompted them to discuss similar foods, traditions, and experiences shared across the class.

When used as mirrors for multifaceted identities and nuanced experiences, inclusive texts infuse children's funds of knowledge from home and prior knowledge from communities in meaningful ways (Herrera, 2016). The IT framework informs this inclusion, particularly starting with students and getting to know the resources they bring to the classroom. With in-depth knowledge about students and focus on the defined objectives, teachers strategically select and use texts to sustain student, family, and community practices. But critical to the framework is not just *reading* inclusive texts but also situating them as a central feature in instruction. Projects and classroom activities emerge from these texts to prompt children to gather information via oral history or tell stories grounded in rich cultural nuance and tradition (see Table 4.1).

Building Community Through Shared Experiences

Texts also serve as mirrors through characters' experiences growing up and maneuvering life inside and outside of school. Spanning fictional genres, story plots allow readers to connect with different occurrences or events in their lives. Texts written for primary and middle-grade students often include common experiences among children, such as making new friends or maneuvering home and school cultures. These texts provide an ideal medium to build classroom community, engaging children with unique identities in meaningful collective dialogue and nurturing feelings of validation

Table 4.1. Strategies to Connect Texts with Funds of Knowledge

Strategy	Description
Artifacts	Students bring artifacts from home in relation to a focal text, such as photographs, recipes, books, clothing, or other objects.
Artwork	Students respond to text in various artistic mediums to portray personal connections, including sketching, painting, or molding clay.
Class Texts	Students respond to a text with their own story, which becomes part of a class book on the topic (e.g., food, family traditions).
Oral History	Students prompt family and community members to recall stories regarding a particular topic from the text (e.g., names, traditions).
Writing Prompts	Students reflect on a predefined prompt and write about particular home and community experiences in relation to a text.

and belonging (Glazier & Seo, 2005; López-Robertson & Haney, 2017; Martínez-Roldán & López-Robertson, 1999; Méndez-Newman, 2012). In this way, students form relationships with one another that stem from the recognition and respect that they have for one another's identities, experiences, emotions, and affinities. As teachers seek to build classroom community, inclusive texts provide an avenue to nurture spaces where children feel safe and comfortable to be themselves and share perspectives.

Bethany is a primary-grade, Spanish-English bilingual teacher. She wanted to enact community circles for learners to openly and honestly discuss events, issues, and feelings. She struggled to get students to participate and turned to a picture book, *The Dog Who Loved Tortillas/La perrita que le encantaban las tortillas* (Alire Sáenz, 2009), since most of her Latinx bilingual learners had animals at home. In the bilingual book, the family adopted a dog from the shelter that became ill, requiring a visit to the veterinarian. During the interactive read-aloud, students connected with the text personally, demonstrating deep concern and sadness and conveying these emotions openly with one another. Bethany first let students take control over the discussions, as was her desire for community circle, and later pointed out to students that they could talk about things that they feel strongly about in the safe environment of the classroom.

When used across units, texts authentically nurture community over time. In the identity unit introduced in Chapter 3, Anne included a wide range of titles for read-aloud selections and book clubs, including *Better Nate Than Ever* (Federle, 2018), *Hello Universe* (Estrada Kelly, 2020a), *Garvey's Choice* (Grimes, 2016), and *Harbor Me* (Woodson, 2018). These texts prompted reflections and discussions on the multifaceted nature of identity, stretching across race, gender identity, and family structure. Each middle-grade novel involved a protagonist feeling different from peers on a journey of self-acceptance. Their experiences differed, such as Nate pursuing his dream of theater and questioning his orientation in *Better Nate Than Ever* and Garvey's weight not fitting his father's athletic expectations in *Garvey's Choice*. Characters also varied in identities, including four kids brought together in friendship and adventure in *Hello Universe* and six classmates experiencing issues ranging from deportation to racial profiling in *Harbor Me*. By reflecting a range of experiences and identities, Anne created space for students to share connections and questions about characters, stories, and one another.

Inclusive texts reflecting children's multifaceted identities and experiences serve as an excellent medium to promote positive and collaborative learning environments. To build community in this way, the key is first finding texts for students to connect in various ways and experience related emotions. The next step is to use the text in classroom instruction to promote reflection, connections, and collaborative dialogue. Table 4.2 provides examples of extension strategies to support personal connections and community-building efforts.

Table 4.2. Strategies to Build Classroom Community With Inclusive Texts

Strategy	Description
Find Someone	Read *The Day You Begin* (Woodson, 2020). Based on students' backgrounds, compile a matrix of experiences that children have in common. Students find others to sign each box, such as speaking another language, having a sibling, living with extended family, celebrating a holiday, attending church, etc.
Identity Poems	Students reflect upon names, backgrounds, and identities and creatively craft poetry to share with others. Sentence stems, predictable patterns, and graphic organizers support students in putting thoughts into poetic form. Examples include *Bio Poems*, *I Am Poems*, and *Where I'm From Poems*.
Identity Webs	Students reflect upon what defines and influences their identities, pinpointing facets such as cultural background, language competencies, family roles, religion, gender and sexual identification, etc. These are compiled and shared via graphic organizers, such as *Identity Webs* and *Circles of Myself*.
Name Exploration	Have students explore their names and identities using seed ideas from various inclusive texts. For example, read *René Has Two Last Names* (Colato-Laínez, 2009) or *Alma and How She Got Her Name* (Martínez -Neal, 2018) and have students share their various names and significances.
Name Songs	Read *Your Name Is a Song* (Thompkins-Bigelow, 2020). Have children explore and share the meaning of their names, along with the accurate pronunciation. Create a class song to capture students' names and stories. Scribe the song on poster paper and hang on the wall with children's pictures.
Personal Traits	Read books that portray kids' character traits and experiences, such as *Just Like Me* (Brantley-Newton, 2020) and *I Am Every Good Thing* (Barnes, 2020). Have students write their name on a piece of construction paper and brainstorm their personal traits and experiences to share with the class.

Supporting Social-Emotional Development

Developing community provides the premise for teachers to support the unique situations of children who may be grappling with complex life events, traumas, and stressors inside and outside of school. Students' lives outside of schools can be difficult, with over half of U.S. schoolchildren having experienced trauma, violence, or chronic stress (Zacarian, Alvarez-Ortiz, &

Haynes, 2017). Certain events occur across the wider student population, such as domestic abuse or a parent struggling with an illness. Others occur with greater frequency within groups of children, such as immigrant-origin students coping with trauma from escaping war, family separations, or stress regarding documentation status (Birman & Tran, 2015), or transgender children facing bullying and harassment from peers (Pampati, Andzejewski, Sheremenko, Johns, Lesesne, & Rasberry, 2020).

Texts and text-based discussions among peers and educators support students in grappling with complex topics and difficult occurrences in their lives (Verden, 2012; Verden & Hickman, 2009). Using books to promote social and emotional well-being centers on awareness of children's lived experiences, as well as available texts that might be appropriate mirrors. But it is also integral to consider your comfort and readiness to have discussions emergent from these texts and follow up with supports, resources, and advocacy efforts. For us, the question is not *if* you have these conversations with students, but *how* you prepare to do so effectively before, during, and after the text. Text selection based on children's experiences is important, as is considering and preparing for the various ways that students may transact with the text. During reading, outlets like journaling or sketching provide students with ongoing ways to reflect and share, which teachers then use to guide the follow-up after reading, which may involve continued dialogue or additional resources from other stakeholders.

Karen taught middle-grade ELA at a school where 90% of students speak languages other than English and whose families come from countries around the world. She crafted a unit on journeys and identity, which involved students selecting texts for literature discussions. She selected book options to reflect the journeys of her students, hoping to facilitate connections. She particularly wanted to reach one student who had come to Chicago from the Congo 2 years prior and remained reserved in the classroom. Karen included the novel in verse *Home of the Brave* by Katherine Applegate (2007), which tells the story of a young boy leaving war-torn Sudan to come to the Midwest. The student eagerly chose this text and regularly brought sketches of the main character, Kek, that she completed at home following reading. In addition to sketches portraying various emotions related to Kek's and her own experiences, she used her French, Swahili, and English to write impassioned and personal poetry with the support of a t-chart prompting words and phrases on the left and emotions on the right. Though she did not regularly share in literature discussions, the sketches and poems provided a space for her to grapple with her experiences and emotions with the support of the teacher.

Karen provides an example of how teachers thoughtfully select and use texts in classroom instruction to allow children to respond in varied ways depending on comfort level. Texts can also be recommended to individual students for independent reading, based on characters and storylines that might sensitively foster self-reflection and dialogue with the teacher. With research indicating that successful students have school-based mentors and confidants with open lines of communication (Suárez-Orozco et al., 2007), inclusive texts serve to initiate relationships and support systems. We see this as fitting into the larger movement of trauma-informed teaching (Zacarian et al., 2017), which is gaining attention and bringing together stakeholders like teachers, social workers, and counselors. Teachers are uniquely situated to support students coping with their social-emotional well-being, and inclusive texts provide an effective vehicle to do this work.

TEXTS AS WINDOWS

Books that serve as *windows* provide insight into wider experiences, places, and people than what might be part of students' direct lived experiences (Sims Bishop, 1990). Window texts allow readers to experience other cultures, races, religions, and lifestyles, opening new worlds beyond what students experience each day to consider multiple perspectives, grapple with how their identities fit into other worldviews, and engage in conversations about a range of topics and identities (Boyd et al., 2015; Gopalakrishnan, 2011). In this section, we consider how to select texts as mirrors to (a) develop sociocultural consciousness, (b) increase empathy, (c) probe sociopolitical issues, and (d) expand worldviews and global mindedness.

Developing Sociocultural Consciousness

Culturally sustaining pedagogies and critical literacy converge around the need to develop sociocultural consciousness. Villegas and Lucas (2002) define *sociocultural consciousness* as "the awareness that a person's worldview is not universal but is profoundly influenced by life experiences, as mediated by a variety of factors, including race, ethnicity, gender, and social class" (p. 31). This means understanding that your worldview is not the same as everyone else's and is certainly not the so-called correct worldview. An individual's biases, assumptions, and prior experiences shape their worldview as well as the process of developing sociocultural consciousness. In this way, it is important for children to (a) learn that their perspective on the world is not shared across society or even with all members of the classroom, (b) deconstruct their worldviews to understand the influence of various factors, and (c) learn about and through the stories, experiences, and perspectives of others.

Socially conscious books introduce children to identities and experiences that differ from their own to promote tolerance, awareness, and empathy (Gopalakrishnan, 2011). Teachers can begin to introduce the concept of multiple perspectives to help young students see different points of view on one occurrence using simple picture books such as *Duck! Rabbit!* (Rosenthal, 2009), *They All Saw a Cat* (Wenzel, 2016), and *Same, Same But Different* (Kostecki-Shaw, 2011). Once students understand the concept of multiple perspectives, teachers build inclusive text sets around different topics to show perspectives of characters with a range of *identities* spanning race, ethnicity, culture, language, religion, gender, orientation, and ability, and *experiences* such as incarceration, poverty, homelessness, and war. By engaging with socially conscious texts through the support of the classroom teacher, students learn that their opinions are not the only ones that exist and that their assumptions may not be correct or just.

Let's revisit Anne's middle-grade classroom, where she frequently uses texts to develop sociocultural consciousness. As a part of her unit on identity, students had explored various texts related to identities and experiences. But Anne wanted to push students to explore experiences different from those represented in the class for students to probe the biases and assumptions that they and others in the school might have about families. Anne used the text *Stella Brings the Family* (Schiffer, 2015), which centers on a Mothers' Day celebration at school. Stella, who had two fathers, was unsure who to bring to the celebration. Through supportive friends and family, she realized she had people in her life who fill the roles that others say their mothers fill, thus celebrating her family structure. Anne shared this text as a read-aloud, resulting in thoughtful dialogue about how people might feel if they differ from what is considered the so-called norm in our country. She was struck by the engagement of her students and noted that the conversation was not uncomfortable, but rather characterized by rich discussion about ways that others might feel different in certain situations.

Following the attack on the U.S. Capitol in January 2021, Anne sought to create space for children to grapple with what they had seen and heard on the news. They had previously read *Something Happened in Our Town* (Celano, 2019), *Breaking News* (Reul, 2018), *Intersection Allies* (Johnson, Council, & Choi, 2019), and *Sometimes People March* (Allen, 2020), which she used to frame the conversation on the following school day. Drawing from Sarah Ahmed's *Being the Change* (2018), Anne modified an activity called *What's in Your News?* She created a graphic organizer for students to write about their news, as well as what they were thinking, questioning, or planning to do with the news that stood out in their minds. Many students chose to write about the Capitol riots and used the space to work through some of their feelings and questions, whereas others wrote about issues related to Black Lives Matter protests, the COVID-19 pandemic, and other things going on in their homes. This exercise helped the students see that because of individuals' experiences, worldviews, and contexts, different occurrences impacted peers in various ways, thus bolstering their sociocultural consciousness.

Increasing Empathy

Classroom discussions surrounding socially conscious books provide space to explore new ideas and experiences, revisit those ideas, and let empathy build over time (Reimer, 2019). Building empathy through texts involves creating opportunities for children to experience a wide range of emotions in an attempt to understand others' emotions and experiences from those points of view, rather than just their own. Empathy-building is important, particularly in societies with widespread and unresolved racism, racial injustice, and prejudice. Children's books can help combat these social issues at an early age by enabling children to learn about people from different identities and backgrounds, rather than growing up with ethnocentric views on the world and people within it (Sims Bishop, 1990, 1997). Both picture books and novels serve as a platform for introducing topics that develop empathy, as readers experience different emotions related to varied events (Nikolajeva, 2013). Novels provide time and space to create rich characters who go through multiple experiences, prompting the reader to experience life alongside that character. Picture books evoke emotional responses not only through the storyline, but also with visual imagery.

Texts that have relatable characters are good choices to begin this work of fostering empathy through inclusion. Reading books and fostering strong, supportive discussion leads students to deeper understandings of one another while also seeing how they connect to one another. When characters in texts face oppression or hardships, readers who have built connections to those characters experience strong feelings of empathy, hope, and longing for action, even if they have not experienced those situations in their own lives (Reimer, 2019). For example, children build empathy as they learn from Khosrou's sensitive, humorous, and unique storytelling about his experience as a refugee from Iran, starting a new life in Oklahoma in the novel *Everything Sad Is Untrue* (Nayeri, 2020). They walk alongside Faizah and Asiya on Asiya's first day wearing her hijab to school and experience her struggles, her strength, and her pride in *The Proudest Blue* (Muhammad, 2019). Books allow children from all backgrounds and identities to experience powerful emotions through the point of view of others.

Anne uses texts and discussions on different family structures as windows to the concept of family. After reading *Stepping Stones* (Ruurs, 2016), a story of a Syrian refugee family's experience, connections and conversations grew in her middle-grade classroom. Since one child came to the United States from Syria as a refugee, Anne spoke with her in advance to ensure that the text would not evoke trauma or discomfort. She encouraged the student to read and talk about the text with her family before Anne shared the text with the whole group. When Anne read the text aloud, the student asked if she could share her story with the class to help her peers understand the realities of being refugees. Other students drew from the text and their classmate's story to thoughtfully ask questions and engage in discussion in both whole- and small-group settings. Following the whole-group read-aloud, students transitioned into small groups to talk about family influences and people's experiences. In this way, a mirror text for one student served as a powerful window text for others, and they all connected through the shared experience of the text.

Lindsay, a multilingual primary teacher serving children with 10 different home languages, uses inclusive texts to develop empathy. For the read-aloud portion of her literacy block, she selected the text *Pancho Rabbit and the Coyote: A Migrant's Tale* (Tonatiuh, 2013), which illustrated the danger and heartache involved with crossing the Mexican border to the United States. Lindsay initially perceived this text as a window for her young learners to engage in a discussion around the contemporary issue of Central American families migrating and crossing the border. One subset of students had not previously discussed the topic and expressed sadness and care for the characters. For those who had previously heard talk on the topic, the text provided a personal perspective to discuss immigration. Some students shared stories about family members' migration journeys. By reading the book aloud, supporting children in dialogue, and nurturing the sharing of thoughts, questions, and connections, students developed empathy and understandings regarding undocumented immigrants.

Probing Sociopolitical Issues and Perspectives

Window texts open the potential to explore sociopolitical issues. Teaching is not a neutral act, but involves elaborate connections between sociopolitical systems, power, and language (Lewison et al., 2002). Teachers can provide children with space and tools to uncover social issues embedded in texts and examine these issues from multiple perspectives. Numerous high-quality texts spanning fiction and nonfiction genres examine issues like racism, poverty, war, immigration, and other topics for both primary and middle grades. For example, *Mama's Nightingale: A Story of Immigration and Separation* (Danticat, 2015) opens space to discuss separation that sometimes occurs within immigrant families, allowing students to both learn and develop empathy. By focusing on sociopolitical issues in classroom instruction, teachers push readers beyond personal responses and connections to texts to examine how systems of power shape people's experiences in different ways (Jewett, 2007).

Sociopolitical texts serve as an excellent medium to introduce concepts of stereotypes, biases, and assumptions. As described in Chapter 2, stereotypes emerge in texts through simplified generalizations about individuals or groups based on identity factors like gender, race, class, ethnicity, orientation, linguistic background, or ability. These stereotypes show up in both narrative and illustrations, including (a) how characters are framed, (b) how they are drawn, (c) the actions they take in the story, and (d) the words the author uses to describe them. In addition to maintaining keen awareness of the potential for essentialized portrayals in texts, practitioners can select texts that encourage students to take this critical lens. All texts have bias, as authors and illustrators craft them using their perspectives, backgrounds, and assumptions (Luke & Freebody, 1997). We help nurture critical readers by making these biases visible to students—both those present in texts, as well as those that readers bring with them to each book.

Text selection in classrooms also stems from assumptions that children espouse about certain identities that require disruption. Mitch is a middle-grade teacher in an elementary school consisting predominantly of children from Eastern European families, where he recognized the need to disrupt stereotypes and assumptions about various cultures and communities. He turned his focus first to Indigenous people and cultures, particularly since his students brought up stories in the news related to the environment and controversies over team names and mascots. From these interactions, Mitch knew that his students had limited knowledge related to Indigenous groups outside of essentializations that had emerged from news coverage.

Mitch designed a unit of study with the goal to disrupt these narrow perspectives and assumptions about Indigenous people and communities. His students began by researching different regions and First Nations to find similarities and differences, subsequently disrupting the simplified narrative of Native American as a singular identity. Mitch pulled in history through texts that countered the watered-down depiction in textbooks, teaching his students about the atrocities committed against Indigenous people throughout history. He created book clubs, with groups of students reading different texts such as *Fatty Legs* (Jordan-Fenton & Pokiak-Fenton, 2010), *When I Was Eight* (Jordan-Fenton & Pokiak-Fenton, 2013), and *We Are Grateful: Otsaliheliga* (Sorell, 2018). These book clubs provoked discussions about historical atrocities like the Trail of Tears and the forced placement of Indigenous students into boarding schools, to which he observed students getting "very fiery." Building off these responses, his students looked toward action, seeking spaces in their local community that honored Indigenous voices and celebrated their resilience and survival despite colonization over time.

After this work, Mitch knew he also needed to disrupt the stereotype that Indigenous people were part of the past, as often framed in curricula and textbooks. Wanting students to understand both traditional and modern aspects of Indigenous cultures, he read aloud various books by Indigenous authors about Indigenous cultures situated in modern settings, including *Jingle Dancer* (Leitich Smith, 2000), *Fry Bread* (Maillard, 2019), and *I Can Make This Promise* (Day, 2020). He forged a partnership with a nearby Indigenous community organization to allow students to meet and interview individuals from various tribes now living in the same urban area. Students shared these rich narratives with their peers in the classroom, making nuanced connections with the characters in texts and related learning (e.g., boarding schools, Indigenous languages). Drawing from students' concerns and responses across the unit, Mitch developed plans to support students in writing letters to policymakers to enact changes regarding product brands, team mascots, and other problematic stereotypes in need of change.

Expanding Worldviews and Global-Mindedness

We live in a global society, and today's children interact increasingly with people from all over the world in various contexts. As educators, we want to prepare students for interactions with people from cultures, language backgrounds, and identities different from their own. Inclusive texts support this work, pushing back against the *single-story* narrative that tends to essentialize people based on ethnicity or culture. In her widely viewed Ted Talk about the danger of a single story, Chimamanda Adichie (2009) reflects upon not seeing herself in texts as a child and being unaware that characters like her existed in literature. Her lack of mirrors means lack of windows for others, resulting in a single story about the continent of Africa in Western literature. Adichie talks about perceptions that others had of her upon learning of her African origins, such as expressing surprise at her English proficiency, making assumptions about her background knowledge and musical tastes, and feeling sorry for her. By reading texts from across the globe, we counter the single-story narrative that has the potential to emerge from traditional curricula.

Global literature consists of books that celebrate, honor, and inform others about cultures around the world, including within the United States (Hadaway, 2007). These texts might capture the nuances of life in specific countries (e.g., *My Day With the Payne*; Charles, 2021), migration between countries (e.g., *Other Words for Home*; Warga, 2019), or cultural communities within the local context (e.g., *Amy Wu and the Perfect Bao*; Zhang, 2019). Texts that promote global-mindedness help students see their connectedness to children in other countries and cultures to make meaning about the world. When selecting global texts, it is important to avoid the caveat of traditional multicultural trade books, typically written by White authors who are not associated with the country or culture being described in the text (Kincade & Pruitt, 1996). We recommend returning to the criteria for authenticity from Chapter 2 to ensure presentation of accurate details, preferably from an author with inside experience in the focal community.

Read-alouds occupy a central role in literacy and content-area instruction in Lindsay's primary classroom of multilingual learners. Lindsay has stocked her library with texts that serve as windows and mirrors for various learners, from which she strategically selects texts to feature as aligned with her instructional goals. As part of an integrated social studies and literacy unit at the beginning of the school year, Lindsay used an informational picture book titled *School Days Around the World* (Ruurs, 2015). Strategically chosen to frame discussion about school rules and procedures, this text supported students in developing global perspectives on educational experiences in other countries. Children in Lindsay's classroom read the text together and created an ongoing list of similarities and differences between their school in the United States and kids' learning experiences in different countries. Written with a global lens, the text supported learning about everyday experiences and how they might differ based on context.

Lindsay also tapped into the rich backgrounds of her students' families to promote global awareness. To begin the school year, she sent home an invitation to parents, guardians, and family members, welcoming them into the classroom to read aloud stories. The structure was flexible—each person chose a book and time, with flexibility to schedule their read-aloud around a special cultural event or holiday or even read in another language. Many parents and grandparents read books from their home countries, including those in Arabic and Polish. Students loved these *guest read-alouds* with glimpses into life around the globe. Even when students did not understand the language, they soaked in the sounds of the language, the reader's enthusiasm, and the vibrant pictures. They opened and closed each read-aloud with a discussion to introduce the context and frame the learning, which allowed learners to ask questions, make connections, and develop understandings beyond their urban U.S. community.

Through supportive dialogue using quality inclusive texts, students can challenge and change perspectives and worldviews as they learn about others' lived experiences. Table 4.3 provides instructional strategies that support students in using window texts to promote critical thinking. Just as Mitch supported students in disrupting assumptions about Indigenous cultures and Anne fostered sociocultural consciousness with students considering different newsworthy events, teachers bring window texts into all aspects of literacy and content-area learning to create space for critical literacy and learning. Using window texts also prompts social action as part of classroom instruction. As students discover how to disrupt the status quo and challenge problematic texts, they can learn to advocate for inclusive representation in school and local libraries, including by writing letters to publishing companies to ask for diverse voices and creating counternarratives in writing to reflect multiple perspectives.

SELECTING MIRROR AND WINDOW TEXTS FOR INSTRUCTION

Readers bring their own identities and experiences to texts, setting up the potential for one book to serve as a mirror to some students and a window

Table 4.3. Strategies for Using Window Texts

Strategy	Description
Color Symbol Image	Have students choose a color, symbol, and image to represent the theme or overall idea in a text. For example, students read *Amina's Voice* (Khan, 2017) and use a color, symbol, and image to represent Amina's experiences holding onto her culture while experiencing a new culture (Project Zero, 2019).
Give One, Get One	Students have a task, such as sharing what they learned on immigration after reading multiple texts. They go around the room to share (give one) with a partner and listen (get one) to a partner share. They do this repeatedly, then consider all the perspectives they got during the activity and how those impact their new overall understandings.
Headlines	Students write headlines for the main idea of a text, then compare one another's headlines to consider how our experiences cause us to focus on a certain aspect more than others, as well as impact the word choice we use (Project Zero, 2019).
How Might They See It?	Choose an event or image from a text. Ask students to consider other characters whose voices were included (or missing) from the text and think about how they might view the event or image. For instance, how might multiple characters view and describe the hotel from *Front Desk* (Yang, 2018)?
Questioning the Author	Have students question who the author is and what their agenda appears to be. For example, students research the background of the author and determine if a text is Own Voices, what experiences the author has related to the text, or what perspective may be missing.
Tug of War	Students identify two opposing sides on a topic (e.g., historical event, opinion on a character, current event). They list *tugs* (reasons) that pull them toward one side, then rank the tugs by strength and record questions that arise (Project Zero, 2019).
Whose Truth?	Students make claims related to a text to share with others. Classmates then question the claim to determine whose truth that is, and whose truth it is not. For example, after reading a range of texts related to different identities, students determine which characters would agree with a claim and which would not (Project Zero, 2019).

to others (Jiménez, 2021). Teachers never know the multifaceted and ever-changing identities of all students, nor how any given student might transact with a text that their teachers select and use in the classroom. Multiple examples in this chapter capture lessons going a different direction than planned or students connecting unexpectedly. Embracing the active role of readers, teachers can select singular texts or text sets for readers to connect in a variety of ways, using texts in ways that allow for varied transactions and diverse responses. Another approach is to maintain well-stocked classroom libraries or provide strategically selected options tied to themes and goals. In this section, we tap into previous classroom examples to expand upon the third IT framework facet of text selection, including singular texts, text sets, and text options.

Selecting Focal Texts

Selecting texts for classroom use centers on relevance and authenticity, as well as alignment to goals. As we discussed in Chapter 2, text selection should emerge from children, including their identities and experiences in homes, communities, and schools. With awareness of students, as well as foresight of instructional goals, teachers select texts that authentically portray the target community and support readers' learning. When selecting singular texts for lessons, teachers should consider students and goals. Lesson objectives related to developing empathy or global-mindedness prompt use of window texts, whereas those related to identity and community require mirror texts. But windows and mirrors vary by text and reader, and teachers never know the full scope of children's lives to know how students might connect with a given text. In this way, singular text selection involves putting relevant and authentic books in front of children and allowing them to flexibly connect and develop understandings.

Throughout this chapter, we have learned from teachers who thoughtfully selected texts for instructional use. Javier opted to read *René Has Two Last Names* (Colato-Laínez, 2009) to facilitate discussion around names and identities. He selected the text to serve as a mirror for his Latinx students with two surnames but happily embraced the multifaceted connections across students as they learned about one another's families and experiences. Anne chose *Stella Brings the Family* (Schiffer, 2015) as a window to expand children's perceptions beyond traditional family structures but found that students connected in various ways while they deepened their understanding of families and communities. In both examples, we see teachers contemplating how texts could serve as mirrors and windows in relation to students and facilitate progress toward goals while allowing readers to make unique and dynamic connections.

Texts with rich storylines open the potential for multiple connection points to provide windows and mirrors for all students. Whereas picture books might be selected as mirrors or windows on focal identities or experiences, chapter books provide multiple layers, characters, and storylines that facilitate varied and dynamic connections. For example, in Charlotte's middle-grade classroom, she read aloud *The First Rule of Punk* (Pérez, 2017). Since all children were new to the 4th- and 5th-grade school building, she recognized the potential for rich dialogue among students maneuvering similar challenges to the protagonist. The text served as a mirror to all students in various ways: all students connected to Malú as the new student maneuvering her identity, some connected to the family separation between Malú and her father, and one connected to her Cuban and Mexican heritage. Since most students were multilingual, she called attention to the use of Spanish in the text, which students enjoyed discussing in the context of their families and home languages. Otherwise, Charlotte left meaning-making open to students, allowing their varied connections and questions to emerge.

Inclusive texts should find their way into every classroom, even in schools that mandate predefined curricula. As described in Chapter 3, critical curricular analysis opens avenues to consider whose voices and stories are prioritized and silenced and where teachers have flexibility to bring in additional texts. In many contexts, teachers can change out texts, replacing those named in the curriculum with ones that align to students but still facilitate progress toward standards. Even in the most rigid curricular contexts, such as those requiring teachers to follow a script, teachers can bring in inclusive texts outside of the literacy block, such as selecting engaging storylines for daily read-alouds. Whenever these opportunities present themselves, strategic text selection can yield rich and varied interactions among all readers.

Using Text Sets

Text sets refer to collections of books and materials organized around topics or themes (Opitz, 1998). Text sets support students in exploring different perspectives, considering different versions of an event or topic, and comparing aspects of theme, author's craft, text structure, and other text elements while reading different types of texts at different levels (Hartman & Hartman, 1994; Opitz, 1998; Tschida & Buchanan, 2015). Text sets disrupt the single-story caveat that comes with sharing singular texts. By engaging with multiple texts within and across identities and communities, children develop nuanced understandings that enhance their sociocultural consciousness, empathy, and worldviews (Newstreet et al., 2018). Additionally, exposure to more books means that more children see their identities and experiences reflected on the pages, which supports progress toward goals for identity and literacy development.

Text sets might center on mirrors, seeking to provide all readers with avenues to connect to focal identities while linking students' experiences with one another. Think back to Susan's text set on children's school-based experiences with names or Sheila's texts on family and food with ties to her students' cultural backgrounds. In these examples, we see how teachers drew from learners' cultural identities and experience in homes and schools to select texts. Whereas these examples center on developing classroom community, text sets can also align with academic goals. In Krista's primary classroom, she selected Cinderella stories to explore story variations, opting for those connecting to students' cultural backgrounds, including tales from Iraq (*The Golden Sandal*; Hickox, 1998), Korea (*Kongi and Potgi*; Han & Plunkett, 1996), Mexico (*Domítila*; Coburn, 2000), and Russia (*Baba Yaga and Vasilisa the Brave*; Mayer, 1994). Children read, discussed, and compared the texts, prompting personal connections and emergent extensions as they sought out information and story variations from family members. In this way, we see how text sets tap into funds of knowledge.

Text sets also provide students with windows into various identities and experiences to develop understandings of focal topics, issues, or events. Research has shown that texts written from different perspectives allow children to deepen insight on a topic and recognize how texts yield multiple meanings based on readers' backgrounds and experiences (Ciardiello, 2004; Papola, 2013). Take, for example, the unit designed by Mitch, who sought to develop students' understandings of Indigenous communities in the United States. He amassed a collection of texts in response to his students' perceptions and in line with his goals to disrupt the simplified narrative around Native Americans and deepen understandings about Indigenous people's multifaceted identities. Whereas Mitch selected texts portraying Indigenous identities, teachers can also weave multifaceted identities (e.g., gender, orientation, ability) around a common disciplinary theme. For example, in a unit on civil rights, teachers could create text sets that portray LGBTQ histories (e.g., *Sylvia and Marsha Start a Revolution*; Ellison, 2020), disability advocacy (e.g., *We Want to Go to School!: The Fight for Disability Rights*; Cocca-Leffler & Leffler, 2021), and current civic movements (e.g., *Sometimes People March*; Allen, 2020) to extend the narrative of civil rights as focused solely on race in decades past.

Whether you design your own units or use prescribed curricula, text sets can enhance your efforts to support students in achieving instructional goals. In an ideal world, you could select all texts and materials in response to your unique students and the objectives that you have defined for instruction. But even if you have a curriculum that you must follow, text sets emerge as a valuable option to link high-quality inclusive texts to required materials. For example, if social studies textbooks provide only one perspective on historical events, then bring in texts for read-alouds or book clubs that provide other perspectives. If the literacy curriculum calls for the use of a particular text, then bring in related texts with diverse protagonists that connect to children's unique identities and experiences. Regardless of the context, text sets provide rich opportunities to deepen readers' perspectives, reflections, and connections.

Providing Text Options

Whereas text sets include books to be read among the entire class across a unit, *text options* bring in the notion of choice. When they have choice in what they read, students tend to (a) have increased motivation to read, (b) report more confidence in reading abilities, (c) put forth more effort, and (d) better understand the text (Gambrell, 2011; Guthrie, Hoa, Wigfield, Tonks, Humenick, & Littles, 2007). From the lens of windows and mirrors, text options emerge as important in increasingly diverse communities and societies as teachers seek to tell multiple stories and allow readers to connect in a multitude of ways. By strategically defining a handful of text options, students self-select texts that they wish to read that align with defined instructional goals.

We have explored several examples of teachers providing text options in this chapter. In the middle-grade identity unit, Anne and her grade-level team selected book club options to reflect an array of identity facets. Starting with students' backgrounds and aligned to goals for developing identity and community, they selected texts that reflected common experiences from a variety of identity lenses. In Karen's unit on journeys, she pinpointed options for literature discussions to reflect the immigrant origins of her students. Texts allowed students to connect in various ways to the characters and storylines while also providing space to learn and appreciate one another's journeys. In both classrooms, student choice drove independent reading and small-group discussions, with children selecting their focal texts after being introduced to each title. By providing multiple genres and rich storylines, teachers allowed readers to access and connect with texts in complex ways around unit goals.

Text options are valuable for bringing multiple voices into instruction, as well as allow varied and dynamic connections; however, this approach typically does not stand alone. Teachers often offer choice during certain components of literacy instruction, such as book clubs or literature discussions, but define common texts read by the whole class for other components. In Anne's units of study, she and her team defined text sets of titles centered on the unit's theme, goals, and essential questions to read aloud with the whole class, as well as text options for students' selection and engagement in book clubs. For Karen, she embraced the use of one common read-aloud to capture the key points of the unit while providing students with novel options and *paired texts* in small groups. In addition to the middle-grade titles that facilitated literature discussions, each group engaged with one related picture book to build background on the focal text and serve as an entry point to practice discussion procedures. Together, purposively selected arrays of inclusive texts in units nurture readers' literacies, identities, and understandings.

THE FRAMEWORK IN ACTION: RESPONDING TO STUDENTS' IDENTITIES AND PERSPECTIVES

Centering students' identities and experiences begins with classroom collections that feature a wide range of high-quality inclusive texts that allow readers to make personal connections, construct meaning, and explore the world. Of course, amassing a rich and diverse array of inclusive texts is no easy task. Teachers often encounter limited funds to purchase texts, subsequently requiring partnerships with stakeholders who hold the budgetary decision-making power, such as administrators and librarians. But we have found that communication is a simple and important advocacy tool for teachers. Stakeholders are often very aware of the diversity within their schools and communities but unaware of the texts and resources that can provide mirrors and windows to students. We encourage you to connect with individuals in your setting to share wish lists for inclusive texts, paired with well-defined rationales for why these texts support the learning and literacy development of children in classrooms.

Selecting inclusive texts also requires us to deconstruct what is considered *appropriate* for children. Inclusive texts often tackle complex topics, which may make teachers uncomfortable, especially if the experiences reflected in texts differ from their own. In our many years of working with educators, we have found that adults are often hesitant to select texts that portray complex circumstances or events, including war, gun violence, drug use, discrimination, and illegal immigration. But it cannot be denied that these things happen in real life. Some of our students have experienced these things directly in their short lifetimes. Many others see portrayals on the news, Internet, movies, shows, and video games. Children are often ready to have these conversations in safe classroom spaces, even when adults are not. As teachers consider texts for classroom use, they should deconstruct this notion of appropriateness, carefully considering and preparing for various factors that may influence students' and their own readiness to engage with related topics.

Teachers can build comfortability about approaching complex topics by developing their own sociocultural consciousness, empathy, and global-mindedness. We discussed these facets of critical literacy earlier in the chapter for students, but teachers should also contemplate the need to deepen these areas themselves before facilitating this work in classrooms. Without this introspection, teachers may rely on personal experiences and make assumptions about students' lives and perspectives, potentially leading to misconceptions and false information (Villegas & Lucas, 2002). In previous chapters, we discussed getting to know children's identities and experiences and interrogating curricula with our unique students in mind. With this, we want you to look *at,* but also *beyond,* individual students to examine inequitable social systems and racist structures, including the roles that schools play in these inequities. By recognizing and working against these systems, as well as viewing students from an asset-based lens, teachers develop sociocultural consciousness, as well as espouse empathy for children's experiences and consider how they may approach reading and learning from unique worldviews.

As you move forward and engage in text selection, we encourage reflective dialogue about appropriateness and comfortability around complex topics. For instance, if you are browsing texts and a voice inside you says that a particular text is inappropriate, go deeper to question from where that conception emerges and the potential reasons for your doubt (e.g., administrative support, parental pushback, ability to facilitate dialogue with students). Whatever the reason, own the hesitation as yours, recognizing that students are likely ready to engage with these contemporary topics that either directly or indirectly influence them or someone they know. If your concerns center on potential pushback, rationalize using these texts in your classroom to approach and inform conversations with families and administrators. If you have concerns about facilitating these conversations with students, connect with colleagues for support or start a book club with other teachers to support one another.

At this point of the text, we have explored the first three facets of the IT framework. Text selection, the focus of this chapter, is not as simple as going to the library and pulling a book off the shelf to read with your class. We start with students—their multifaceted identities, varied experiences, and unique perspectives on the world—and then critically consider and define goals to develop literacies, identities, and understandings. We then strategically select relevant and authentic texts that elevate the voices and perspectives beyond canonical literature and canned curricula. By encouraging identity exploration with mirror texts and probing their biases and assumptions with window texts, we challenge students to think beyond their own worldview to see multiple perspectives and lived experiences in local communities and around the world. In upcoming chapters, we move on to the final facet of incorporating texts into instruction.

QUESTIONS AND ACTIVITIES FOR PROFESSIONAL DEVELOPMENT

1. Think about your own identity, considering the facets of your background and experiences that influence who you are as a person and practitioner. Use the Internet and your local library to find a text that reflects you. What stands out to you in the text? Why does the text resonate with you? How does it feel to see yourself in the text?

2. Guide students through a similar process. Have them reflect on their identities, using an identity web, poem, or related activity. Then encourage each learner to find a text in your classroom or school library that reflects their identity. What stands out in the text? Why is the text a mirror? How does it feel to be reflected in a text?

3. Think about your lived experiences and identities. How have these shaped your own viewpoints on the world and on other cultures and backgrounds? What assumptions, biases, and stereotypes do you hold about certain identity groups? Evaluate these perspectives and consider ways to disrupt them through texts.

4. Support students in evaluating texts by asking questions like: Who is included and who is missing in this text? How are groups and individuals represented? What does the author want us to think or believe about this topic? What are other perspectives on this topic? Once students begin to use this lens, they can seek texts that disrupt the status quo. Challenge them to find texts about identities or experiences different from their own. Create a space for students to reflect and share these texts with one another.

5. Critically consider the texts and resources available to your students in the classroom and school. Do texts reflect your students in a variety of ways? Do texts open windows to various identities and experiences that may differ from your students? Are there mirrors or windows missing from your collection? Add to your book wish list.

CHAPTER 5

Supporting Language Development
Literacy and Biliteracy Instruction

Each word, each language has its own magic.

—From *The Upside Down Boy / El niño de cabeza*,
by Juan Felipe Herrera (2000, pp. 23)

In the previous chapters, we shared how children's books serve as mirrors and windows, creating valuable opportunities for building identity and community, as well as widening worldviews and deepening understandings about communities and society. In this chapter, we expand on those ideas as applied to language and literacy development. In the fourth and final component of the Inclusive Texts (IT) framework, we prioritize the purposeful incorporation of high-quality texts into classroom curriculum. As has been reiterated across this book, the goal is to not simply have these amazing texts on the shelves of classroom libraries, but to use them in daily instruction to nurture students' literacies, identities, and understandings.

Literacy instruction with inclusive texts supports learners in developing as readers and writers while building identities and critical literacy skills (Christ et al., 2018; DeNicolo & Franquiz, 2006; Ebe, 2010; McCullough, 2013). Mirror texts allow readers to bring cultural knowledge to meaning-making, deepening comprehension of texts and concepts (Christ et al., 2018; Schrodt, Fain, & Hasty, 2015). Inclusive texts belong across the literacy block, including read-alouds (Ryan & Hermann-Wilmarth, 2019), small-group reading and literature circles (DeNicolo & Franquiz, 2006; Fain, 2008; Jocius & Shealy, 2017), and literature extensions (Schrodt et al., 2015). Teachers can also use students' home languages for reading and learning. In the passage from *The Upside Down Boy / El niño de cabeza*, we hear an immigrant father's response to his son's developing bilingualism, who uses Spanish at home while learning English in school. For him, words across languages hold magic by facilitating communication and connections with one another. We agree and embrace inclusive texts as an important resource to nurture students' home language and biliteracy development (Freeman & Freeman, 2007; Schrodt et al., 2015). When teachers embrace linguistic funds of knowledge, readers deepen connections with texts and languages, leading to greater comprehension and engagement (Ebe, 2012; Giroir, Grimaldo, Vaughn, & Roberts, 2015).

The purpose of this chapter is to feature how inclusive texts, including those written in multiple languages, enhance the literacy block or language-arts classroom to facilitate students' learning and literacy development. We start by considering key levers that influence children's engagement and motivation: text selection and linguistic medium. When we dive into using inclusive texts across the various components of reading and writing work-shops, we weave in these lenses on literacy and biliteracy development.

KEY LEVERS FOR LITERACY ENGAGEMENT AND MOTIVATION

Think about what motivates you to read a book. Usually the text stands out to you for some reason: relevance to you and your own interests, connections to certain aspects of the story, or your desire to learn something. You probably embrace the potential to *choose* what you read by browsing the shelves at your local library or bookstore, or by visiting an online site. If the book resonates and hooks you with the characters and storyline, you likely cannot wait to suggest the title to friends and neighbors to have conversations in the future.

Just like us, students demonstrate motivation to read if (a) the book feels relevant to their lives, (b) they have a wide selection of texts from which to choose, and (c) they talk with peers about what they read (Gambrell, 2011). Purposeful selection of texts to share with students, as well as consideration of the languages used in texts, can be two powerful approaches to fostering engagement and motivation in literacy.

Selecting Texts to Engage and Motivate Readers

Inclusive texts engage readers via relevance and authenticity, providing space to interact with texts in deeper and more meaningful ways than low-level texts that focus solely on building basic reading skills (Tatum, 2000). Inclusive texts can foster a strong affinity for reading in students and promote engagement, which subsequently bolsters reading achievement (Freeman & Freeman, 2004; Gambrell, 2011; Guthrie & Wigfield, 1999). In other words, engaged readers maintain motivation to read and subse-quently become better readers. Given a range of texts across genres that serve as windows and mirrors, as well as space in the classroom for mean-ingful and authentic dialogue about those texts, children feel motivated to read and engage with books, further supporting literacy development.

Fostering literacy motivation and engagement connects back to the first part of the IT framework—getting to know students. The more teach-ers learn about their students, the better they connect each student with relevant, meaningful, and interesting books. As described in the previous chapter, using texts as mirrors allows readers to tap into funds of knowledge and establish connections to dynamic lived experiences (Tschida, Ryan, & Ticknor, 2014). When teachers incorporate mirror texts into their classroom collections and literacy curricula, personal connections with texts allow students to (a) construct meaning and visualize texts through familiarity with aspects of the content or storyline, (b) make meaningful predictions and inferences due to relevance and familiarity to their lives, (c) develop as strong readers who see their identities and experiences on the pages of texts, and (d) understand texts more fully and subsequently deepen engagement and motivation (Freeman & Freeman, 2004; Tatum, 2000).

Whereas mirror texts motivate students through reflections of themselves, window texts pique curiosities to learn about others' identities and experiences. Reading high-quality window texts positions children as active readers who make their own connections to social issues based on their lived experiences (Freire & Macedo, 1987). Research has shown that texts tackling sociopolitical issues increase engagement due to students' direct interest and connections with poignant topics in communities and the world around them (DeNicolo & Franquiz, 2006; Newstreet et al., 2018). Think back to Mitch's classroom, where students wanted to learn more about Indigenous tribes after reading various inclusive texts. Through discussions in the classroom, students developed interest in current events influencing Indigenous communities, leading them to seek changes in policies and disrupt stereotypes. By finding authentic window texts that match students' interests, teachers tap into motivation already present, leading to deeper engagement with reading, texts, and literacy instruction.

As described in Chapter 2, Anne begins each year getting to know students, including their interests, identities, and experiences. In addition to her identity unit, she gives students an interest inventory at the start of the year to get to know things they like to read and like to do, and other information about them. She makes notes of these interests as she builds her text collection for students, finding mirrors to match the students' identities as well as windows to match areas they want to learn more about. Anne personalizes text recommendations during reading conferences, where she and the student discuss both current and future texts. She prioritizes their identities and interests over reading levels; in fact, she does not level her books as a way for them to select texts to read. Instead, if a student wants to read a book that is too challenging to read independently at that time, she uses scaffolding strategies to provide access, such as using audio-recorded text or building background knowledge.

Using Multiple Languages in Literacy Instruction

The linguistic medium of texts also influences children's engagement, motivation, and comprehension, particularly for multilingual learners. Students enter classrooms with an array of language backgrounds, competencies, and preferences. In bilingual classrooms, children often use the same languages (e.g., Spanish, English) but vary in regional dialect, proficiency level, and home-language literacy ability. In English-medium classrooms, students come from various linguistic backgrounds, including Indigenous and immigrant languages and language varieties like African American Vernacular English. Regardless of classroom context, teachers can leverage and maintain children's rich language competencies. By embracing children's linguistic resources and providing texts and opportunities to respond to texts in multiple languages, teachers build readers' confidence, as well as enhance *literacy* (i.e., reading and writing in one language), *biliteracy* (i.e., reading and writing in two languages), and even *multiliteracies* (i.e., reading and writing in multiple languages; Hornberger, 2004).

Literacy skills *transfer* across languages, which means children need to learn to read in only one language and then apply those skills when reading in other languages (Cloud, Genessee, & Hamayan, 2009). Logically, students learn to read most efficiently in languages that they have used since birth, drawing from the sounds, letters, and words across their early childhood to crack the code and read texts. Not only do early readers benefit from home-language materials for reading, but so do primary and middle-grade multilingual learners. Research has shown that the most successful multilingual readers are those who recognize and use the connection between their languages while reading (Jiménez & Gámez, 1996). This *metalinguistic awareness* (Nagy & Anderson, 1995) facilitates the transfer of literacy skills between languages. Bilingual texts support metalinguistic awareness, as children see both languages on the same page. Think back to Javier's bilingual read-aloud with *René Has Two Last Names/René tiene dos apellidos* (Colato-Laínez, 2009). By reading the text in both languages, he allows children to tap into linguistic strengths to comprehend the story while calling attention to similarities and differences between languages. In this way, teachers build bridges between languages, pushing back against common practices that treat languages as separate entities that operate in seclusion.

But practitioners often enact linguistic transfer and metalinguistic awareness to promote literacy in Standard English, tapping into children's home languages but only as a means to yield assimilative practices in line with mainstream schooling expectations (Alim & Paris, 2018). Another pedagogical approach, *translanguaging*, offers teachers across classroom contexts the opportunity to embrace and sustain children's linguistic competencies. Translanguaging pedagogy centers not only on named languages but also on how individuals dynamically use and socially construct languages (García, 2009). Rather than rigidly defining the language of instruction, teachers encourage students to use their many linguistic competencies and repertoires while learning and engaging in the classroom. Think back to

Karen's ELA classroom and her student's creative responses to *Home of the Brave* (Applegate, 2007), merging Swahili, French, and English words and sketches to respond to the text and uniquely engage in literature discussions with her peers. Teaching in an English-medium classroom, Karen does not need to speak French or Swahili to recognize the value of translanguaging in enhancing literacy engagement and comprehension. By embracing other languages and language varieties and encouraging children to use these many linguistic resources in the classroom, teachers open a multitude of opportunities to develop multiliteracies and multifaceted identities.

In addition to shifting mindsets about which languages belong in classrooms, practitioners can nurture multiliteracies with bilingual and translingual texts. *Bilingual books* in different languages foster literacy and biliteracy development with all children, with options to use the English text, non-English text, or build bridges across languages. *Translingual books* mirror the authentic language practices of multilingual learners, where authors translanguage in the narrative to enhance students' interaction and comprehension with the text (Flores, 2019). Multilingual texts exist across genres, including fiction, nonfiction, and poetry, as well as tools like dictionaries and multimedia resources. It is important to note that just because a text is *bilingual* does not mean the text is *bicultural* or that it serves as a mirror to users of that language. Many times, prepackaged reading programs translate texts from English to other languages but maintain focus on dominant cultures and identities. For example, a translated text about a White family living on a farm likely does not serve as a mirror to a Spanish-speaking Latinx child living in the city. Authentic inclusive texts embrace children's language *and* culture, as well as other facets of their identities and experiences.

Lindsay embraces her young learners' multilingualism in all aspects of her classroom, beginning with the texts in her library that get incorporated throughout the school day during literacy and content-area instruction. She constantly seeks to build her collection with texts written in the languages used by students and families. Most of her students speak Spanish, Polish, or Arabic, so she has worked to procure bilingual texts in these languages, as well as authentic Spanish-, Polish-, and Arabic-medium texts from other regions of the world. In addition to formal data on home languages, Lindsay maintains frequent communication with families, gathering dynamic information on children's experiences to incorporate titles that align with interests and abilities. For example, some students attend Polish school on Saturdays, so she uses Polish-medium texts to reflect their home language and provide consistency across language learning experiences, as well as demonstrate similarities and differences between Polish and English reading to promote transfer of literacy skills between languages. But Lindsay does not restrict children to reading in prescribed languages. She frequently observes children's curiosity about books in different languages and encourages their multilingual exploration.

In sum, literacy instruction holds numerous opportunities to integrate inclusive texts, including those in multiple languages. Building classroom libraries stocked with mirror and window texts accessible to students is a start. But in addition to gathering inclusive mirrors and expansive windows, we want to use these texts to enhance and shift instruction. Simply using an inclusive during a read-aloud, for example, does not have the same impact as facilitating important conversations around that text to foster critical consciousness and encourage deep questioning and analytical thinking (Wood & Jocius, 2013). When intertwined with the multiple facets of literacy instruction, the use of inclusive, multilingual texts has deep and wide impact. In the next section, we explore ways to develop literacy and biliteracy by incorporating inclusive texts into the different components of readers' and writers' workshop.

READERS' WORKSHOP AND LITERACY INSTRUCTION

Readers' workshop is an instructional model that allows teachers to flexibly provide instruction to reach individual students through authentic reading experiences (Serafini, 2001). Workshops take on different structures and formats (e.g., Daily Five, literacy centers) but often consist of similar activities. Each day, classrooms might feature read-alouds, mini-lessons, guided reading, book clubs, and independent reading, among other activities focused on language, decoding, and vocabulary (Serafini, 2001). In this section, we look at how inclusive texts fit into these aspects of literacy instruction. All components offer opportunities for the use of inclusive texts to disrupt the status quo and provide opportunities for students to learn through high-quality mirror and window books (see Table 5.1).

Interactive Read-Alouds

Daily read-alouds are a commonplace activity in elementary classrooms (Fisher, Flood, Lapp, & Frey, 2004). More specifically, teachers often engage in interactive read-alouds with frequent opportunities to pause, reflect, think aloud, and encourage dialogue from students. Read-alouds give the whole class access to the same text, regardless of children's reading skills or abilities, creating space for teachers to (a) share reading strategies, (b) explore authors' craft, (c) model fluent reading, (d) introduce vocabulary, and (e) invite students to reflect and share (Hoyt, 2016). Additionally, read-alouds provide opportunities for students, including multilingual learners, to use language in meaningful and authentic ways, drawing from the discourse

Table 5.1. Literacy Instruction With Inclusive Texts

Strategy	Description Using Inclusive Texts
Interactive Read-Aloud	During read-aloud, pause to model critical literacy lens through questioning the author's intent, looking for representation in texts, interrogating texts for stereotypes, and building conversation around sociopolitical issues.
Mini-lessons	Targeted lessons on topics such as using a critical lens when reading, learning how to have discussions about texts, and looking for representation in texts.
Guided Reading	Supporting students with the skills and strategies they are expected to learn using inclusive texts with BIPOC characters, social issue topics, or identities that are often underrepresented.
Literature Circles/ Book Clubs	Provide space for students to choose a text and participate in conversations with peers around the texts that foster empathy, identity, self-efficacy, and critical literacy lens.
Author/Genre Studies	Intentional inclusion and study of BIPOC authors, inclusive identities in all genres, and Own Voices authors and illustrators.
Writing	Using mentor texts to promote engaged writing about self-identities or use of inclusive texts to model author's craft.

of the text, author, and teacher to practice, extend, and develop their own language (Christ & Cho, 2021). During interactive read-alouds, children collaboratively use their languages to make sense of the text, ask questions, and share connections.

Read-alouds offer space to foster thinking about representation, identity, and social justice issues that impact children's everyday lives (Meller, Richardson, & Hatch, 2009). Text selection makes visible and embraces different stories, highlights voices and identities traditionally excluded, and focuses on justice issues in communities and society (Harste, 2000; Leland, Lewison, & Harste, 2018). In an effective read-aloud, the text itself is a medium for the rich discussion that takes place during and after reading, which involves the teacher posing purposeful questions for learners to reflect, respond, and engage with one another (Meller et al., 2009). In Chapter 4, we shared strategies and prompts to build critically literate conversations around inclusive texts (see Table 4.3). These conversations provide opportunities for children to practice critical questioning, interrogate texts, and experience texts as both mirrors and windows through dialogue with one another.

Read-aloud texts carry across learning objectives, pique varied critical conversations, and serve as a touchstone for ongoing learning. When used in this longitudinal way, the book becomes an anchor text read multiple times to support learning across the school year. An anchor text becomes the central text on which to build a text set around topics, themes, or genres. You might select an anchor text that provides mirrors or windows for students or because the text structure aligns to reading objectives like analyzing character development or determining the central idea. Because the text connects to students' experiences, they can engage with the story to enhance comprehension. Additionally, inclusive texts as read-alouds show students the multitude of identities and experiences deemed valuable to include in the curriculum (Ryan & Hermann-Wilmarth, 2019). The read-aloud then connects to future lessons around the text, such as recalling character development when introducing character traits. You can reread the text for author's craft during writing lessons, or perhaps use the text to spur discussion during content-area instruction. In this way, future lessons and learning are *anchored* to the read-aloud.

Let's go back to Anne's middle-grade classroom to see strategic use of inclusive texts for read-alouds. She selected *The Proudest Blue: A Story of Hijab and Family* (Muhammad, 2019) to read early in the school year to kick off conversations around identity. This became an anchor text that the class returned to throughout the school year for different purposes, such as finding themes of texts and analyzing color representations in stories. As Anne got to know her students, read-aloud selections centered on students developing identities, building community, and taking perspectives. She selected *Fish in a Tree* (Hunt, 2017), a text about a young girl with dyslexia, to support learners with inferring character traits as aligned to Common Core standards, as well as to begin conversations about disabilities and learning differences. One child connected to the text because of his own dyslexia, opening up with the class about his experiences with reading and learning. When kids left for lunch after the read-aloud, the child approached Anne and shared his excitement to see himself in the book read to the class.

Read-alouds do not solely involve text selection but also how teachers and students use the text to engage in rich discussion. As exemplified in Anne's classroom, we see how texts serve as both mirrors and windows depending on the reader, which enriches dialogue among communities of learners as they listen to one another's perspectives and connections. By facilitating the emergent discussions following read-alouds, teachers allow learning to occur not just from the text and teacher but from one another. Interactive read-aloud time is an ideal place to begin weaving inclusive texts into the classroom, as even teachers with mandated curricula typically select their own books for read-alouds. By strategically selecting and using texts based on students and goals, teachers create space during read-aloud time for children to connect and engage in these invaluable conversations with one another.

Mini-lessons

Mini-lessons refer to 10- to 15-minute lessons explicitly focused on one skill, strategy, or topic in reading, writing, or language (Fountas & Pinnell, 2018). These often take place in the whole-group setting, with foci emergent from learning goals, standards, curriculum, or students' needs (Atwell, 2017). Unlike read-alouds, mini-lessons are short and targeted to a specific aspect of literacy, often using a brief passage to model a strategy, rather than a full text. Mini-lessons might focus on finding the main idea, looking at figurative language, or comparing and contrasting texts. Teachers often look at students' abilities, combined with learning outcomes for their grade level, to plan these short lessons (Fountas & Pinnell, 2018). Mini-lessons allow the whole class to receive instruction on the same focus before providing individualized opportunities to practice and apply skills (Atwell, 2017).

Mini-lessons can center inclusive texts that tap into children's funds of knowledge to develop language and literacy skills. Tori teaches in a primary, dual-language classroom where she uses Spanish and English instruction to support her students' biliteracy development, including mini-lessons to develop metalinguistic awareness. Recognizing the importance of cognates for Spanish-English bilingual readers, she designed a mini-lesson that encouraged students to recognize cognates in texts. *I Love Saturdays y domingos* (Ada, 2004) alternates between English and Spanish to capture authentic activities with the protagonist's English- and Spanish-speaking grandparents, with the author explicitly using cognates to allow all readers to comprehend both languages. For example, on Saturday the protagonist watches a circus video with lions, tigers, giraffes, and elephants, while on Sunday she visits the real *circo* with *leones*, *tigres*, *jirafas*, and *elefantes*. Using a portion of the text, the class went on a guided cognate scavenger hunt, listing and discussing the similar words that they encountered. Tori informed her language detectives that cognates help them to be effective and efficient readers, encouraging them to use this biliteracy skill in their small-group and independent reading.

In addition to developing literacy and biliteracy skills, mini-lessons with inclusive texts can tackle critical literacy skills, such as disrupting biases and assumptions, breaking stereotypes, probing the author's positionality, taking social action, and providing multiple perspectives. For example, in *Milo Imagines the World* (de la Peña, 2021), the protagonist imagines the lives of the people he encounters on the subway, where he makes assumptions about their backgrounds and lives. Engaging with the text requires inferring skills to make informed guesses based on observable traits of people and visual literacy to examine the illustrations where Milo disrupts his assumptions to reimagine other possible lives for those same people. When strategically selected and used in mini-lessons, this and other inclusive texts serve to disrupt potential biases and develop critical literacy skills for reading texts and the world.

Small-Group and Guided Reading

Elementary teachers often spend time working with small reading groups, often called *guided reading* or *small-group reading*. This small-group instruction allows for focused support and guidance in helping students develop a range of reading strategies and skills (Fountas & Pinnell, 2012). In traditional guided reading, teachers flexibly group four to six students based on reading levels, abilities, interests, and needs. After selecting texts to match the students and goals of the reading group, the teacher guides readers through thinking about the text before, during, and after reading. These small-group lessons are an important approach for teachers to differentiate instruction and provide support in a smaller setting (Serafini, 2001).

Small-group reading begins with students. Drawing from formal and anecdotal data sources, teachers can use their knowledge of children's abilities, strengths, and interests. When planning small-group reading instruction, keep in mind asset-based approaches to instruction (Alim & Paris, 2018; Moll et al., 1992), as well as the research indicating enhanced reading comprehension when using relevant texts (Ebe, 2010; McCullough, 2013; Perez, 2004). Whereas small-group reading often targets students' needs (i.e., deficits) and dictates text selection by reading level, inclusive texts allow teachers to focus on students' strengths and leverage resources to foster rich connections, conversations, and comprehension (Fountas & Pinnell, 2012). In this way, reading groups move beyond rote reading levels to instead center on children's identities and experiences, mediated by mirror texts that value and sustain their funds of knowledge while offering opportunities to practice reading skills and strategies.

In Tori's primary dual-language classroom, she uses inclusive texts across her literacy block, including in guided reading groups. Her curriculum provides authentic Spanish and English books for small groups, rather than translated, decodable readers with stories from dominant cultures common in other curricula. Tori recognizes that these books serve as windows and mirrors, including those about Latinx legends and celebrations, as well as characters from cultures around the world. In one unit on communities, her curriculum prompts children to recognize the character's point of view and compare and contrast communities. During guided reading, she designed lessons that targeted these skills using textual mirrors. For example, students read *Trouble at the Sandbox* (Simpson, 2016) and *Chato y su cena* (Soto, 1997), which center around the theme of communities. Readers made connections to their own communities, eventually holding a food drive to donate to a local food pantry to reinforce the concept of working together with community resources. Tori noted the students' enhanced engagement and interest when they read these inclusive and relatable texts in both Spanish and English.

One obstacle we often hear from teachers relates to leveled readers in their school's reading program as not being inclusive or allowing for critical conversations. Some publishers are starting to consider this lens for these types of texts. For example, Lee & Low Books, a publisher that prioritizes BIPOC authors, characters, and storylines, has created book rooms with culturally relevant and bilingual leveled texts. Additionally, more inclusive early readers have emerged on the market, including series like *Princess Truly* (Greenwalt, 2020), *Juana and Lucas* (Medina, 2019), and *Ty's Travels* (Lyons, 2020), which center on BIPOC characters. These and other inclusive options might shift small-group reading instruction beyond the often culturally neutral texts provided in prepacked curricula (Sims-Bishop, 1997).

Literature Discussions

In addition to teacher-guided, small-group instruction, book clubs (Raphael & McMahon, 1994) and literature circles (Daniels, 2002) are excellent spaces to incorporate discussion around inclusive texts. In both formats, students read, write, and orally discuss one common text in a small-group setting. Unlike teacher-led groups, students lead conversations, prompting relevant and authentic dialogue about texts that simulate discussions we often have outside of classrooms about texts that we read, enjoy, and reflect upon with others. When teachers plan literature discussion groups using inclusive texts, students engage in deep conversations resulting in enhanced literacy and language development (Jocius & Shealy, 2017).

Book clubs can focus on sociopolitical issues and multifaceted identities and experiences, hinging on accountable student talk (Mills & Jennings, 2011). Conversations about texts should welcome multiple perspectives within safe and respectful contexts, which requires modeling for learners to see these authentic and autonomous discussions in action. Teachers might first model how to have discussions about books in the whole-class setting, defining norms to encourage respectful dialogue that leads to deeper thinking. From here, teachers move into partner reading, where children practice discussion skills with another student in a smaller context. During partner reading, teachers prompt students to share thoughts using sentence stems (e.g., I noticed, I was surprised by, I connected to this by) or with strategies like *Say Something* (Short, Harste, & Burke, 1996) to encourage periodic stops to share thoughts, questions, connections, or reactions to the text with one another. Many teachers use partner reading for weeks or months as they apprentice learners into literature discussions.

Literature discussion groups can be organized in various ways. Some teachers prefer to assign roles to students, such as summarizer, question-generator, connection-maker, story-mapper, or vocabulary expert (Daniels, 2002; Leland et al., 2018). While students take on these roles or engage in organic conversation without assigned roles, teachers rotate between groups and support deeper discussion when needed, prompting students to say more or consider another perspective. Students might use specific strategies such as identity webs, personal traits, headlines, or questioning the author (see Tables 4.3 and 4.5 in Chapter 4). Once students grow comfortable in literature discussions, they consider multiple perspectives, share connections between texts and sociopolitical issues that impact their lives, affirm their identities and experiences, and learn about others around them (Leland et al., 2018).

Anne chooses inclusive texts for her book clubs, giving students as much choice as possible so that they select something that feels like a mirror to them or a window to an identity they want to know more about. In their unit on equality, Anne offers students book-club choice titles like *Amina's Voice* (Khan, 2017), *Amal Unbound* (Saeed, 2018), *Front Desk* (Yang, 2018), *Wishtree* (Applegate, 2017), *Ghost Boys* (Parker Rhodes, 2019), and *I Am Malala* (Yousafzai, 2016). She coaches students through critical conversations where they dig deeper into identities explored in the novels and prompts sharing of connections to texts. Over time, children take ownership of book clubs, leading conversations where they question the author's intent, explore related texts for deeper understanding of content, and listen to multiple perspectives from peers about different issues. Learners deeply engage in book clubs and make meaningful and authentic connections to the texts, other parts of literacy instruction, and peers through these conversations. For example, when discussing *Amina's Voice*, students (a) connected to their cultural identities, (b) discussed how family members either maintained their culture or tried to assimilate, and (c) interrogated these decisions from various lenses. These rich connections took place *while* Anne's middle-grade students learned the required standards and reading skills.

Author Studies

Author studies support students in studying the craft of particular authors, analyzing the works of focal authors to make connections, compare different texts, explore their writing style, and increase enjoyment and motivation to read (Fox, 2007; Jenkins, 2006). Studying authors helps readers analyze across texts by a single author, looking for commonalities in style, topics, or characters. During author studies, students delve into the author's background, getting to know the person behind the stories. These varied activities support readers' excitement around reading, as well as nurture overall literacy development (Fox, 2007).

Author studies also foster critical conversations with lenses on diversity and inclusion (Fox, 2007). Through intentional decisions to include BIPOC and LGBTQ creators, as well as authors and illustrators with disabilities, teachers ensure wider representation of identities for children to explore. Many author-study websites feature authors from dominant identity groups, mainly White, English-dominant, cisgender males without disabilities. For example, in primary grades, we often see Eric Carle, Mo Willems, Dr. Seuss, and Kevin Henkes as suggested author studies. These authors are also those whose works are revered as the *classics* of early grades. While some of these works provide fun contributions to the classroom, the continued overreliance on these authors reinforces the need to intentionally seek out BIPOC, LGBTQ, and disabled authors, as well as others from traditionally marginalized identity groups.

In her school, where more than 80% of the students identify as Black, Latinx, or multiracial, Felisha consistently searches for mirror texts for her middle-grade students while encouraging critical analysis of the inclusion and exclusion of voices in the curriculum. Though her literacy curriculum does not include author studies, Felisha designed and incorporated author-focused units using text sets by BIPOC authors, including Grace Lin and Jacqueline Woodson, for her students to explore. She selected these authors because their work served as mirrors for many students, but also windows to new identities and experiences. Her students responded with interest, noticing similarities in topics, craft, and themes across each author's texts and expressing the desire to read more texts by these focal authors. Tapping into the consistent instructional lenses on culturally sustaining and critical literacy, children noticed and sought to learn more about the BIPOC authors' backgrounds, identities, and experiences.

WRITING INSTRUCTION AND WRITING WORKSHOP

Writing workshop has been widely used for decades to organize writing instruction in elementary classrooms (Fletcher & Portalupi, 2001). In this approach, teachers support student writers by (a) teaching short mini-lessons on specific skills or strategies, (b) providing time for their own individual writing, and (c) creating space for sharing finished pieces. Teachers often hold individual and small-group conferences to provide individualized lessons while the rest of the class works independently (Fletcher & Portalupi, 2001).

Whether due to writing curricula or expectations from standards, writing instruction often focuses heavily on conventions, including grammar and spelling, linear and fixed steps of the writing process (i.e., brainstorming, drafting, revising, editing, publishing), and formulaic approaches to organization (e.g., five-paragraph essay). These rigid approaches to writing disengage learners from developing passion and care about writing and limit their abilities and ways to express themselves (Cutler & Graham, 2008).

Alternatively, inclusive texts provide a medium to center children's identities and experiences while developing the skills possessed by successful writers. In this section, we highlight two approaches used during writing workshop: using mentor texts in mini-lessons and supporting students' independent writing.

Inclusive Mentor Texts in Mini-lessons

When thinking about creating a specific type of writing for the first time (e.g., graduate school paper, grant application), you likely benefit from seeing an exemplar text to emulate and align to your own writing style. In K–12 classrooms, teachers use models in the form of *mentor texts* across literacy and content-area instruction to exemplify types of writing for various purposes (Gallagher, 2011). Mentor texts in writing instruction provide strong examples of authors' craft, allowing learners to focus on specific strategies or aspects of their writing. Teachers use mentor texts to encourage children to take risks and try new things in their writing, which nurtures feelings of authenticity and empowerment as authors (Gainer, 2013).

Mentor texts frequently mediate writing mini-lessons (Fletcher & Portalupi, 2001). By using inclusive texts as mentor texts, writers simultaneously learn about writing skills while centering traditionally marginalized identities (Beschorner & Hall, 2021). Knowing children's identities and choosing relevant and authentic texts to model aspects of writing yield powerful results. For instance, you might teach a mini-lesson about adding details to create the setting of a story. Amid the many texts featuring strong settings with rich word choice, select mentor texts that capture students' lived experiences, such as *Last Stop on Market Street* (de la Peña, 2015) and *My Papi Has a Motorcycle* (Quintero, 2019) for urban and suburban settings or *The Christmas Gift/El regalo de Navidad* (Jiménez, 2000) and *At the Mountain's Base* (Sorell, 2019) for rural settings. Please visit this book's supplemental website (inclusivetexts.weebly.com) for ideas on using inclusive texts as mentors for common writing mini-lesson topics.

Anne consistently centers children's identities and experiences during writing mini-lessons using inclusive mentor texts. She was excited to find *I Am Every Good Thing* (Barnes, 2020), a lyrical picture book highlighting a young Black boy who proudly embraces who he is, while also pushing back on who he is not. She selected the text to simultaneously serve as a mirror and window and subsequently engage all students as they connected to the protagonist. During one mini-lesson, Anne read the mentor text aloud, aiming for students to write their own poems or passages connected to their identities. She highlighted the text's "I am, I am not" framework (p. 3), prompting students to actively notice how that framework supported the text. Writers then used these as sentence starters to dig into self-ascribed identities as well as those often placed on them by others. Anne modeled her own sentences using this same framework to reflect on her identities for students.

Linking Mini-lessons to Student Writing

After selecting strong inclusive texts to use for mini-lessons during writing, teachers support students in using aspects of these books in their own writing pieces (Gallagher, 2011). Using mentor texts to guide writing helps students develop confidence, take risks, and apply individuality to their work (Marchetti & O'Dell, 2015). Teachers explicitly model how to apply the writing style from a mentor text to their own writing through think-alouds, shared writing with students, and coaching in small-group and individual settings.

Writing workshop should also allow space for multiple languages and identities to be part of both process and product. By encouraging students to write in their home languages and language varieties, teachers reinforce cultural and linguistic diversity as valuable (Lee & Handsfield, 2018). This multilingual lens on writing instruction includes various dialects and forms of English that differ from Standard English, such as African American Vernacular English. To facilitate and model writing with multiple languages and language varieties, teachers deliberately select mentor texts in writing that have characters that disrupt the status quo for language. For example, teachers might use *Chess Rumble* (Neri, 2007), *Dear Primo: A Letter to My Cousin* (Tonatiuh, 2010), or *We Are Grateful: Otsaliheliga* (Sorell, 2018) to show characters using a variety of languages or dialects (Beschorner & Hall, 2021; Hartman & Machado, 2019). Multilingual learners use the texts as exemplars to see how authors weave multiple languages throughout one story, followed by using their language competencies in writing.

In Anna's middle-grade, Spanish-English dual-language classroom, she and her students express themselves flexibly in multiple languages. Though bilingual classrooms tend to compartmentalize languages, encouraging the use of Spanish or English only depending on the content area (García, 2009), Anna encourages learners to tap into their competencies in all languages throughout the school day, including during writing instruction. To start the school year, Anna reads *Marisol McDonald Doesn't Match/ Marisol McDonald no combina* (Brown, 2011) as the mentor text to initiate writing workshop. The book explores the protagonist's bicultural identity, prompting conversations about students' identities and experiences of being bilingual. Students create writing pieces about their identities and ways they might not match, as well as various cultural and linguistic influences on their lives. Of utmost importance, Anna models and encourages children to use Spanish, English, and potentially other languages and language varieties in their writing. As students share their writing and experiences with one another, they make connections and celebrate the uniqueness and diversity they all bring to the classroom.

Tapping into children's multilingualism in writing does not require multilingual teachers. After Anne used *I Am Every Good Thing* (Barnes, 2020) to highlight text structure, children's identities emerged in writing with products tackling issues of race, religion, culture, language, academic abilities, athletic abilities, and gender expression. Anne noticed strong, passionate writing pieces of which students were proud and subsequently shifted her personal-narrative unit to connect to the theme of identity woven across her language-arts curriculum. She incorporated mentor texts with depictions of identity development, such as *My Name Is Sangoel* (Williams & Mohammed, 2009) and *Stepping Stones* (Ruurs, 2016), to exemplify how to capture stories and memories related to children' identities. One student wrote about a memory from 2 years prior when a new student spoke primarily Assyrian. When the new student cried on her first day, this student used Assyrian to comfort the new student, sparking a beautiful friendship. As Anne's student recalled this memory, the student inquired if she could write part of the story in Assyrian since she used Assyrian to think about the story. Anne happily agreed, and this resulted in a meaningful piece of writing for this child, who had previously struggled during writing instruction. By using inclusive texts in writing instruction, children can explore and sustain their identities and languages (Flores, 2018).

PUTTING IT ALL TOGETHER IN THE CLASSROOM

Jenny is a middle-grade teacher at a school with 92% BIPOC students, including 45% Black, 23% Latinx, 17% Asian, and 6% multiracial. She blends the various components of literacy instruction with her students by exploring identity twice per school year—once at the beginning to develop concepts as they get to know one another and later in the year when students feel comfortable with one another and have melded into a class community. Deeper conversations emerge as they feel safe to share more about themselves. She reads aloud books that focus on a range of identities, noting the students' favorite as *Crown: An Ode to the Fresh Cut* (Barnes, 2017). To support her multilingual learners, she strategically introduces vocabulary associated with identity and community during read-aloud time, with follow-up supports during targeted mini-lessons. She provides spaces for oral language development as children use the new vocabulary discussing their own identities and those of characters in the texts she shares.

In small groups, Jenny pulls in many inclusive texts for book clubs and guided reading, selecting texts like *One Crazy Summer* (Williams-Garcia, 2011) or *Maybe Something Beautiful* (Campoy & Howell, 2016). She uses these learner-centered spaces to guide students in discussing the texts, using their concepts and related vocabulary on identity and community. Jenny also guides readers in small groups to look at who is telling the stories, noting how stories differ when told from a different perspective, or from someone inside the community versus an outsider's viewpoint. In this way, small-group literacy instruction not only focuses on standards-based reading skills but also authentically integrates opportunities for critical literacy.

In her writing instruction, Jenny consistently uses inclusive texts. To initiate the personal-narrative unit, she shares several poetry books and short stories by BIPOC authors, with texts highlighting personal identity (e.g., *Hope Nation;* Brock, 2018; *Woke: A Young Poet's Call to Justice;* Browne, Acevedo, & Gatwood, 2020). Students engage and connect with texts, expressing how they love the various ways to celebrate different identities. Texts serve as mentor texts for children to write about their own identities, where pride and joy emerge in her students' writing. Jenny later uses biographical immigration stories, leading students to interview family members who immigrated to the United States. Students then turn interviews into pieces of writing.

Finally, Jenny pulls all facets of literacy instruction together by providing students with opportunities to engage in reflective dialogue around inclusive texts. These whole- and small-group discussions merge and develop children's reading, writing, speaking, and listening about justice-oriented topics emergent from inclusive texts, such as the Black Lives Matter movement. They discuss identities, communities, and social justice while pulling in nonfiction texts, news articles, video clips, and historical fiction to enrich conversations and deepen understandings. Jenny encourages children to tap into their multiple languages, identities, and experiences to mediate literacies and their larger understandings of the world.

THE FRAMEWORK IN ACTION: NURTURING STUDENTS' LANGUAGE AND LITERACY

As awareness grows about the widening array of high-quality inclusive texts, more teachers like Jenny, Anne, Anna, Lindsey, and Tori have prioritized integration of these texts into literacy and language-arts instruction. When strategically selected based on students, goals, and authenticity, inclusive texts mediate literacy and language development while sustaining identities and promoting critical consciousness and worldviews. But this work is not without its obstacles, and each teacher should find appropriate and flexible spaces in their curricula to weave in diverse voices to enrich the literacy block. The primary pitfall of this work lies in rigid interpretations of mandated standards and curricula, with stakeholders framing these documents as scripts to follow rather than using them to guide teachers' expert decision-making based on the unique learners in classrooms. As we explored in Chapter 3 and noted throughout this chapter, every teacher has the agency to select texts that nurture children in learning, reading, and growing as human beings.

Let's connect back to the ideas that we explored in Chapter 3. Literacy standards and curricula often focus on isolated skills and concepts, prompting interpretation as the need to move back to basics with whole-class instruction using canonical literature rather than centering children's identities (Papola-Ellis, 2014). But standards are simply guideposts for the scope and sequence of literacy development, and curricula provide resources to promote progress toward those goals. Teachers have the agency and expertise to select and use inclusive texts that align with students and goals. Think back to Anne's literacy instruction addressing the standard of determining the theme of a text, where she selected a text serving as a window for some and a mirror for others, creating space for students to discuss the theme together. Even with predefined curricula, teachers can use texts aligned to students' identities, experiences, and perspectives. Whether you use original units or prescribed basals, use the tools in Chapter 3 to analyze curricula to find space for inclusive texts to enhance literacy engagement and development.

Inclusive texts do indeed provide effective tools to facilitate children's learning as a part of culturally sustaining pedagogy and critical literacy instruction. But the linguistic medium of those texts, as well as the discussions, reflections, and writings that emerge from those texts, also play an integral role, particularly for multilingual learners. All children bring rich resources into classrooms, with a large and growing number of students who speak, read, and write in languages other than English. After recognizing standards as guideposts for children's learning, teachers can embrace roles as active decision-makers who use children's rich linguistic resources to reach English-focused literacy goals in the standards, as well as more pluralist goals for developing and maintaining rich competencies in multiple languages (Alim & Paris, 2018). Whether in English-medium or bilingual classrooms, teachers can integrate opportunities for children to use their home languages to support literacy and biliteracy development. Reflect upon what this asset-based approach to multilingual learners might look like in your classroom context, potentially exploring professional literature in more depth (e.g., García, Ibarra Johnson, & Seltzer, 2017). Then consider how inclusive texts springboard this work, tapping into both bilingual resources and those written in the languages used by your students.

Throughout this chapter, you have read ideas and examples of inclusive text integration in the literacy block. This focus on purposeful integration of inclusive texts in the curriculum rounds out the four-part IT framework. As you consider applications in your literacy instruction, remember to start with students, such as making space for children's home languages and cultures in classrooms. From Lindsay's inclusion of multilingual books to Anne's encouragement of biliteracy in writing, intentional choices embrace and tap into children's assets and identities. You might start small rather than trying to tackle your entire literacy curriculum. For example, consider the texts you use for each component of literacy instruction (e.g., read-aloud, guided reading, writing) and try replacing one existing text with a high-quality inclusive text that serves as a mirror or a window for the unique learners in your class. See how your students respond, and draw from their interactions and recommendations to select additional texts that deepen their literacy engagement and development.

The literacy block is an excellent place to begin weaving inclusive texts into your regular repertoire of classroom practice; however, content-area instruction is also ripe for inclusion of these texts, allowing students to hear multiple perspectives and see diverse identities while learning throughout the school day and across the curriculum. In the next chapter, we continue to explore this fourth facet of the framework on instructional implementation by looking at inclusive texts in social studies, science, mathematics, and special areas.

QUESTIONS AND ACTIVITIES FOR PROFESSIONAL DEVELOPMENT

1. Think about the home languages of your students. Are these welcomed and supported in your classroom? In what ways? Locate books that feature your students' languages to include in the classroom library and/or support students in including multiple languages in their writing. What do you notice about students' literacy engagement?

2. Look at the mentor texts that you use to teach writing. Would you consider these books to be inclusive? Do they serve as models for writing while also centering traditionally excluded voices and identities (e.g., BIPOC, LGBTQ)? Also consider language in your writing workshop. Are students allowed to write freely in multiple languages and language varieties? Do conventions (e.g., grammar, punctuation, spelling) typify your writing instruction, or do you support students with word choice, focusing ideas, and adding details? Challenge yourself to include all identities and languages in writing workshop and consider how inclusive texts might facilitate students' multilingual and translingual writing.

3. Choose one aspect of your language and literacy instruction. What is one change you could make immediately to use more inclusive texts or strategies? Share this idea with a colleague and have a discussion after making the change. How did students react and respond? What was student engagement and learning like with the inclusive text?

CHAPTER 6

Deepening Understandings

Inclusive Texts Across Disciplines

> Katherine told mission control, "You can count on me." She rolled up her
> sleeves, took a deep breath, and began doing the math.
>
> —From *Counting on Katherine: How Katherine Johnson*
> *Put Astronauts on the Moon,* by Helaine Becker (2018, p. 25)

When we discuss the use of inclusive texts in classrooms, the logical focus is on literacy and language arts. But with high-quality texts exploring a vast array of topics, stories, and perspectives, the potential expands for inclusion in social studies, mathematics, science, and the special areas (e.g., art, music, physical education). In Chapter 1, we discuss how the literary canon maintains White, male, heteronormative, and other dominant voices. Content-area curricula often reflect the same trends, such as the history textbook written from the White male perspective or the science textbook prioritizing contributions of homogenous scientists, leading students to feel excluded by not seeing themselves and people like them as integral contributors. But every discipline has been enriched and shaped by diverse individuals, and curricula should include the contributions of innovators like African American mathematician Katherine Johnson. By using inclusive texts like *Counting on Katherine* across elementary and middle-school curricula, students can develop nuanced and accurate understandings of the disciplines.

In contrast to literacy and language arts, the use of inclusive texts in the content areas is relatively understudied. Nonetheless, existing research converges around its efficacy in enriching students' perspectives and understandings of focal disciplinary topics. Many studies investigate students' learning in response to a particular text, such as *The Legend of St. Ann's Flood* in social studies (Jacob, 2005, as cited in Fry, 2009), *The Space Traders* in science (Bell, 1992, as cited in Laughter & Adams, 2012), and *My Granny Went to Market* in mathematics (Blackstone, 2005, as cited in Iliev & D'Angelo, 2014). These texts, commonly referred to as *trade books*, accompany content-area textbooks and curricula and prompt students to think of disciplinary concepts in larger societal concepts and in their own lives. While multicultural literature has often been the concentration of content-area integration (e.g., McCarty, 2007), inclusive texts provide nuanced, relevant, and authentic accounts of diverse individuals and communities. With a growing number of disciplinary-themed inclusive texts, teachers can enrich content-area instruction by purposefully integrating relevant narratives and authentic perspectives.

This chapter explores using inclusive texts to develop and deepen students' learning, understandings, and engagement in content-area instruction. Using the Inclusive Texts (IT) framework, texts become a consistent and central feature of the disciplinary curriculum, rather than using one or two texts across the school year and subsequently perpetuating the single story. We begin by detailing available genres and applications in each content area and then present strategies for incorporating texts into instructional design in disciplinary units and lessons. The goal is for readers to build familiarity with the rich array of texts available and consider ways to formally enact these resources to push forward students' learning in the classroom.

INCLUSIVE TEXTS BEYOND THE LITERACY BLOCK

Incorporating inclusive texts across the curriculum means extending children's exposure to windows and mirrors in ways that purposively tap into background knowledge, deepen understandings, and promote criticality (Saint-Hilaire, 2014; Vasquez, 2017). Fortunately, more texts are published each year that reflect our students and their world with disciplinary themes that widen the possibilities for use in content-area instruction. In this section, we explore how inclusive texts enhance teaching and learning in social studies, science, mathematics, and special areas. We consider uses of inclusive texts in each discipline and provide text and classroom examples to enhance connections to practice. Visit the book's supplemental website (inclusivetexts.weebly.com) for detailed lists of text ideas by content area.

Exploring Authentic Perspectives: Focus on Social Studies

In social studies instruction, inclusive texts provide windows to learn beyond students' known world, as well as mirrors for readers to relate content to personal, familial, cultural, and community experiences. Outside of the literacy block, social studies has the largest array of inclusive texts for integration into classroom instruction, which is not surprising due to the broad disciplinary focus on how people live and interact with one another in both past and present (Cruz & Thornton, 2013). Trade books provide multiple narratives and perspectives on historical and current events that may be excluded from social studies textbooks that often center on dominant perspectives (Loewen, 2018). High-quality inclusive texts, those that reflect the criteria for relevance and authenticity discussed in Chapter 2, are available to tackle an array of topics, time frames, contexts, and people spanning the domains of the C3 Social Studies Standards, including civics, economics, geography, and history (NCSS, 2013). Both nonfiction and fiction texts can mediate disciplinary understandings and civic values to yield active citizens in a participatory democracy (NCSS, 2021).

Numerous texts provide nonfiction accounts of social studies topics, offering nuanced portrayals and authentic perspectives often left out of the curriculum. In our review of high-quality inclusive texts for K–8 classrooms, two categories of nonfiction emerge: those focusing on individuals and those probing larger events, locations, or movements. Personal perspectives and authentic accounts emerge in well-researched *biographies* on leaders in politics and history (e.g., *Before She Was Harriet*; Cline-Ransome, 2018) and *memoirs* of various known and unknown individuals (*Coat of Many Colors*; Parton, 2016). *Narrative nonfiction* provides in-depth exploration of events (e.g., *Unspeakable: The Tulsa Race Massacre*; Weatherford, 2021), legislation (e.g., *Lillian's Right to Vote: A Celebration of the Voting Rights Act of 1965*; Winter, 2015), and movements (e.g., *Sylvia and Marsha Start a Revolution*; Ellison, 2020). Nonfiction texts come in various formats that lend themselves to different applications during instruction. For example, biographical picture books make for engaging read-alouds, such as *That's Not Fair/No es justo: Emma Tenayuca's Struggle for Justice* (Tafolla & Teneyuca, 2008), whereas biographies for early readers (e.g., *The Story of Barack Obama*; Leslie, 2020) and middle-grade readers (e.g., *Hidden Figures: Young Readers' Edition*; Shetterly, 2016) mediate small-group and independent inquiry.

Fictional texts also play an integral role in social studies instruction, specifically historical and realistic fiction. These texts provide rich and relatable context on historical and contemporary contexts beyond the rigid dates and details provided in textbooks. Typically written from the perspective of protagonists who are children or adolescents themselves, fictional texts allow students to step into the story to experience the historical event or contemporary issue alongside the characters to promote deeper empathy and understanding (Sims Bishop, 1990). *Historical fiction* tells stories set in the past, which naturally align with inquiry into historical events both at home (e.g., *Indian No More*; McManis & Sorell, 2019) and abroad (e.g., *Brother's Keeper*; Lee, 2020). *Realistic fiction* involves stories that could occur in current contexts, which allow students to explore topics like immigration and refugees (e.g., *A Journey Toward Hope*; Hinojosa & Voorhees, 2020) and the fight for racial justice through the Black Lives Matters movement (e.g., *A Good Kind of Trouble*; Ramée, 2019). Both historical and realistic fiction can be used across grade levels, with text options written in a variety of formats, including picture books, chapter books, graphic novels, and novels in verse.

Let's look at a classroom example to see how inclusive texts enhance social studies instruction. In Anna's dual-language classroom, social studies units across the academic year focus on Indigenous perspectives. Using the social studies standard of *Communities Near and Far* to organize the curriculum, the grade-level team has designed bilingual units to spotlight Indigenous populations in the Midwest, where the school is located, as well as Latin America, where many students' families have roots. Since units need to alternate by language medium, Anna teaches about Midwestern tribes in English and Latin American tribes in Spanish, as well as encouraging contrastive analysis across units and bridging between languages. Whenever possible, she taps into inclusive texts to get at authentic stories from various tribes of the Midwest, such as *Bowwow Powwow* (Ojibwe; Child, 2018), *The Water Walker* (Ojibwe; Robertson, 2017), *The Christmas Coat* (Sioux; Sneve, 2011), and *Meet Christopher* (Osage; Simermeyer, 2008). Anna has struggled to find Spanish-medium texts authentically portraying Indigenous populations in Latin America and instead engages students in writing to take the perspective of Incan children in Peru, for example. She has found that her young learners embrace different perspectives and make powerful connections, such as one child who recognized the influence of colonization on his family's hometown in Puerto Rico.

In Anne's middle-grade classroom, she integrates social studies and language arts to allow students more time to dig into inclusive texts and explore pertinent topics that cut across historical and current events. Anne aspires to craft curriculum that responds to her students' richly diverse cultural and linguistic backgrounds as well as promotes critical literacy into events and circumstances that influence their families and communities. In one of the four units that span the school year, her students explore the concept of equal rights with continued inquiry around the essential question: How and why do people struggle for social justice? Beginning with the Civil Rights movement, moving into the Farm Workers Movement, and then building into current events, students engage in deep exploration of authentic perspectives and nuanced stories. Anne strategically amasses inclusive texts to provide authentic perspectives on various efforts to secure rights by race, ethnicity, class, gender, and ability, as well as span genres to mediate inquiry during whole-group read-alouds and small-group book clubs (see Figure 6.1). Anne uses these high-quality inclusive texts as the primary curriculum, rather than a supplement to an existing basal or textbook. In addition to the texts themselves, she incorporates strategies to support children in digging into the text, including graphic organizers such as circle of viewpoints and think-puzzle-explore.

Figure 6.1. Text Examples from Anne's Equal Rights Units

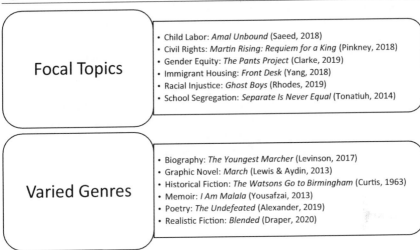

Focal Topics

- Child Labor: *Amal Unbound* (Saeed, 2018)
- Civil Rights: *Martin Rising: Requiem for a King* (Pinkney, 2018)
- Gender Equity: *The Pants Project* (Clarke, 2019)
- Immigrant Housing: *Front Desk* (Yang, 2018)
- Racial Injustice: *Ghost Boys* (Rhodes, 2019)
- School Segregation: *Separate Is Never Equal* (Tonatiuh, 2014)

Varied Genres

- Biography: *The Youngest Marcher* (Levinson, 2017)
- Graphic Novel: *March* (Lewis & Aydin, 2013)
- Historical Fiction: *The Watsons Go to Birmingham* (Curtis, 1963)
- Memoir: *I Am Malala* (Yousafzai, 2013)
- Poetry: *The Undefeated* (Alexander, 2019)
- Realistic Fiction: *Blended* (Draper, 2020)

Probing Problems and Contributions: Focus on Math and Science

Science and math instruction aims to nurture real-world problem-solvers who engage in inquiry that mirrors authentic practices of scientists, mathematicians, and engineers (NGA & CCSSO, 2010c; NGSS Lead States, 2013). To this end, inclusive texts provide a powerful medium to invoke the *lived curriculum* over the *paper curriculum*, where children probe and solve real-world problems in their lives rather than rote equations or multiple-choice questions on the pages of content-area textbooks (Vasquez, 2017). Although typically taught in separate blocks of time, math and science have similar themes and uses of inclusive texts, which is why we merge them here. Previous work in both fields has emphasized inclusive texts as a concrete way to connect curriculum to students' background knowledge, lived experiences, and interests, as well as promote inquiry into scientific and mathematical concepts (Leonard, Moore, & Brooks, 2014; Saint-Hilaire, 2014). When teachers incorporate nonfiction and fiction texts, students deepen understandings within and across life science, physical science, earth and space science, engineering and scientific explorations, and mathematics.

Nonfiction texts provide nuanced accounts of individual contributors to STEM fields, as well as provide real-world applications of math and science concepts. Biographies of women and BIPOC individuals offer mirrors for students to see scientists, engineers, and mathematicians who look like them, as well as windows into different careers and trades in STEM (e.g., *The World Is Not a Rectangle: A Portrait of Architect Zaha Hadid*; Winter,

2017). By reading about the storied lives of astronauts, biologists, chemists, doctors, engineers, mathematicians, and paleontologists, children develop nuanced perspectives on applications of and careers in STEM fields, including those in multiple contexts (e.g., in the field, in the lab). Narrative nonfiction spotlights real-world applications of math, science, and engineering. By sharing accounts and perspectives related to focal events around the world, these inclusive texts invoke critical dialogue about using STEM understandings and concepts to solve problems and promote change. For example, children learn about the centrality of water to our lives and the need to protect this pertinent natural resource through texts like *We Are Water Protectors* (Lindstrom, 2020) and *The Water Princess* (Verde & Badiel, 2016). Based on actual events in the world, these texts give glimpses into communities to understand efforts to protect water and sustain life.

Fictional texts also play an integral role in the math and science classroom, particularly those with storylines that invoke using mathematical and scientific concepts to consider and solve everyday problems. For example, *Grandma and Me at the Flea/Los meros meros remateros* (Herrera, 2013) involves a colorful trip to the local flea market, which provides a rich context to explore money and estimation in primary grades. *Blackout* (Rocco, 2011) tells the story of a family who experiences a blackout during a summer storm, which frames inquiry into energy transfer through electric currents in middle grades. In math and science instruction across grade levels, picture books frame instruction in real-world events and prompt application of mathematical or scientific concepts. A related application but separate genre, folktales and myths encourage children to think about math and science concepts outside of academic content, using texts that explore various phenomena from the perspectives of Indigenous communities (e.g., *The Girl Who Helped the Thunder and Other Native American Folktales*; Bruchac & Bruchac, 2008) and cultures around the world (*Head, Body, Legs: A Story from Liberia*; Paye, 2005).

Let's explore examples to see how teachers incorporate inclusive texts to support STEM learning. Bridget teaches science to 60 students from culturally and linguistically diverse backgrounds as part of a departmentalized middle-grade team. She uses picture-book biographies tied to units of study to broaden perceptions of scientists. For example, an earth science unit employs *Mary Anning and the Sea Dragon* (Atkins, 2012), *Solving the Puzzle Under the Sea: Marie Tharp Maps the Ocean Floor* (Burleigh, 2016), *The Boy Who Harnessed the Wind* (Kamkwamba & Mealer, 2016), and *The Librarian Who Measured the Earth* (Lasky, 1994). Each week, Bridget reads one book aloud and then engages students in creating a web of character traits about that scientist, which then gets added to a "mega web" of all scientists. She prompts them to make connections and draw conclusions about scientists, using scaffolded questions to encourage students to extend characterizing scientists beyond being smart and successful. Later in the school year, after having profiled many scientists through this approach, Bridget recalls adding to the web when one student shouted, "Well *of course* they were hard-working and creative! They were a scientist!" Through these windows into the lives of diverse contributors and careers in the sciences, her students transformed their views of what it meant to be a scientist and pinpointed key traits that they could emulate.

Whereas Bridget incorporated an array of inclusive texts into her classroom, Luke struggled to find texts for algebra instruction with his first- and second-generation immigrants at the middle school across the street. Luke looked to word problems as potential inclusive texts, seeing them as a lever to promote culturally relevant and authentic problem-solving. He modified an existing rubric for cultural relevance (Paulsen & Freeman, 2003) for students to analyze word problems in the curriculum. Using the provided prompts, students reflected upon if and how the word problems connected to people, places, problems, and experiences in their lives. Despite the curriculum being packaged as problem-centered to promote inquiry, students found the problems to be generic, boring, and unconnected to their lives. In response to these findings, Luke scoured resources and discovered Mathalicious, a website providing engaging problems situated in the real world. Students embraced the opportunity to apply mathematical learning while deeply engaged with topics such as income inequality, police violence, and school lunch distribution. By selecting and crafting word problems to connect with his students' lives and learning goals, Luke enacted a unique disciplinary genre of inclusive texts.

Examining Identity and Society: Focus on Athletics and the Arts

Inclusive texts also enhance instruction beyond the traditional academic curriculum. Often referred to as *special areas*, art, music, dance, and physical education often occur outside the self-contained classroom with specialty teachers trained in the focal area. However, classroom teachers should not skip over this section, as incorporating texts and themes related to the arts and athletics provokes powerful transdisciplinary instruction, particularly during literacy, social studies, and social-emotional learning. Inclusive texts in the special areas provide children with windows and mirrors into the lives of artists and athletes, as well as provoke thinking about arts and athletics in real-world contexts. Texts provide a medium to explore and challenge stereotypes, such as those by gender or ability, as well as consider how art, dance, music, and athletics serve as a form of resistance (Vasquez, 2017). Across special areas, high-quality inclusive texts enhance instruction and deepen critical connections to self and society, including both nonfiction and fiction with four emergent themes for application.

Nonfiction texts in the special areas serve to provide rich and important context that situates the arts and athletics in our larger history and society.

Similar to themes in inclusive texts shared in previous sections, *biographies* and *memoirs* provide windows into the lives of artists and athletes. In addition to those profiling well-known individuals, such as Frida Kahlo or Michael Jordan, inclusive texts tell the stories of lesser-known people who inform children's thinking about key concepts and character traits. For example, *Fauja Singh Keeps Going: The True Story of the Oldest Person to Ever Run a Marathon* (Singh, 2020) tells the story of Fauja's lifelong courage and determination to overcome physical and emotional challenges and commit to long-distance running past the age of 100. In addition to spotlighting individuals, inclusive texts probe the role of art, music, dance, and sports in society and the world through *narrative nonfiction* texts, including those that capture social, cultural, historical, and political themes. Consider the text *Baseball Saved Us* (Mochizuki, 1993), which situates baseball as the centerpiece of the story about a boy living in the Japanese internment camps in the United States during World War II. Weaving critical literacy into the special areas, inclusive texts like this one prompt thinking about the bigger picture beyond a particular game or activity.

Fictional texts also encourage students to connect personally with themes related to the arts and athletics. Identities intersect with art, music, dance, and athletics, both in how we see ourselves in relation to those areas as well as how we tap into those areas to define who we are as individuals. In other words, being an artist, musician, dancer, or athlete may be a defining facet of someone's identity. Additionally, art, music, dance, and athletics serve as an outlet for sharing unique identities with the world. Inclusive texts provoke that connection, having students explore their own identities in connection with these themes. For example, *Cuando amamos cantamos/ When We Love Someone We Sing to Them* (Martínez, 2018) tells the story of a boy whose father teaches him the significance of serenading someone you love. Written in rhythmic bilingual poetry alongside the gorgeous artwork of Maya González, the book uses musical tradition to capture cultural identity, as well as orientation as the protagonist reveals his desire to sing for a boy he loves. The exploration of identity also disrupts stereotypes, such as those attributed by gender or ability in the areas of arts and athletics. In the text *I Will Dance* (Flood, 2020), a young girl with cerebral palsy sees herself as a dancer and finds a way to express herself through dance from her wheelchair. When used in the special areas, inclusive texts promote self-exploration and counter prevalent stereotypes within arts and athletics.

Drawing from these themes, teachers can deepen connections and understandings by incorporating texts into instruction. Take, for example, an art unit on identity and self-portraiture, where texts encourage children to think about intersectional identities and how colors and textures represent individuals. Strategically selected picture books allow students to consider various shades of color (e.g., *Magnificent Homespun Brown*; Doyon, 2020), connect color to larger life experiences (e.g., *My Colors, My World/Mis*

Colores, Mi Mundo; González, 2013), disrupt preferred colors by gender (*Pink Is for Boys*; Pearlman, 2018), and explore sensory experiences beyond the ability to see color (*What Color Is the Wind?*; Herbauts, 2016). The teacher reads texts aloud, with frequent prompts for students to consider how the author and illustrator use colors to capture facets of the character's identity. These texts become seed ideas for students' portrayals of themselves in self-portraits. Following the read-aloud, students head to art tables to mix paints to make different colors and try out brushes for various textures to portray one facet of the self-portrait (e.g., face, hair, clothes, background). The culminating project is the full self-portrait, crafted after multiple rounds of read-alouds, guided reflections, and experimentation with color and texture to explore and capture identities.

This unit's focus on illustrations serves as an important reminder of the opportunity that picture books hold. Inside and outside the art classroom, students look aesthetically at the artwork in picture books to deepen comprehension and engagement, as well as understandings that the text provokes (e.g., identity and self-portraiture). But artwork can be considered alone, encouraging students to inquire into illustrators' identities to explore artistic choices. For example, Ed Young grew up in Shanghai and Hong Kong, and influences of Chinese literature and folk art come through in his illustrations that use various colors and textures. Jerry Pinkney aims to capture historical accuracy in his watercolor paintings that have expanded the portrayals of African American characters and families (Erbach, 2008). In addition to drawing and painting, illustrators tap into multiple mediums, such as the poignant photography of George Ancona (e.g., *Pablo Remembers: The Fiesta of the Day of the Dead*; Ancona, 1993), Geronimo García's use of clay (e.g., *A Gift from Papá Diego/Un regalo de papá Diego*; Alire Sáenz, 1998), or the cut-paper art of Carmen Lomas Garza (1999) in *Magic Windows/Ventanas mágicas*. Teachers can discuss the artwork of picture books, considering illustrators' cultural backgrounds, identities, and reasons for using a particular medium, as well as using those mediums (e.g., photographs, clay, cut paper) as extensions to facilitate learning following the text.

Art-based extensions have been shown to support meaning-making around texts, providing research-based strategies for teachers across content areas. Children draw, paint, and mold clay in response to text, using artwork to reflect upon texts and connect to their own lives (Carger, 2004). Drama-based strategies prompt students to espouse different perspectives and engage in critical dialogue about inclusive texts, such as *writing-in-role* of characters, putting students on the *hot seat* as characters to answer questions from their peers, and creating a still-frame *tableau* of a poignant event in the story (Medina, 2004). Music taps into the oral tradition prevalent in various cultures and communities, such as using hip-hop and rap music to connect with the African American oral tradition of storytelling through music (Grace, 2004). Whether focusing on reading comprehension, providing multiple perspectives on historical events, considering the contributions of scientists and mathematicians, or exploring the role of arts and athletics in society, arts-based strategies and inclusive texts foster development of identity, languages and literacies, and disciplinary understandings.

INCORPORATION INTO CURRICULUM AND INSTRUCTION

In the IT framework, one critical component lies in the meaningful incorporation of texts into curriculum and instruction. Through formal and purposeful instructional design, teachers expose children to brilliant and beautiful literature while mediating learning. Previous framework facets have supported consideration of the students in the classroom, goals for instruction, and suitable texts to push forward learning. Now attention shifts to using these texts in meaningful ways. Whether planning original units or enhancing existing curricula, the goal is to incorporate texts to facilitate connections, engagement, and conceptual understandings. In this section, we demonstrate how to feature inclusive texts in content-area instruction through planning at the unit level and lesson level, and in broader supplemental resources available in the classroom.

Designing Units of Study

Today's classrooms typically organize content-area curriculum into a series of units across the school year. Units center on a particular theme or area of study and have clear goals defined for students to reach by their culmination (Wiggins & McTighe, 2005). Many teachers design their own units of study, using knowledge of students and learning goals to plan responsive instruction that engages learners and promotes learning (Heineke & McTighe, 2018). When planning original units of study, teachers can embark upon the design process with inclusive texts at the forefront. In this way, units of study center on inclusive texts, using them as a consistent medium for facilitating learning in daily instruction. This *text-centered* approach is most feasible in literacy and social studies due to the quantity and quality of inclusive texts for various students and learning goals. The goal is to craft units that deepen understandings and critical literacy through multiple voices, stories, and perspectives.

For an example of a text-centered unit, let's return to Anne's classroom, where students engage with social studies themes as a part of language arts. In an 8-week unit titled *Faces of Immigration* (see Table 6.1), she uses texts to facilitate reading, writing, language arts, and social studies goals. Starting with students and aligning with unit goals, Anne selects high-quality texts for daily read-alouds and three rounds of literature discussions. She wants

Table 6.1. Text-Centered Unit of Study

Faces of Immigration Unit (8 weeks)		
Essential Questions	**Academic Language**	**Social Studies Standards**
What defines the immigrant experience? What challenges do immigrants face? What is the history of immigration? How do immigrants contribute to their new countries?	Genre-specific text structures and features Words: ancestor, conflict, citizen, culture, customs, document, hardship, heritage, immigrant, navigate, refugee, unfamiliar, visa	SS.G.4.5: Environment comparisons SS.EC.1.5: Individuals around world SS.H.3.5: Causes and effects of U.S. history
Reading Standards	**Writing Standards**	**Supporting ELA Standards**
RL 5.2—Theme/ Summary RL 5.5—Structure SL 5.1—Collaborative Discussions L 5.4—Vocabulary RI 5.2—Main Idea/ Details and Summary RI 5.3—Explaining Relationships	W 5.4—Clear and Coherent Writing W 5.2—Expository Performance Task: Create pamphlets for immigrant families enrolled at the EL Center	RL.5.1 & RI.5.1— Quote, infer RI5.5—Informational Text Structures RI.5.7—Draw on information from multiple print or digital sources RI.5.9—Integrate information from several texts on the same topic
Texts for Read-Aloud & Shared Reading	**Texts for Book Clubs**	**Other Texts and Activities**
A Different Pond (Phi, 2017) *All the Way to America* (Yaccarino, 2014) *Carmela Full of Wishes* (de la Peña, 2018) *Dreamers* (Morales, 2018) *Grandfather's Journey* (Say, 2008) *Here I Am* (Kim, 2015) *Islandborn* (Díaz, 2018)	*Amina's Voice* (Khan, 2017) *Escape from Aleppo* (Senzai, 2020) *Esperanza Rising* (Muñoz Ryan, 2002) *Inside Out and Back Again* (Lai, 2013) *A Long Walk to Water* (Park, 2011) *Lucky Broken Girl* (Behar, 2017) *Refugee* (Gratz, 2017)	Regular Procedures: • Read-Aloud/Shared Reading • Book Clubs • Journal Reflections Thinking Routines: • What Makes You Say That? • Step Inside • Sentence-Phrase-Word • Headlines • Circle of Viewpoints Paired Texts/Activities: • Oral Interviews— Scholastic

(continued)

Table 6.1. Text-Centered Unit of Study (Continued)

Faces of Immigration Unit (8 weeks)		
Texts for Read-Aloud & Shared Reading	Texts for Book Clubs	Other Texts and Activities
Life at Ellis Island (Isaacs, 2001)	*The Night Diary* (Hirandani, 2019)	• *Discover* Magazine: Immigration #23
Mama's Nightingale (Danticat, 2015)	*The Only Road* (Diaz, 2016)	• Ellis Island informational text
Marwan's Journey (de Arias, 2018)	*The Red Pencil* (Pinkney, 2014)	• Family members' immigration stories
Other Words for Home (Warga, 2019)	*Return to Sender* (Alvarez, 2009)	• "Where I'm From" poems
Stepping Stones (Ruurs, 2016)	*Shooting Kabul* (Senzai, 2010)	
The Journey (Sanna, 2016)	*When Stars Are Scattered* (Jamieson & Mohamed, 2020)	
The Keeping Quilt (Polacco, 2001)		
The Lotus Seed (Garland, 1997)		
The Name Jar (Choi, 2001)		
We Are Like the Clouds (Argueta, 2016)		

children to build literacy skills while probing the immigrant experience beyond the traditional Ellis Island narrative, using mirrors and windows to explore and compare immigrant stories, contexts, contributions, and challenges. Unit texts include immigrant stories from various countries of origin, including those of students (e.g., Mexico, Vietnam) and others in the community (e.g., Italy, Poland). She selects poetry (Argueta, 2016), nonfiction (Isaacs, 2001), and fiction from various subgenres, including wordless text (Kim, 2015), graphic novel (Jamieson & Mohamed, 2020), and novel in verse (Pinkney, 2014). With consistent routines to use these texts in whole- and small-group settings, texts support nuanced inquiry into immigration.

Whereas Anne has the flexibility to craft her own curriculum centered on inclusive texts, other teachers use curricular programs that have been purchased and encouraged—perhaps even required—for use. Other contexts use teacher-designed units of study, but those units may have been planned without the lens on inclusive texts. In Chapter 3, we discussed analyzing curricula for students in your classroom, as well as the relevancy and authenticity of texts and materials. By recognizing where existing units do and do not sustain and engage students, teachers can supplement inclusive texts to enhance instruction and learning. In this *text-supplemented* approach, teachers select texts in response to students and objectives and then incorporate texts and related tasks into the learning trajectory. This approach is commonly used across content areas, including social studies, science, math, and the special areas.

Camille, a principal at a K–8 school with 60% White, 20% Latinx, 10% Asian, 6% multiracial, and 4% Black students, sought to model how to supplement existing units with texts. Teachers at the school used Understanding by Design (UbD; Wiggins & McTighe, 2005) to plan original units of study, but most units had been drafted years before, without lenses on cultural relevancy or critical literacy. Using a unit on U.S. westward expansion from the UbD text (Wiggins & McTighe, 2011), Camille selected books that provoked inquiry related to unit essential questions and served as windows and mirrors for students. After brainstorming titles spanning multiple genres, she sequenced texts into the learning trajectory, with tasks to deepen understandings in relation to unit goals. Across the revised unit, students read and discussed *The Birchbark House* (Erdrich, 2002) alongside excepts from the originally slated *Little House on the Prairie* (Wilder, 1992), allowing them to compare the perspectives of White and Indigenous authors and critically probe the portrayal of Indigenous communities in the texts. Additionally, use of other texts across the unit prompted connections, understandings, and reflections (see Table 6.2). Through the process of supplementing an existing social studies unit, Camille modeled how to engage learners with inclusive texts woven into content-area instruction.

Featuring Texts in Lessons

After considering where inclusive texts fit into broader units of study, teachers then look to incorporate texts into lessons. We have found that lesson-level incorporation is valuable for teachers with existing curricula, as they seek to supplement existing materials with relevant and engaging examples rooted in real-world practice. Earlier in the chapter, we explored genres and uses for texts in each content area, such as biographies of individuals engaged in the work, real-world applications of disciplinary concepts, fictional depictions of historical or current events, and folklore from various cultures. Knowing the array of texts available, teachers select texts that enhance the curricula. But as has been emphasized before, it is not just about supplementing the text, but also using the text in meaningful ways to promote students' connections, engagement, understandings, critical thinking, applications, and reflections. Here we explore ways to use inclusive texts at different points of a lesson, including warming up, facilitating learning, and wrapping up (see Table 6.3).

Table 6.2. Text-Supplemented Unit of Study

Essential Questions		
• Why do people move? • What happens when cultures and communities interact?		• What does it mean to be a pioneer? • How do our experiences impact the way we tell a story?

Texts	Genre	Incorporation into Unit Learning Trajectory
My Diary From Here to There/ Mi diario de aquí hasta allá (Pérez, 2009)	Memoir	Interactive read-aloud at the beginning of unit to access students' background knowledge and experiences about why people move: In small groups, students use graffiti board to share responses, connections, and ideas from the text.
The Arrival (Tan, 2007)	Graphic novel	Close reading and analysis of selected excerpts from the graphic novel: In dialogue journals, students reflect on cultures and communities interacting.
Overground Railroad (Cline-Ransome, 2020)	Historical fiction	Interactive read-aloud to connect with previous unit of study and extend to why people move: After modeling by teacher with 4-square graphic organizer, pairs conduct research on migration, resources, geography, and interaction.
Pancho Rabbit and the Coyote: A Migrant's Tale (Tonatiuh, 2013)	Allegorical picture book	Shared reading to connect and grapple with current events: Engage students in critical dialogue about migrants from Central America to build empathy and understandings around essential questions (e.g., Why do people move?).
Brave Girl: Clara and the Shirtwaist Makers' Strike of 1909 (Markel, 2013)	Historical fiction	Close reading of text to understand with cause-and-effect graphic organizer: Students explore the events around the strike and probe Clara's role. Teacher prompts connections to essential question: What does it mean to be a pioneer?
Look Up! Henrietta Leavitt, Pioneering Woman Astronomer (Burleigh, 2013)	Biography	Interactive read-aloud to connect to other examples of pioneers: Make a class web of terms to describe Henrietta, who was a pioneer in astronomy. In small groups, students select and explore other pioneers and add to identity webs.
All texts across unit	All	Picture-cued small-group discussion: At the end of the unit, students sort and discuss photocopied illustrations from texts to respond to essential questions.

Table 6.3. Using Inclusive Texts in Lessons

Timing in the Lesson	Purposes for Inclusive Text Use	Related Instructional Strategies
Warming Up	• Hooking interest and engagement • Accessing background knowledge • Building background on the topic	• Artifacts: Share perceptions of realia, illustrations, or photos related to the topic and text (e.g., immigration, environment) • Graffiti: Respond to thought-provoking prompts on poster paper • Prompted Pairings: Share connections with partner or group • Sketch to Stretch: Graphically capture and describe responses to text • Word Splash: Brainstorm words that come to mind from text.
Facilitating Learning	• Offering nuanced perspectives • Exploring concepts and ideas • Providing real-world examples	• Gallery Walk: Explore and respond to photos and perspectives • Hot Seat: Take on characters or personae to interact with peers • Story Map: Capture integral components of a given text • Timeline: Follow the important timeline of events in a text • Webbing: Pull out key ideas, attributes, and themes from text
Wrapping Up	• Supporting text-to-self connections • Promoting text-to-world connections • Encouraging reflection on learning	• Blogs: Draft perspectives on public site for classmates • Journals: Respond creatively in any written format or language • Poetry: Use haiku or other formats to creatively connect with text • Social Media: Craft a post to capture thoughts and applications • Tableau: Enact moments in story or event in still form with bodies

When starting lessons, texts tap into background knowledge and hook engagement. For example, lessons might begin with read-alouds prompting initial connections and thoughts. In Javier's bilingual classroom, he selected *Too Many Tamales* (Soto, 1996) to read aloud with Latinx students to start a math lesson on fractions. He recognized children's funds of knowledge of cooking at home with family members, as well as academic knowledge on measuring volume from a previous unit. In a lesson on fraction partitions (e.g., halves, thirds, fourths), Javier followed up the text by mixing the ingredients for the tamale dough with his class. As they measured the flour, broth, baking powder, and spices, he introduced the terminology for fraction partitions in English and Spanish (e.g., half cup, *media taza*). This experience served as a springboard into the rest of the lesson, where students worked collaboratively to discuss and label partitioned shapes. Using the text prompted excitement for learning and supported conceptual understanding by tapping into prior knowledge.

Texts also mediate learning during lessons with the text as the focal point to prompt exploration of perspectives, disciplinary concepts, and real-world applications. In Bridget's middle-grade classroom, she designed a lesson centering on *One Grain of Rice* (Demi, 1997) to teach exponents (see Table 6.4). In this folktale from India, a clever girl devised a plan to feed her village by asking the selfish raja, who typically kept the rice for himself, to continually double the grains of rice given to villagers. Bridget set up the lesson with a similar problem (i.e., *The Djinni's Offer;* Illustrative Mathematics, 2016) to hook engagement by making predictions about the outcome. She then did an interactive read-aloud with *One Grain of Rice* and had students work collaboratively to make text-to-text connections between

Table 6.4. Sample Disciplinary Lesson

Established Goals	Learning Objectives
6.EE.A.1 Write and evaluate numerical expressions involving whole-number exponents.	• Unit Transfer Goal: Use expressions and equations to solve problems. • Essential Questions: How are exponents useful in solving problems? • Learning Objective: Solve problems using exponential expressions.

Check for Understanding	Other Evidence
• Think-and-Draw: On a notecard, students respond to the essential question through drawing and spatial organization of ideas, numbers, and words.	• Observations during think-pair-share • Observations during interactive problem solving • Artifacts from student practice with exponents

Learning Trajectory
• Hook: Introduce the *The Djinni's Offer* (Illustrative Mathematics, 2016) • Think-Pair-Share, Round 1: Make predictions as to the better offer presented by the Djinni • Read-Aloud: *One Grain of Rice* (Demi, 1997) • Think-Pair-Share, Round 2: Make connections between *The Djinni's Offer* and *One Grain of Rice* • Interactive Problem Solving: Learn about exponents while solving the *The Djinni's Offer* • Student Practice: Paired or independent work with exponential expressions

the two problems and ultimately solve using exponents. Bridget described engagement at an all-time high for a lesson focus that did not always yield excitement. Indian students eagerly contributed background information emergent from the text illustrations, such as the Indian word for the protagonist's scarf (*dupattā*) and the cultural significance of animals like elephants and peacocks. Other students connected to folktales and trickster tales told in their families. Used as a central mediator of the lesson, the text engaged students and facilitated conceptual development by providing a rich context for meaning-making.

Finally, texts can close lessons to encourage reflection and transfer to lives outside the classroom. As described above, many trade books provide real-world problems and applications for disciplinary concepts. When used at the end of a lesson, texts connect classroom learning with real-world practice to encourage thinking beyond the scope of the lesson. In her primary bilingual classroom, Tori read *Rocket Says Clean Up!* (Bryon, 2020) to close a lesson in her unit on Earth and human activity (NGSS Lead States, 2013). They had been discussing solutions to reduce people's impact on the environment, such as through recycling and reusing materials. The lesson focused on tangible applications to sustain the environment, and she wanted students to see themselves as part of the solution. In the text, the young protagonist visits family in Jamaica and, after finding garbage all over the beaches, initiates collaborative efforts to clean up and protect local wildlife. After reading the text, Tori prompted reflection and sharing ways to help the environment. Ideas connected to the text with children considering problems with garbage and pollution in their community, as well as places where they visit family, such as Mexico and Puerto Rico. Students continued to talk about plans to help the environment for weeks after the lesson.

Providing Supplemental Texts for Learning

Along with use in content-area units and lessons, disciplinary-focused inclusive texts enrich literacy and learning in other ways. In this chapter, we have focused on incorporation of texts to enhance content-area curriculum and instruction. By integrating texts into units and lessons, teachers center traditionally marginalized voices and show the applications of concepts in global and community contexts. But despite our focus on formal integration into instruction, we do not want to ignore the value of having texts available for students to engage with outside of the disciplinary curriculum. A growing number of texts spanning genres feature lenses on the disciplines to incorporate in informal and transdisciplinary ways.

To begin, teachers and librarians can stock libraries with relevant and authentic materials for independent reading. In addition to providing texts in the subgenres of historical and realistic fiction, which we discussed early in the chapter, teachers can explore fantasy and science fiction titles, particularly those that feature BIPOC protagonists like *Aru Shah and the End of Time* (Chokshi, 2018) and *Lalani of the Distant Sea* (Estrada Kelly, 2020b). A growing number of fictional reading series, particularly transitional chapter books, depict disciplinary applications among female and BIPOC characters like Jada Jones (Lyons, 2017), Jasmine Toguchi (D. M. Florence, 2017), Lola Levine (Brown, 2015), and Sadiq (Nuurali, 2021). Nonfiction reading series also provide balance of genre for students, including Biographies for New Readers (e.g., Leslie, 2020; Rockridge Press), the Citizen Kid collection (e.g., Ruurs, 2015; Kids Can Press), and the Mothers of Xsan series (e.g., Huson, 2018; Highwater Press). With various genres and titles available, students self-select texts based on identities and interests.

Another step is considering how to use disciplinary texts across the school day, rather than maintaining siloed content areas. In self-contained elementary classrooms, teachers might struggle to find time to engage students in science and social studies, given the emphasis on literacy. But literacy instruction should infuse disciplinary concepts and related texts, which results in powerful transdisciplinary instruction where students read and write to learn. As described above, Anne's classroom exemplifies integration of social studies and language arts. Her literacy instruction centers on social studies themes (e.g., immigration, equal rights) with read-alouds, literature circles, and writing workshop using inclusive texts to promote children's literacy development, disciplinary understandings, and social action. As you reflect upon your classroom instruction and consider potential uses of inclusive texts, consider how a transdisciplinary approach might maximize inquiry into pertinent themes, topics, and ideas both within and across content areas—as well as outside the formal curriculum.

THE FRAMEWORK IN ACTION: PROMOTING STUDENTS' DISCIPLINARY UNDERSTANDINGS

Envision a classroom that features inclusive texts across the school day and curriculum to nurture disciplinary understandings and self-esteem. Imagine seeing children's eyes light up as they make sense of math problems that tap into their cultural ways of knowing, see scientists and engineers with similar identities, and learn various perspectives on historical, social, and political issues that impact their community and world. Inclusive texts hold great potential in content-area instruction, but this is often the last place where we see their use. Children's books logically play a role in literacy instruction, where most attention and time often get exerted in elementary classrooms. State and local policies influence the emphasis on literacy, but elementary teachers might also espouse anxieties around teaching content areas like math and science, which results in less confidence to maneuver the curriculum (Avery & Meyer, 2012; Hadley & Dorward, 2011). Even within the literacy block, educators might feel wary of using informational texts grounded in disciplinary concepts (Reutzel, Jones, Clark, & Kumar, 2016).

Deconstructing perceptions of disciplinary teaching and children's literature is a good first step. Begin by considering your disciplinary teaching, probing how different factors like policies, previous experiences, and self-efficacy influence how you teach every day. How much time is dedicated to disciplinary learning (e.g., math, science, social studies)? Do you feel confident to flexibly shape the content for unique learners, or do you stick to the predefined curriculum? These reflections open the door to considering how and where inclusive texts support content-area instruction. Perhaps time is an issue, as your administration insists upon a lengthy literacy block that leaves limited time for other subjects, so you might consider integration like Anne's interdisciplinary units in social studies and language arts. Perhaps you feel less confident in teaching math and science, so you might take some time with your team and instructional coaches to probe the curriculum, deepen your understandings, and consider where inclusive texts might enhance not only students' learning but also your comfort in disciplinary teaching. Carving out time for disciplinary learning is integral to nurturing critical, creative, mathematical, and scientific thinkers, as is flexibly shaping the curriculum to respond to students' identities and perspectives to reach learning goals.

This integration of literacy and content-area instruction requires challenging the institutionalized siloes that often typify schools, where educators approach content areas as separate blocks of instructional time. We have seen some schools shift to transdisciplinary and interdisciplinary learning through initiatives such as the International Baccalaureate and project-based learning, which more aptly and authentically reflect real-world and 21st-century problem-solving. But these purposeful interconnections do not have to be limited to niche sites, as the new standards that most practitioners use to guide instruction also align with interdisciplinary teaching and learning (Heritage et al., 2015). Literacy standards push for the predominance of informational texts, opening the door to using inclusive texts with disciplinary themes in literacy instruction. Math and science standards prompt rich disciplinary language use, which inclusive texts foster in content-area instruction. By leveraging the current policy context, educators seek out spaces in their classrooms and schools to simultaneously support children's disciplinary learning and language development. Inclusive texts play a crucial role in these efforts, deepening children's engagement, learning, and literacy skills.

After deconstructing these larger ideas around inclusive texts within disciplinary teaching and learning, dig into the IT framework to put these ideas into practice. Return to Chapter 3 to critically interrogate content-area goals and curricula, using students' identities and experiences as a backdrop for analysis. Then consider how and where inclusive texts might support work to make curricula relevant, engaging, and effective for students. How might you tap into texts to sustain children's identities and backgrounds in the disciplines? How might texts engage learners in critical thinking and dialogue about pertinent disciplinary topics in communities and society? You might use the different themes, genres, and text examples in this chapter as a starting place to select relevant and authentic texts to try out in content-area instruction. Think about how these texts facilitate learning in relation to goals and then strategically incorporate them into lessons and units. During instruction, observe how students respond and engage with the texts. These anecdotal data provide a valuable starting place for you and your colleagues to discuss the integration of inclusive texts across the school day.

This chapter has sought to provide actionable ideas, examples, and next steps to use inclusive texts across the content areas. With this focus outside the literacy block, we seek to harness the power of including and elevating voices, perspectives, and stories across the school day so that children have a multitude of windows and mirrors through which to learn and develop as individuals, as well as discover and interrogate the world. This work is further enhanced when educators across schools embrace inclusive texts. In this way, learners are not limited to having these rich learning experiences in one classroom, but experience them across their learning trajectory in the school. In the next chapter, we discuss how to extend these efforts across schools, tapping into your expertise and advocacy to seek support for these efforts.

QUESTIONS AND ACTIVITIES FOR PROFESSIONAL DEVELOPMENT

1. Across this text, you have been exploring and amassing texts to use in your classroom instruction. Return to that list and add titles for each content area that you teach. Be sure to seek out a variety of genres, including a balance of fiction and nonfiction, that tackle topics within and across various disciplines. Return to your students' identities, experiences, and worldviews to select meaningful mirrors and windows for potential use in your disciplinary instruction.

2. Think about your current approach to instructional design for each discipline that you teach (e.g., mathematics, science, social studies). If you have prescribed curricula that you use for any content area, use the criteria provided in Chapter 3 to analyze the integration of inclusive texts. If you design your own curriculum, think about your existing unit or lesson plans to evaluate where and how inclusive texts currently occupy space in classroom instruction. Then explore titles and resources to consider how you

might expand the use of inclusive texts in disciplinary instruction to enhance students' learning, understandings, and engagement.

3. Special-area teachers (e.g., art, health, music, physical education, technology) play an integral role in the holistic development of children in schools. Nonetheless, professional texts often focus primarily on classroom teachers. If you are a special-area teacher, think about how inclusive texts might enhance your work to support your students. If you are a classroom teacher, consider how you might share key ideas from this chapter and the rest of the text that might be of value to special-area teachers. If you are a school leader, consider how you might use inclusive texts as a cross-school initiative to promote all educators' responsive and critical practice.

CHAPTER 7

Expanding the Reach of Inclusive Texts

Advocacy Work Beyond the Classroom

un sueño	a dream
lo soñamos	we dream
solos	alone
la realidad	reality
la soñamos	we dream
juntos	together

—"Soñando Juntos / Dreaming Together" from *Poems to Dream Together/ Poemas para soñar juntos,* by Francisco X. Alarcón (2005, p. 32)

Throughout this book, we have explored ways to incorporate inclusive texts to promote identity development, social-emotional well-being, critical literacy, language development, and disciplinary learning. We have centered on teachers embracing their agency to critically reflect and make informed decisions regarding texts for classroom use. Exemplified by the innovative work by teachers in urban and suburban schools in the greater Chicago area, the Inclusive Texts (IT) framework detailed across this text seeks to challenge the prevalence of canonical texts to reflect the students in today's classrooms and elevate often-marginalized voices and experiences. The framework guides work to (a) start with students' rich backgrounds and experiences, (b) critically probe existing standards and curricula, (c) select high-quality, relevant, and authentic texts, and (d) incorporate texts across literacy and content-area instruction.

But this work should not be limited to the four walls of a classroom. Children move from classroom to classroom in any given day, year, or schooling experience, and they should engage with inclusive texts across contexts. By limiting exposure to inclusive texts in one classroom, we risk perpetuating the single story—where the canon continues as the norm and diverse voices remain the outlier. By expanding this work across schools, we increase both the quality and quantity of texts, including mirrors for children to see themselves and windows to learn from and about others (Sims Bishop, 1990). To accomplish this, schools can take action to support teachers, such as purchasing high-quality texts and providing related professional development. As reflected in the poignant words of Francisco X. Alarcón, we accomplish more together: All members of a school community should come together and aspire to transform who and what children see in the texts that define and drive their educational experiences.

This culminating chapter supports readers in thinking through how efforts across schools enhance the use of inclusive texts. Using examples from three schools, we detail four facets to build capacity across schools: (a) amassing inclusive resources, (b) supporting curricular design, (c) building professional capacity, and (d) using texts with stakeholders. In each example, you see how one key stakeholder, such as the assistant principal or instructional coach, advocates to concentrate on inclusive texts and leads capacity-building efforts. In sum, it starts with just one person with passion and expertise to promote broader change that influences every student in the school. With that in mind, we close the chapter and text by discussing how to use the framework to advocate for inclusive texts in your community.

AMASSING INCLUSIVE RESOURCES

The first step to prioritizing inclusive texts in schools involves amassing inclusive texts and resources for teachers' use. In this way, teachers have large collections of high-quality texts reflective of the community and the world to explore, select, and incorporate into instruction spanning literacy and the content areas. For the person or team leading these efforts in schools, this step involves building and maintaining resource libraries with an array of texts, authors, and topics reflective of the school, the community, and the world.

Building Resource Libraries

This work begins with students. Using the IT framework that has been detailed throughout this text, readers initiate collections by first considering children's identities, experiences, and perspectives. Begin by pondering: Who are the students in your school and community? Whose stories, experiences, identities, and perspectives may not be reflected in the currently available texts and materials? Chapter 2 provides various tools and approaches for classroom teachers to get to know students. Whereas teachers might use anecdotal data to get at individual nuances, initial efforts to build school libraries start broadly with formal data to understand the cultural backgrounds, home languages, gender identities, family structures, and (dis)abilities across the school. Drawing from data-based understandings of the school land-scape, seek out high-quality texts that are representative of the population. We recommend using the criteria in Chapter 2 to secure relevant and au-thentic texts written from insider perspectives.

In addition to texts representative of the population, resource libraries should consider the school's programs and grade ranges. Our framework aims to make inclusive texts a central feature of the curriculum, rather than one book on a shelf or for a random read-aloud. To encourage this, texts should align with the programs, curricula, and instruction. Following initial exploration with the lens on students, consider how learning occurs in the building: What texts would support learning within programs and curricula in your school? Do you have texts across genres and content areas? Do you have texts in multiple languages? Chapter 3 provides resources for readers to consider how texts support learning in line with existing standards and supplement existing curricula to provide diverse stories and perspectives. Leaders can enhance teachers' incorporation of texts by securing texts that enhance curricula across content areas, as well as ensuring availability of high-quality texts and resources in all languages of instruction.

Let's explore an example of school-level work. Baker School (a pseud-onym) has worked to prioritize inclusive texts for the past 8 years, with efforts led by the bilingual instructional coach. At this PK–8 school of 800 students, 80% of students speak a multitude of languages, includ-ing Spanish, Arabic, Tagalog, Farsi, Urdu, Malayalam, Russian, Swahili, Thai, Burmese, and French. Karen had recently shifted roles at the school from middle-school ELA teacher to instructional coach supporting mul-tilingual learners. She initiated efforts to build school and classroom col-lections to reflect learners' cultural and linguistic backgrounds. Through a partnership between Baker and our university, Karen worked with us to find mirror texts written by BIPOC authors, such as *Lakas and the Manilatown Fish* (Robles, 2003), *Hush! A Thai Lullaby* (Ho, 2000), and *Night of the Moon: A Muslim Holiday Story* (Khan, 2008). With 75% of students coming from Spanish-speaking families from Mexico, Central America, the Caribbean, and South America, Karen sought a diverse array of texts to represent Latinx experiences. With many texts in their collec-tion portraying Mexican immigrant and Mexican-American characters, she sought out the work of award-winning authors from Puerto Rico, the Dominican Republic, and Guatemala, such as Judith Ortiz-Cofer, Julia Alvarez, and Luis Garay.

Following the initial work of seeking out mirrors to reflect students' diverse backgrounds and experiences, Karen shifted to focus on texts to mediate students' progress toward learning goals. In line with state policy, Baker School had used transitional bilingual education for years to serve its large Spanish-speaking population. Spurred by Karen's leadership, the school had embraced and implemented dual-language education with the goal of nurturing children's bilingualism and biliteracy. One thing Karen quickly identified was the dearth of inclusive texts written in Spanish. They had some bilingual texts, primarily from the first round of purchases to provide mirrors for Latinx students, as well as translated texts like Harry Potter. But Karen recognized the need for high-quality, Spanish-medium texts to use across the curriculum in dual-language classrooms. She sought out resources from Books del Sur, a company that curates authentic Spanish-language texts written by Latin American authors spanning grades, genres, and disciplines. She also found a local bookstore owner who regularly traveled to South America to purchase books for schools, particularly hard-to-find, content-focused texts for math and science. These partnerships aided her efforts to secure Spanish-medium texts that teachers could incorporate into their units of study in dual-language classrooms.

This example provides ideas on how to prioritize and carry out the procurement of texts for schoolwide collections reflective of students and programming. It also demonstrates how this initial work to build school collections is both exciting and daunting. Like Karen, remember to draw from existing resources and available partnerships so that this work does not feel like an overwhelming, individual endeavor. With this book, we provide numerous examples of high-quality inclusive texts, both across the chapters and on the supplemental website (inclusivetexts.weebly.com). Additionally, we have shared our favorite organizations, publishers, and awards to consult when seeking out the latest and greatest titles and authors (see Table 2.6 in Chapter 2). Leaders also might forge partnerships with local bookstores and other companies that specialize in procuring texts for schools, such as those described above. In the spirit of collaboration and shared commitment to meaningful change in schools, we recommend using all available resources to alleviate the workload involved in building an inclusive library.

Ongoing Reflection on Texts

After starting an initial collection, the work to ensure inclusivity and representation continues over time in response to changing communities, society, and texts. To provide mirrors for all students, educators must continually ponder students' dynamic identities, experiences, and circumstances, seeking to amass multiple stories, perspectives, and topics to reflect diverse realities. Additionally, as the world transforms with new events and occurrences, teachers need contemporary mirrors to promote critical literacy and explore societal issues like the COVID-19 pandemic and social movements for racial justice. To enrich school collections with nuanced mirrors and contemporary windows, educators can monitor recently published texts, authors, and illustrators. Paired with ongoing reflection on the changing contexts of the community and world, school teams can continue to bring new titles into the collection.

Situated in the same neighborhood as Baker, Hillside School (a pseudonym) exemplifies this ongoing reflection. This work began over 10 years ago with the hiring of Kyla as assistant principal, a literacy expert with experience working with multilingual learners. At a school where multilingual learners comprised half of the population, she quickly got to work in extending the school's text collection to reflect students. Like Karen, she began by amassing texts reflective of the 900 PK–6 students, including authentic stories of immigrants, refugees, newcomers, children learning a new language, bicultural families, and various family structures. Over time, Kyla expanded collections to ensure "more than a single story" for any community. She scoured their growing collection, looking to provide nuanced portrayals reflective of the community and society. For example, Hillside welcomed families from the Middle East, with Arabic being the second most prevalent home language after Spanish. But Kyla realized their collection featured many texts about Muslims but none about Arab Christians. She worked with her contact at the Junior Library Guild to find titles to fill these gaps as they were discovered.

But Kyla did not maintain this work on her own. She regularly sought the input of teachers, students, and families to build Hillside's collection to respond to dynamic identities and situations. Kyla modified the *Classroom Library Questionnaire*, available online from Lee & Low Books (2017), to gather data to guide her expansion of the school's collection. The survey prompted teachers to review their classroom libraries and reflect upon the availability of texts based on (a) representation of characters and authors (e.g., BIPOC, LGBTQ, individuals with disabilities), (b) diversity of lived experiences (e.g., family structures, socioeconomic status, religious diversity), (c) disruption of dominant curricular foci (e.g., immigration beyond Ellis Island, Black contributions beyond the Civil Rights movement), and (d) relevance to Hillside students (e.g., topics children face, community diversity, cultures and languages). Teachers rated each statement (e.g., *My library contains numerous books that explore religious diversity*) on a five-point Likert scale (i.e., strongly agree, agree, neutral, disagree, and strongly disagree). The most recent iteration of the teacher survey yielded insight across prompts, with a glaring need for more authentic Indigenous voices. Kyla then worked to secure related texts, specifically seeking out those written with the authentic voices of BIPOC and LGBTQ authors.

In addition to teachers' perspectives, Kyla encouraged students and families to share ideas for texts. After a decade of doing this work, educators had fostered self-advocacy among students and families to assert what kinds of books they wanted to see in classrooms. Kyla recalled multiple parents approaching her with their children before or after school to request books, such as those with characters exploring gender identity and expression. She used these reflections and requests to expand available texts, and used her own continued analyses as the community and world evolved. For example, to support conversations about the contemporary Black Lives Matter movement, she prioritized texts with Black protagonists situated in the current day (e.g., *All Because You Matter*; Charles, 2020) in addition to existing portrayals of historical figures like Ruby Bridges (Coles, 1995) or Martin Luther King Jr. (King, 2012).

It is important to close this section by discussing funding for efforts to expand libraries with high-quality, inclusive texts. Whether you are a teacher or an administrator, the question likely arose as you were reading the above-described examples: How did they pay for all of this? Both schools described above are urban public schools, which are known as being underfunded in contrast to their neighboring suburban schools. But school leaders recognize inclusive texts as effectively pushing forward the learning of their highly diverse population and subsequently prioritize funding to support these efforts. At both schools, one pertinent decision has freed up a significant amount of funding: rather than purchasing prepackaged curricula, which often cost tens of thousands of dollars, administrators use funds to purchase inclusive texts for teachers to design their own units of study in response to students in classrooms. These schools have also used outlets like Donors Choose and Amazon Wish Lists, but funds primarily come from various lines of the school budget (e.g., Title 1, Title 3) for curricular and learning materials.

SUPPORTING CURRICULAR DESIGN

Having an extensive collection is the first step for schools seeking to promote this work at a larger scale. But having texts in the building is not enough, as we ultimately want them in classrooms with students. Stakeholders can support teachers in selecting and using texts from the school's collection by strategically connecting texts with the curriculum. For the person or team leading these efforts in schools, the work begins by determining how inclusive texts fit into teachers' efforts to either design their own instruction or implement prescribed curricula.

Teacher-Designed Units of Study

The first approach involves integrating inclusive texts into original curricular design. Many schools recognize their teachers as pedagogical experts and leverage this expertise by having them plan instruction to support their unique students in reaching learning standards and goals. In Chapter 6, we explored how teachers use backward design of units and lessons to strategically incorporate inclusive texts. Each of these examples occurred in schools where teachers design their own curriculum using UbD (Wiggins & McTighe, 2005). For schools that engage in this work, inclusive texts should infuse into these efforts, particularly when designing the learning trajectory (i.e., Stage 3) to yield learning goals (i.e., Stage 1). At this stage of instructional design, teachers have clearly defined the learning goals and seek to brainstorm and organize various tasks and texts that support students in achieving those objectives.

At Baker, teachers work in grade-level teams to design original units of study. Over the years, they have developed and refined an instructional planning template that integrates the principles of backward design (i.e., learning objectives, followed by assessment and instruction), as well as the school's priorities to promote social action and language development. As a part of the team's curricular design work, Karen ensured an emphasis and integration of inclusive texts. In her capacity as instructional coach, she worked with grade-level teams to refine units using authentic texts, which now included balance between English- and Spanish-medium texts. Teams met with Karen for work sessions, alongside the stacks of books that they had secured from various sources and collaboratively matched texts to units. They sought to ensure that every unit had authentic texts in both languages and purchased additional books when holes emerged. Teachers then used these authentic texts to collaboratively revise units with a clear charge from Karen: Centralize inclusive texts in instruction to promote progress toward learning goals, language development, and social action.

For readers who engage in original curricular design, we encourage making inclusive texts an integrated component of these larger efforts. As emphasized throughout this text, inclusive texts should not be a stand-alone feature in classrooms, where books sit on a shelf for occasional use during independent reading or read-aloud. We want these texts, which have demonstrated efficacy to support multiple facets of learning and development, to be integrated in meaningful ways into instruction. Ensuring that inclusive texts occupy a central space in instruction begins with an explicit focus during instructional design. In an upcoming section, we explore the professional learning trajectory at Hillside School, where Kyla develops teachers' expertise for inclusive texts and purposefully embeds that focus within their larger work of using UbD to design culturally sustaining practice (Heineke & McTighe, 2018). The connection between inclusive texts and instructional design is integral.

Existing Programs and Curricula

The second approach includes analyzing and situating inclusive texts within existing programs and curricula. For decades, schools have looked to educational publishing companies for resources to support teachers in implementing classroom instruction. Companies like McGraw Hill, Houghton Mifflin Harcourt, Scholastic, and Heinemann produce detailed curriculum guides and materials written broadly for a national audience. Other entities provide frameworks to guide implementation, such as balanced literacy (Fisher, Frey, & Akhavan, 2019), workshop models (Calkins, 2001), and The Daily CAFE (Boushey & Moser, 2006). Inclusive texts should be woven into existing curricula, seeking to enhance instruction by responding to students. In Chapter 3, we explored how to analyze existing programs as a starting place for selecting and incorporating inclusive texts. When engaging in this work at the school level, school leaders should initiate and facilitate these analyses, encouraging critical lenses on existing curricula to see where and how to incorporate texts that enrich learning experiences.

Courtney is the principal at Bingham Elementary School (a pseudonym), where 500 students attend 1st through 5th grades. Situated in a community that immigrant and refugee families from around the world call home, the district prioritizes culturally sustaining practice in its strategic plan and subsequently engages educators in efforts to review all curricula with that lens and supplement as needed. Whereas the district uses prescribed curricula, including the Journeys Reading Program (published by Houghton Mifflin Harcourt) and Eureka Math (published by Great Minds), Courtney encourages teachers to use these materials as supplemental resources. Both she and the librarian work with grade-level teams to critically consider relevance and representation of the curriculum and make subsequent revisions to purposively include inclusive texts. For example, the 2nd-grade team worked collaboratively with the librarian to revise a fractured fairy tale unit during their weekly meetings. Keeping in mind the nuanced identities of their students, teachers noticed that many children could likely not tap into their background knowledge to make meaning of the various fractured fairy tales. With the help of the librarian, they discovered additional texts to incorporate into the unit.

One key tenet must be reinforced when integrating inclusive texts into existing curricula: Teachers have the agency to make changes to existing curricula. Stakeholders must collectively agree and consistently emphasize that curriculum guides, basal readers, and textbooks are resources rather than scripts (Wiggins & McTighe, 2005). Teachers must know and feel safe in the fact that they have the flexibility to change texts in response to students in classrooms (Framework Facet 1) while seeking to achieve designated learning goals (Framework Facet 2). School leaders, instructional coaches, and librarians can support teachers in making these decisions by providing high-quality inclusive texts and modeling decision-making processes with the focal curriculum, as illustrated in the example at Courtney's school. This work occurs in grade-level teams or professional development, which is the focus of the next section.

BUILDING PROFESSIONAL CAPACITY

As with any effort across schools, professional development is typically needed to support practitioners in this work. In this section, we share our approach for equipping teachers with expertise to select and incorporate inclusive texts into instruction. The learning trajectory, which aligns with the framework and organization of this text, applies to both university and school settings. Sessions can maintain an explicit focus on inclusive texts or be couched within larger efforts, such as instructional design or culturally sustaining pedagogy.

Pertinent Features and Facets

Professional development starts by building awareness and urgency around the need for inclusive texts. We like to begin by exposing the racism inherent in canonical literature, using the annual data on representation in texts from the Cooperative Children's Book Center (e.g., Huyck & Dahlen, 2019) alongside demographic data of the student population. This prompts teachers to critically reflect on their use of texts in classrooms, as well as interrogate biases that may unknowingly guide text selection (Ebarvia, Germán, Parker, & Torres, 2020). Following this macro lens to disrupt larger institutional ideologies, we take a micro lens on children's experiences with texts in classrooms. We introduce the concepts of windows and mirrors (Sims Bishop, 1990), including an overview of the research on how inclusive texts support students and anecdotal stories of children both seeing and not seeing themselves in texts.

After securing buy-in to the work's importance, the next goal is to develop criteria to find and select high-quality texts. Drawing from the key ideas outlined in Chapter 2, we engage in guided exploration of texts for relevance and authenticity. After problematizing traditional multicultural texts and considering what makes texts relevant and authentic, we provide examples (i.e., relevant and authentic texts) and non-examples (i.e., irrelevant and inauthentic texts) for comparison and discussion. Strategically selected texts typically prompt meaningful conversations about the author as insider versus outsider, the authentic or inauthentic use of language, and the potential promulgation of cultural stereotypes. This then equips teachers to take a critical lens on texts in their libraries and curricula, using a nuanced lens on the relevance to students in classrooms, as well as the authenticity of the portrayals. After sharing findings across the group, we provide time for teachers to explore an array of texts and authors, as well as provide resources to aid in finding texts in the future (i.e., book awards, organizations, publishers; see Table 2.6 in Chapter 2).

At this point in the learning trajectory, the passion and excitement for inclusive texts are palpable. Teachers recognize their importance and find amazing texts to bring into classrooms. But this is where the work often stops, which is why the next facet of professional development is integral: incorporating texts into curriculum and instruction. We designed the IT framework in response to this exact hurdle, as the four facets emphasize selecting and using texts as connected to learning goals. When used in professional development, the framework supports selecting texts to support learning objectives and incorporating texts into instruction in meaningful ways. Teachers receive guidance and support in designing units or lessons with inclusive texts, which they then return to classrooms to implement and reflect upon its efficacy. In subsequent sessions, teachers share reflections and detail students' responses, which allows the professional development to emphasize the value of incorporating inclusive texts to bolster learning.

Finally, any professional development trajectory should be open-ended to encourage ongoing reflection over time. This work is dynamic by nature: students change, teachers change, texts change, and the world changes. At the same time, the deep-seated ideologies that influence the availability, selection, and incorporation of inclusive texts remain ever-present, requiring the need for continuous interrogation of this work. We encourage you not to engage in this work alone, but to form community with colleagues, community members, authors, and others who collaboratively push forward and advocate for inclusive texts in schools.

One School's Learning Trajectory

In addition to sharing the learning trajectory that we regularly incorporate in university courses and school settings, we wanted to highlight the ongoing capacity-building work of an exemplar school with long-term commitment to inclusive texts. Hillside School has been used as an example throughout this chapter, as the school's teachers and leaders have collaboratively worked over the last decade to use inclusive texts to enhance practice. Efforts started with targeted focus on reading instruction and extended beyond to other disciplines, maintaining the lens on using inclusive texts to promote culturally sustaining pedagogy for Hillside students.

The professional development trajectory began with a deep dive into the literacy block at this K–6 school. Kyla started with an explicit focus on guided reading, an important and tangible time of the school day where teachers worked closely with individual learners. She first engaged teachers in critically probing their perceptions of readers. At a school where over half of students are multilingual learners from an array of language backgrounds, she wanted staff to interrogate assumptions about what students should read and consider how texts used in guided reading might support or deter readers (e.g., required background knowledge, interest, language). This set the stage to introduce teachers to the power of inclusive texts. Working within the structure of The Daily CAFE (Boushey &

Moser, 2006), where students read in different contexts (e.g., independently, paired), teachers learned how to select texts with relevance to kids. Kyla incorporated Sims Bishop's framework (1990) to encourage selection of texts as mirrors and windows and then prompted analysis of text authenticity by reading aloud excerpts of examples and non-examples. While serving as the primary facilitator of the sessions, she centered her sessions on the voices and experiences of her teachers.

The initial focus on the reading block provoked teachers' interest and passion for finding and utilizing inclusive texts in classrooms. The leadership team wanted to harness this excitement to begin looking at content-area curricula. While analyzing and selecting texts, practitioners had recognized that existing curricula did not reflect and represent the diverse population at Hillside. The school embraced UbD for teachers to design their own units of study, specifically incorporating lenses on language and culture across instructional design to tap into students' backgrounds and abilities (Heineke & McTighe, 2018). Professional development sessions delved into each stage of instructional design, including incorporation of inclusive mentor texts. With an expanding school collection, teachers explored and selected texts to design learning trajectories. These efforts occurred across disciplines, as whole-school sessions transitioned into grade-level and departmental teams collaboratively designing curricula. On professional development days when the full faculty gathered, teachers shared units, data, and reflections to promote ongoing dialogue and refinements to instruction.

In addition to capacity-building efforts through professional development, Hillside has prioritized recruiting and hiring BIPOC teachers. Kyla has found that this enhances the buy-in for this work immediately, as teachers have typically experienced White-washed curricula and embrace the opportunity to disrupt the canon and integrate inclusive texts with students. She sees these efforts as positively influencing children's self-perceptions and learning experiences in schools. Not only do readers get to see themselves in texts, but they get to see themselves in their teachers. In this way, centering the school's curriculum around inclusive texts elevates diverse voices in two ways: through the authors who write the texts and the teachers who read them with learners. We encourage other schools to follow Hillside's lead in using inclusive texts as a key lever to promote meaningful school change for children, families, and communities.

USING TEXTS WITH STAKEHOLDERS

Learning does not only need to be *about* inclusive texts, but can occur *through* inclusive texts. In this way, stakeholders read and engage with inclusive texts as a medium of collaborative learning. High-quality texts written for children and adolescents have been used to push forward educators' thinking in book clubs and literature discussions, particularly centered on educators' work with multilingual learners (e.g., Florio-Ruane, 2001; Martínez-Roldán & Heineke, 2011; Nathenson-Mejia & Escamilla, 2003). Inclusive texts also serve to meaningfully engage families in schools, inviting them to read and respond to texts alongside their children that allow them to collectively embrace personal, familial, cultural, and linguistic identities (Dávila, Noguerón, & Vásquez-Dominguez, 2017; Flores, 2018; López-Robertson, 2017). Using texts with educators and parents provides opportunities for authentic exploration and engagement as described throughout this text, and demonstrates approaches to reading in classrooms and homes.

Focus on Teachers and Candidates

In research and practice, we have found inclusive texts to be one of the most powerful mediums to push forward teachers' and teacher candidates' professional learning. Because inclusive texts authentically reflect and portray an individuals' lived experiences with rich nuances, educators take the perspective and empathize with the characters and begin to grapple with the complexity of various circumstances and occurrences. Whether using poems from *My Name Is Jorge on Both Sides of the River* (Medina, 1999), a picture book on school bullying like *My Name Is Bilal* (Mobin-Uddin, 2005), a middle-grade novel on identity like *Amina's Voice* (Khan, 2017), or a graphic novel on changing schools in *The New Kid* (Craft, 2019), educators can (a) develop nuanced understandings of their students, (b) critically consider their roles as educators, and (c) gain exemplars for using inclusive texts in classrooms.

Implementing this approach is relatively straightforward given structures already in place in schools. Teachers regularly come together in professional learning communities (PLCs) to engage in interactive dialogue with one another, often using a professional text that has been preselected by the team, school, or district. The mediating text that all PLC members read and use does not *have* to be a professional text. Just as children learn through inclusive texts, adults connect, make meaning, and change their thinking from engaging with authentic texts that provide windows into the lived experiences of their students (Sims Bishop, 1990). In this way, teachers and stakeholders might select focal inclusive texts that reflect students in their building (Framework Facet 1) and align to goals for professional learning (Framework Facet 2). Teachers then use the strategically selected text or text set (Framework Facet 3) with literature discussion strategies that promote personal reflection, active participation, and purposeful connections to classroom practice (Framework Facet 4).

This last component is integral to meaningful discussions and subsequent professional learning. As has been emphasized throughout this text, we don't want to stop at selecting high-quality texts and simply making them available or reading them aloud. We want to make texts central via integration into instruction and professional development. At our university, we use inclusive texts to mediate discussions about multilingual learners, including children's nuanced experiences in homes, communities, and schools and teachers' integral role in nurturing their development. Our research (e.g., Heineke, 2014; Papola-Ellis & Heineke, 2019) has indicated the need to use literature strategies to promote rich discussions around texts. Without these strategies, text-based discussions often remain at the surface level, with participants discussing what they liked or didn't like about the book, rather than using the text to connect with students and probe their roles as teachers. Table 7.1 shares strategies for teachers'

Table 7.1. Strategies to Mediate Teachers' Literature Discussions

Comparisons: Chart similarities and differences between the main character(s) and students in your classroom. Consider historical and political contexts, cultural and linguistic backgrounds, plot and sequence of events, and more. Use the chart to determine how the text provides windows into the lives of characters as students—both generally and specifically.

Connections: As you read, jot down stories or experiences that the text makes you think about, both personally and professionally. In the group, share your connections and talk about how the connections relate to the text and teaching multilingual students.

Prompts: To prepare for the literature discussion, flag and respond to parts of the text that:

- Portray culture or language in an authentic or inauthentic manner.
- Reminds you of a particular student and/or event in your classroom.
- Made you rethink a particular concept or approach in the classroom.
- Made you rethink a particular notion, topic, or idea in the world.
- Reminds you of another text or artistic creation (e.g., art, drama).
- Allow you to step inside the text to make meaning of the described realities.
- Your students might connect to and find relevance to their lives.

Roles: In advance of reading, each teacher selects a role to participate in the discussion.

- Discussion Director: Look for big ideas and questions to mediate discussion.
- Classroom Connector: Consider connections to classroom practice, including how students would connect with the text and possible uses in the classroom.
- Character Captain: Share observations and traits about characters that inform understanding of social, emotional, cultural, linguistic, and academic facets.
- Discourse Analyst: Look for ways that language is utilized and reflected in the text to inform understanding and thinking about linguistic repertoires.
- Literacy Luminary: Flag and read aloud powerful or puzzling parts of the text to discuss, specifically those that highlight unique nuances and experiences.
- Sociohistorical Sleuth: Research the social, historical, and political realities of the time period and context to frame, critique, and connect to the text plot.

literature discussions, which draws from those originally designed for students (Short et al., 1996).

Focus on Parents and Families

Using inclusive texts with parents, guardians, and family members is a powerful strategy to enhance authentic engagement and involvement in schools. In addition to inviting adults into the classroom like Lindsay's in Chapter 4, stakeholders have found success in using inclusive texts with families outside of classrooms, providing opportunities to read, interpret, and respond to texts collaboratively with children (Flores, 2018; López-Robertson, 2017). These interactions allow adult readers to (a) see their backgrounds, identities, and experiences reflected in texts; (b) build awareness about inclusive texts and the authors who write them; and (c) provide ideas for how to introduce and use these texts at home with their children.

At Baker, Karen embraced the use of inclusive texts in her work with the schools' bilingual parent advisory committee. Per Illinois state policy, schools must host quarterly meetings for bilingual program parents, guardians, teachers, and community members. Recognizing the same handful of parents in attendance at each meeting, Karen aspired to infuse life into the group with a different approach—using inclusive texts with adults in similar ways to their children in bilingual classrooms. Using word-of-mouth invitations on the playground before and after school, she welcomed parents to join Baker's multilingual book club, where they would read and discuss a bilingual picture book to then take home to enjoy with their children. Karen received an overwhelming response, with 35 parents signing up for the book club. With funds for only 30 texts per quarter in the committee budget, Karen worked with her principal to cover the cost and allow all to participate. In the first session, they read *René Has Two Last Names/René tiene dos apellidos* (Colato-Laínez, 2009) and engaged in an impassioned discussion about their names, families, cultures, and identities.

Word about the book club spread around the school. In addition to Spanish-speaking parents with children in the bilingual program, Arabic-speaking parents with children in EL programming also joined the book club. For the next meeting, Karen provided copies of *Golden Domes and Silver Lanterns: A Muslim Book of Colors* (Khan, 2012), and, after getting things started, she handed off facilitation to a mother from Algeria. Participants collaboratively read the text and engaged in conversation about Ramadan by questioning, comparing, and connecting to other holiday traditions. Karen described the book club as the most powerful moment of her teaching career, as Spanish- and Arabic-speaking parents who had not previously interacted in the school forged authentic bonds and relationships. Participants expressed joy in seeing their cultures reflected in texts, as well as excitement to use texts at home with their children. By prioritizing selection of bilingual texts, Karen prompted key connections with the school's dual-language program and goals to promote students' biliteracy.

In summary, inclusive texts hold value beyond classroom use. Their incorporation within existing structures, such as PLCs or parent committees, provides tangible ways to promote culturally sustaining pedagogies and critical literacy with stakeholders across schools. In addition to providing space for their own reflection and development, educators, parents, and family members can experience and learn about methods and materials that nurture children's identity exploration, language and literacy development, and conceptual understandings. When schools commit to the work of ensuring a wide array of high-quality texts reflective of the community and world, stakeholders use these texts in creative ways inside and outside of classrooms to yield meaningful learning, engagement, collaboration, and relationships.

THE FRAMEWORK IN ACTION: PROMOTING CHANGE IN SCHOOL COMMUNITIES

Throughout this text, we have asked you to visualize classrooms that buck traditional norms for text selection to develop authentic curricula that tap into children's identities, experiences, and perspectives. In each chapter, teachers like Anne, Felisha, Javier, and Lindsay have demonstrated how to enact these visualizations into practice: finding space and flexibility in the curriculum, making decisions rooted in students' strengths, and thoughtfully weaving an array of high-quality texts to nurture children's learning and engagement. In this chapter, you have seen how schools like Baker, Bingham, and Hillside support educators in challenging the canon and embracing inclusive texts to sustain children's multifaceted identities, as well as promote literacy development and disciplinary learning. Cited throughout the text, research has consistently indicated that inclusive texts develop children's identities, critical consciousness, empathy, literacy engagement, reading comprehension, and disciplinary learning. With this text, we sought to provide actionable ways for practitioners to reap these benefits and incorporate inclusive texts to better serve students in today's classrooms.

But this work does not come without challenges. The canon is not simply a suggested text list, but a deeply ideological conception of what should be taught in schools and whose voices belong in the formal curriculum. This institutionalization means that many educators, parents, and policymakers tacitly accept the canon as the norm, which requires interrogation and deconstruction to yield real change in schools. As reiterated throughout this book, this work is not about adding a *multicultural* or *diverse identities* book bin to libraries, which continues to marginalize BIPOC, LGBTQ, and disabled children, authors, and communities. If we seek to avoid this limited and disparaging outcome when incorporating inclusive texts, educators must recognize and negotiate the normative and racist curricular practices that pervade U.S. schools. Even the most woke of educators can fall into the trap of dominant ideologies and practices, perhaps assuming students' need to assimilate to White, English-dominant norms, lamenting top-down mandates to teach rigidly interpreted standards, agreeing to teach the so-called classics, and only suggesting inclusive texts to children for independent reading. We all must continually deconstruct the impact of these institutional ideologies on our biases, assumptions, and approaches to teaching and learning.

Despite the value of incorporating inclusive texts into classrooms, described across the pages of this text, we do not wish to portray this as the silver bullet that transforms schools and disrupts systemic racism, classism, ableism, and sexism. As Gloria Ladson-Billings (2014) has asserted, simply having books with BIPOC characters in your classroom does not signify the presence of culturally relevant pedagogy. Nonetheless, inclusive texts provide an entry point—a foot in the door to bring theory into practice and begin the work to disrupt dominant ideologies and practices in classrooms. By bringing inclusive texts into classrooms, we begin to resituate curricula to build from children's identities and elevate diverse voices, rather than provide scaffolds to the so-called mainstream curriculum written for White, English-dominant, middle-class children in the name of equity and access.

This can start small. Perhaps one teacher brings one book into their literacy block, which leads to another, then another, and then another. After seeing the incredible response in students' engagement, reading comprehension, and overall joy to see themselves in the curriculum, the teacher incorporates diverse voices and perspectives into the content areas—interrogating multiple perspectives in social studies, seeing diverse contributions in STEM, and disrupting stereotypes in the arts, athletics, and society. They engage colleagues across their school and district, prompting wide procurement of resources, professional development, and prioritization of inclusive texts across classrooms, grade levels, and content areas. Not only does this teacher reach the individual child who previously felt a lack of belonging and engagement in school, but collectively they and their colleagues sustain the identities and challenge the perspectives of thousands of children who pass through their school. They then share these approaches, collaborations, and success stories at conferences and via social media, subsequently extending inclusive texts into more classrooms, schools, and communities.

Now the system continues to damper this work, most recently with talk, threats, and even policies seeking to quell discussions on race and racism in schools, which might deter this teacher from ever initiating this chain of events. But we contend that selecting texts that allow children to see themselves should not be political—and certainly should not be prohibited. Unless legislators dare to enact policies insisting that texts have White,

English-speaking, cisgender, heterosexual protagonists without disabilities, then inclusive texts have a place in classrooms. Fear and intimidation should not stop teachers from nurturing children's literacies, identities, and understandings, goals that likely led them to the profession of teaching in the first place. By situating children at the center of what we do—seeking to provide welcoming learning spaces and practices that foster their learning and development—we maintain the pedagogical rationale despite the ideological battles going on around us. As we collectively seek to disrupt systemic racism more broadly across the educational institution, take small steps to enact change in your classroom. Just one text that you bring into the classroom might connect with one student, encourage them to love themselves, read more expansively, and be kind to others. That matters.

As you move forward from this book, think about how you plan to find space to do this work in your classroom in your own way to reach your unique students. It takes one person to promote change, and your expertise and advocacy might be the key lever to initiate this work in your school, district, and community. Perhaps awareness is the issue, and a text wish list with a strong rationale grounded in research and school demographics is all the convincing your administrator needs to procure and encourage use of inclusive texts. Maybe your colleagues lack comfort in flexibly interpreting and maneuvering the standards and curricula, and sharing examples of your lessons with inclusive texts piques their interest in trying new approaches to literacy instruction. Or perhaps you see the larger ideological challenges and take your voice to the school board or state legislature, using authors' words from poignant inclusive texts to demonstrate the need to maintain their use in classrooms. Regardless of how you choose to approach this work—in the classroom, schoolhouse, or statehouse—embrace your agency and define action to promote change for children and the world.

QUESTIONS AND ACTIVITIES FOR PROFESSIONAL DEVELOPMENT

1. Critically analyze and reflect upon your school's curricular resources and text collections using the following questions: Are our students authentically represented in the texts that we have? Do we have inclusive texts aligned to standards and other learning goals? What resources can we secure to reflect students and support learning? How can we integrate inclusive texts into our existing curricula?

2. Seek out the perspectives of your colleagues in relation to the above questions. Draft a survey for teachers to analyze their classroom materials and provide feedback on the texts that they have available to them for classroom use. Discuss these findings as a leadership

team or full faculty to drive the procurement of inclusive texts moving forward.

3. Talk one-on-one with various students and families to gather anecdotal data on their perceptions and interactions with texts at the school. Do they see themselves in texts? What other types of texts or characters would they like to see in libraries?

4. Consider other sources of collaboration and support to sustain this work. Explore local businesses, organizations, and universities who might collaborate around these efforts for inclusive texts (e.g., professional development, text procurement, family engagement). Use social media to build community more broadly and stay in touch with authors, publishers, and others seeking to incorporate inclusive texts in classrooms.

5. Start a journal to capture your practice with inclusive texts over time. You might (a) note poignant stories of students engaging with inclusive texts, (b) reflect on text selection and students' responses, (c) consider various nuances of students' identities and experiences and reflect upon the mirrors that texts provide, and (d) grapple with current events and find texts that promote children's critical literacy and understandings.

References

Children's Books Cited

Ada, A. F. (2004). *I love Saturdays y domingos*. Atheneum.

Alarcón, F. X. (2005). *Poems to dream together/Poemas para soñar juntos*. Lee & Low.

Alexander, K. (2016). *Booked*. HMH Books.

Alexander. K. (2019). *The undefeated*. Versify.

Alire Sáenz, B. (1998). *A gift from Papá Diego/Un regalo de papá Diego*. Cinco Puntos Press.

Alire Sáenz, B. (2009). *The dog who loved tortillas/La perrita que le encantaban las tortillas*. Cinco Puntos Press.

Allen, T. (2020). *Sometimes people march*. Balzer & Bray.

Alvarez, J. (2002). *How Tía Lola came to (visit) stay*. Yearling.

Alvarez, J. (2004). *Before we were free*. Ember.

Alvarez, J. (2009). *Return to sender*. Yearling.

Ancona, G. (1993). *Pablo remembers: The fiesta of the Day of the Dead*. HarperCollins.

Applegate, K. (2007). *Home of the brave*. Feiwel & Friends.

Applegate, K. (2017). *Wishtree*. Feiwel & Friends.

Argueta, J. (2016). *Somos como las nubes/We are like the clouds*. Groundwood Books.

Atkins, J. (2012). *Mary Anning and the sea dragon*. CreateSpace.

Banks, L. R. (1980). *The Indian in the cupboard*. Doubleday.

Barnes, D. (2017). *Crown: An ode to the fresh cut*. Agate Bolden.

Barnes, D. (2020). *I am every good thing*. Nancy Paulsen Books.

Bateson-Hill, M. (1998). *Shota and the star quilt*. Zero to Ten.

Becker, H. (2018). *Counting on Katherine: How Katherine Johnson saved Apollo 13*. Henry Holt and Company.

Behar, R. (2017). *Lucky broken girl*. Puffin Books.

Blackburne, L. (2021). *I dream of Popo*. Roaring Book Press.

Blackstone, S. C. (2005). *My granny went to market: A round-the-world counting rhyme*. Barefoot Books.

Blume, J. (1970). *Are you there, God? It's me, Margaret*. MacMillan.

Boelts, M. (2009). *Those shoes*. Candlewick.

Boelts, M. (2018). *A bike like Sergio's*. Candlewick.

Brandt, L. (2014). *Maddi's fridge*. Flashlight Press.

Brantley-Newton, V. (2020). *Just like me*. Knopf.

Brock, R. (Ed). (2018). *Hope nation*. Philomel Books.

Brown, B. (2015). *Lola Levine is not mean!* Little Brown Books.

Brown, M. (2011). *Marisol McDonald doesn't match/Marisol McDonald no combina*. Children's Book Press.

Browne, M. L., Acevedo, E., & Gatwood, O. (2020). *Woke: A young poet's call to justice*. Roaring Book Press.

Bruchac, J., & Bruchac, J. (2008). *The girl who helped the thunder and other Native American folktales*. Sterling.

Bryon, N. (2020). *Rocket says clean up!* Random House.

Bunting, E. (2006). *One green apple*. Clarion Books.

Burleigh, R. (2013). *Look up! Henrietta Leavitt, pioneering woman astronomer*. Simon & Schuster.

Burleigh, R. (2016). *Solving the puzzle under the sea: Marie Tharp maps the ocean floor*. Simon & Schuster.

Burnett, F. H. (1911/1985). *The secret garden*. HarperCollins.

Callender, K. (2018). *Hurricane child*. Scholastic.

Campoy, F. I., & Howell, T. (2016). *Maybe something beautiful: How art transformed a neighborhood*. HMH Books.

Celano, M. (2019). *Something happened in our town*. Magination Press.

Charles, T. (2020). *All because you matter*. Orchard.

Charles, T. (2021). *My day with the panye*. Candlewick.

Child, B. J. (2018). *Bowwow powwow*. Minnesota Historical Society Press.

Choi, Y. (2001). *The name jar*. Dragonfly Books.

Chokshi, R. (2018). *Aru Shah and the end of time*. Rick Riordan.

Clarke, C. (2019). *Pants project*. Sourcebooks.

Cleary, B. (1955). *Beezus and Ramona*. HarperCollins.

Cline-Ransome, L. (2018). *Before she was Harriet*. Holiday House.

Cline-Ransome, L. (2020). *Overground railroad*. Holiday House.

Coburn, J. R. (2000). *Domítila*. Shen's Books.

Cocca-Leffler, M., & Leffler, J. (2021). *We want to go to school!: The fight for disability rights*. Albert Whitman.

Colato-Laínez, R. (2009). *René has two last names/René tiene dos apellidos*. Arte Publico Press.

Coles, R. (1995). *The story of Ruby Bridges*. Scholastic.

Craft, J. (2019). *New kid*. HarperCollins.

Curtis, C. P. (1963). *The Watsons go to Birmingham*. Yearling.

Danticat, E. (2015). *Mama's nightingale: A story of immigration and separation*. Dial Books.

Davis-Williams, N., & Davis-Williams, S. (2018). *Umi and Uma: The story of two mommies and a baby*. Wooden Roses.

Day, C. (2020). *I can make this promise*. Heartdrum.

de Arias, P. (2018). *Marwan's journey*. Minedition US.

de la Peña, M. (2015). *Last stop on Market Street*. G. P. Putnam's Sons.

de la Peña, M. (2018). *Carmela full of wishes*. G. P. Putnam's Sons.

de la Peña, M. (2021). *Milo imagines the world*. G. P. Putnam's Sons.

Delacre, L. (2016). *Olinguito, from A to Z! Unveiling the cloud forest*. Children's Book Press.

Delaunois, A. (2017). *Water's children: Celebrating the resource that unites us all.* Pajama Press.

Demi. (1997). *One grain of rice.* Scholastic.

Diaz, A. (2016). *The only road.* Simon & Schuster.

Díaz, J. (2018). *Islandborn.* Dial Books.

Dionne, E. (2020). *Lifting as we climb: Black women's battle for the ballot box.* Viking.

Doyon, S. C. (2020). *Magnificent homespun brown.* Tilbury House.

Draper, S. (2012). *Out of my mind.* Atheneum.

Draper, S. (2018). *Blended.* Atheneum/Caitlyn Dlouhy Books.

Edwardson, D. D. (2004). *Whale snow.* Charlesbridge.

Eggers, D. (2018). *What can a citizen do?* Chronicle.

Ellison, J. M. (2020). *Sylvia and Marsha start a revolution.* Jessica Kingsley Publishers.

Erdrich, L. (2002). *The birchbark house.* Hyperion.

Estrada Kelly, E. (2020a). *Hello universe.* Greenwillow Books.

Estrada Kelly, E. (2020b). *Lalani of the distant sea.* Greenwillow.

Faruqi, R. (2015). *Lailah's lunchbox: A Ramadan story.* Tilbury House Publishers.

Federle, T. (2018). *Better Nate than ever.* Simon & Schuster.

Fitzgerald, F. S. (1925). *The great Gatsby.* Charles Scribner's Sons.

Flood, N. B. (2020). *I will dance.* Atheneum.

Florence, D. M. (2017). *Jasmine Toguchi.* Farrar, Straus & Giroux.

Garland, S. (1997). *The lotus seed.* HMH Books.

Garza, C. L. (1990). *Family pictures/Cuadros de familia.* Children's Book Press.

Garza, C. L. (1999). *Magic windows/Ventanas mágicas.* Children's Book Press.

Gephart, D. (2018). *Lily and Dunkin.* Yearling.

Gholz, S. (2019). *The boy who grew a forest: The true story of Jadav Payeng.* Sleeping Bear Press.

Gino, A. (2022). *Melissa.* Scholastic.

Golding, W. (1954). *Lord of the flies.* Faber & Faber.

Gonzales, M. (2017). *Yo soy Muslim.* Salaam Reads / Simon & Schuster.

González, M. C. (2013). *My colors, my world/Mis colores, mi mundo.* Lee & Low.

Gratz, A. (2017). *Refugee.* Scholastic.

Greenwalt, K. (2020). *Princess Truly series.* Scholastic.

Griffith, G. (2013). *When Christmas feels like home.* Albert Whitman & Company.

Grimes, N. (2016). *Garvey's choice.* Wordsong.

Guidroz, R. (2019). *Leila in saffron.* Salaam Reads.

Hall, M. (2015). *Red: A crayon's story.* Greenwillow Books.

Han, O. S., & Plunkett, S. H. (1996). *Kongi and Potgi.* Dial Books.

Harrington, J. N. (2019). *Buzzing with questions: The inquisitive mind of Charles Henry Turner.* Calkins Creek.

Herbauts, A. (2016). *What color is the wind?* Enchanted Lion Books.

Herrera, J. F. (2000). *The upside down boy / El niño de cabeza.* Children's Book Press.

Herrera, J. F. (2004). *Featherless/desplumado.* Children's Book Pess.

Herrera, J. F. (2013). *Grandma and me at the flea/Los meros meros remateros.* Lee & Low.

Hickox, R. (1998). *The golden sandal.* Holiday House.

Hinojosa, V., & Voorhees, C. (2020). *A journey toward hope*. Six Foot Press.

Hirandani, V. (2018). *The night diary*. Kokila.

Ho, M. (2000). *Hush! A Thai lullaby*. Scholastic.

Hoffman, S. (2014). *Jacob's new dress*. Albert Whitman & Company.

Hunt, L. M. (2017). *Fish in a tree*. Puffin Books.

Huson, B. D. (2018). *Mothers of Xsan series*. Highwater Press.

Isaacs, S. S. (2001). *Life at Ellis Island*. Heinemann/Raintree.

Jacob, D. (2005). *The legend of St. Ann's flood*. Macmillan Caribbean.

Jamieson, V., & Mohamed, O. (2020). *When stars are scattered*. Dial Books/Penguin Random House.

Jiménez, F. (2000). *The Christmas gift*. Houghton Mifflin Harcourt.

Johnson, C., Council, L., & Choi, C. (2019). *Intersection allies: We make room for all*. Dottir.

Jordan-Fenton, C., & Pokiak-Fenton, M. (2010). *Fatty legs*. Annick Press.

Jordan-Fenton, C., & Pokiak-Fenton, M. (2013). *When I was eight*. Annick Press.

Joy, A. (2020). *Black is a rainbow color*. Roaring Book Press.

Kamkwamba, W., & Mealer, B. (2016). *The boy who harnessed the wind*. Puffin Books.

Keats, E. J. (1962). *The snowy day*. Puffin Books.

Khan, H. (2008). *Night of the moon: A Muslim holiday story*. Chronicle.

Khan, H. (2012). *Golden domes and silver lanterns: A Muslim book of colors*. Chronicle.

Khan, H. (2017). *Amina's voice*. Salaam Reads/Simon & Schuster Books.

Khan, H. (2019). *Under my hijab*. Lee & Low.

Kim, P. H. (2015). *Here I am*. Picture Window Books.

King, M. L. (2012). *I have a dream*. Schwartz & Wade.

Kostecki-Shaw, J. S. (2011). *Same, same but different*. Henry Holt and Co.

Kurusa. (1995). *The streets are free*. Annick.

Lai, T. (2013). *Inside out and back again*. HarperCollins.

Lasky, K. (1994). *The librarian who measured the earth*. Little Brown Books.

Lee, H. (1960). *To kill a mockingbird*. J.B. Lippincott Co.

Lee, J. (2020). *Brother's keeper*. Holiday House.

Leitich Smith, C. (2000). *Jingle dancer*. Heartdrum.

Leslie, T. (2020). *The story of Barack Obama*. Rockridge Press.

Levinson, C. (2017). *The youngest marcher: The story of Audrey Faye Hendricks, a young civil rights activist*. Atheneum.

Lewis, C. S. (1950). *The lion, the witch, and the wardrobe*. Geoffrey Bles.

Lewis, J., & Aydin, A. (2013). *March*. Top Shelf.

Lin, G. (2007). *The year of the dog*. Little Brown Books.

Lin, G. (2001). *Dim sum for everyone!* Knopf.

Lindstrom, C. (2020). *We are water protectors*. Roaring Brook Press.

Love, J. (2018). *Julián is a mermaid*. Candlewick.

Lukoff, K. (2019). *When Aidan became a brother*. Lee & Low.

Lyon, G. E., & Tillotson, K. (2011). *All the water in the world*. Atheneum/Richard Jackson.

Lyons, K. S. (2017). *Jada Jones series*. Penguin Workshop.

Lyons, K. S. (2020). *Ty's travels*. HarperCollins.

Maillard, K. N. (2019). *Fry bread: A Native American family story*. Roaring Brook Press.

Markel, M. (2013). *Brave girl: Clara and the shirtwaist makers' strike of 1909*. Balzer & Bray.

Marks, J., Chester, H., Katzeek, D., Dauenhauer, N., & Dauenhauer, R. (Eds.). (2017). *Shanyaak'utlaax/Salmon boy*. Sealaska Heritage Institute.

Martínez, E. J. (2018). *Cuando amamos cantamos/When we love someone we sing to them*. Reflection Press.

Martínez-Neal, J. (2018). *Alma and how she got her name*. Candlewick.

Mayer, M. (1994). *Baba Yaga and Vasilisa the brave*. Morrow.

McHugh, M. L., & Lo, B. (2010). *Ka's garden*. Universal Human Publishing.

McManis, C. W., & Sorell, T. (2019). *Indian no more*. Tu Books.

Medina, J. (1999). *My name is Jorge on both sides of the river: Poems in English and Spanish*. Wordsong.

Medina, J. (2019). *Juana and Lucas*. Candlewick.

Medina, M. (2020). *Merci Suárez changes gears*. Candlewick.

Melleby, N. (2019). *Hurricane season*. Algonquin Young Readers.

Metcalf, L. H. (2020). *No voice too small: Fourteen young Americans making history*. Charlesbridge.

Mobin-Uddin, A. (2005). *My name is Bilal*. Boyds Mills.

Mochizuki, K. (1993). *Baseball saved us*. Lee & Low.

Morales, Y. (2018). *Dreamers*. Neal Porter.

Mosca, J. F. (2017). *The girl who thought in pictures: The story of Dr. Temple Grandin*. The Innovation Press.

Mosca, J. F. (2018). *The girl with a mind for math: The story of Raye Montague*. Innovation Press.

Muhammad, I. (2019). *The proudest blue: A story of hijab and family*. Little Brown Books.

Muñoz Ryan, P. (2002). *Esperanza rising*. Scholastic.

Muñoz Ryan, P. (2005). *Becoming Naomi León*. Scholastic.

Nayeri, D. (2020). *Everything sad is untrue*. Levine Querido.

Neri, G. (2007). *Chess rumble*. Lee & Low.

Nuurali, S. (2021). *Sadiq* series. Picture Window Books.

Ostertag, M. K. (2018). *Witch boy*. Graphix.

Parish, P. (1963). *Amelia Bedelia*. Harper & Row.

Park, L. S. (2005). *Bee-bim bop!* Clarion Books.

Park, L. S. (2011). *A long walk to water*. HMH Books.

Parker Rhodes, J. (2018). *Ghost boys*. Little Brown Books.

Parton, D. (2016). *Coat of many colors*. Grosset & Dunlap.

Paul, M. (2015). *Water is water*. Roaring Brook Press.

Paul, M. (2015). *One plastic bag: Isatou Ceesay and the recycling women of Gambia*. Millbrook.

Paulsen, G. (1986). *Hatchet*. MacMillan.

Paye, W. (2005). *Head, body, legs: A story from Liberia*. Square Fish.

Pearlman, R. (2018). *Pink is for boys*. Running Press Kids.

Pérez, A. I. (2009). *My diary from here to there/Mi diario de aquí hasta allá*. Children's Book Press.

Pérez, C. C. (2017). *The first rule of punk*. Puffin.

Phi, B. (2017). *A different pond*. Capstone Young Readers.

Pinkney, A. D. (2014). *The red pencil*. Little Brown Books.

Pinkney, A. D. (2018). *Martin rising: Requiem for a king*. Scholastic.

Polacco, P. (2001). *The keeping quilt*. Simon & Schuster/Paula Wiseman Books.

Polacco, P. (2009). *In our mothers' house*. Philomel.

Quintero, I. (2019). *My Papi has a motorcycle*. Kokila.

Ramée, L. M. (2019). *A good kind of trouble*. Balzer & Bray.

Rawls, W. (1961). *Where the red fern grows*. Doubleday.

Reul, S. L. (2018). *Breaking news*. Roaring Book Press.

Robertson, D. A. (2016). *When we were alone*. Highwater Press.

Robertson, J. (2017). *The water walker*. Second Story Press.

Robles, A. (2003). *Lakas and the Manilatown fish*. Children's Book Press.

Rocco, J. (2011). *Blackout*. Little Brown Books.

Rosenthal, A. K. (2009). *Duck! Rabbit!* Chronicle.

Ruurs, M. (2015). *School days around the world*. Kids Can Press.

Ruurs, M. (2016). *Stepping stones: A refugee family's journey*. Orca Book Publishers.

Saeed, A. (2018). *Amal unbound*. Nancy Paulsen Books.

Saeed, A. (2019). *Bilal cooks daal*. Salaam Reads.

Salinger, J. D. (1951). *The catcher in the rye*. Little Brown Books.

Sanders, R. (2019). *Stonewall: A building, an uprising, a revolution*. Random House.

Sanna, F. (2016). *The journey*. Flying Eye Books.

Say, A. (2008). *Grandfather's journey*. Sandpiper.

Schachner, J. (2003). *Skippy Jon Jones*. Dutton.

Schiffer, M. B. (2015). *Stella brings the family*. Chronicle.

Scieszka, J. (1989). *The true story of the three little pigs*. Viking.

Senzai, N. H. (2010). *Shooting Kabul*. Simon & Schuster.

Senzai, N. H. (2020). *Escape from Aleppo*. Simon & Schuster/Paula Wiseman Books.

Shamsi-Basha, K., & Latham, I. (2020). *The cat man of Aleppo*. G. P. Putnam's Sons.

Shetterly, M. L. (2016). *Hidden figures: Young readers' edition*. HarperCollins.

Shraya, V. (2016). *The boy and the bindi*. Arsenal Pulp Press.

Sidney, R. (2015). *Nelson beats the odds*. Creative Medicine.

Simermeyer, G. (2008). *Meet Christopher: An Osage Indian boy from Oklahoma*. Council Oak Books.

Simpson, P. (2016). *Trouble at the sandbox*. Scott Foresman.

Singh, S. J. (2020). *Fauja Singh keeps going: The true story of the oldest person to ever run a marathon*. Kokila.

Sloan, H. G. (2018). *Short*. Puffin Books.

Sneve, V. D. H. (2011). *The Christmas coat: Memories of my Sioux childhood*. Holiday House.

Sorell, T. (2018). *We are grateful: Otsaliheliga*. Charlesbridge.

Sorell, T. (2019). *At the mountain's base*. Kokila.

Sorell, T. (2021). *We are still here! Native American truths everyone should know*. Charlesbridge.

Soto, G. (1996). *Too many tamales*. Puffin Books.

Soto, G. (1997). *Chato y su cena*. Puffin Books.

Stoddard, L. (2018). *Just like Jackie*. HarperCollins.

Tafolla, C., & Teneyuca, S. (2008). *That's not fair/No es justo: Emma Tenayuca's struggle for justice*. Wings Press.

Tafolla, C. (2009). *What can you do with a paleta?* Penguin Books.

Tan, S. (2007). *The arrival*. Arthur A. Levine.

Telgemeier, R. (2010). *Smile*. Graphix.

Thompkins-Bigelow, J. (2020). *Your name is a song*. The Innovation Press.

Thompson, L. A. (2015). *Emmanuel's dream: The true story of Emmanuel Ofosu Yeboah*. Schwartz & Wade.

Tolkien, J. R. R. (1954). *Lord of the rings*. Allen & Unwin.

Tonatiuh, D. (2010). *Dear primo: A letter to my cousin*. Abrams.

Tonatiuh, D. (2013). *Pancho rabbit and the coyote: A migrant's tale*. Abrams.

Tonatiuh, D. (2014). *Separate is never equal: Sylvia Mendez and her family's fight for desegregation*. Abrams.

Twain, M. (1885), *The adventures of Huckleberry Finn*. Charles L. Webster & Company.

Verde, S., & Badiel, G. (2016). *The water princess*. G. P. Putnam's Sons.

Warga, J. (2019). *Other words for home*. Balzer & Bray.

Weatherford, C. B. (2021). *Unspeakable: The Tulsa race massacre*. Carolrhoda Books.

Wenzel, B. (2016). *They all saw a cat*. Chronicle.

Whitley, J. (2014). *Princeless: Save yourself*. Action Lab Entertainment.

Wilder, L. I. (1932). *Little house in the big woods*. HarperCollins.

Wilder, L. I. (1935, 1992). *Little house on the prairie*. Harper & Brothers.

Williams, K., & Mohammed, K. (2009). *My name is Sangoel*. Eerdmans.

Williams-Garcia, R. (2011). *One crazy summer*. Quill Tree Books.

Winter, J. (2015). *Lillian's right to vote: A celebration of the Voting Rights Act of 1965*. Schwartz & Wade.

Winter, J. (2017). *The world is not a rectangle: A portrait of architect Zaha Hadid*. Beach Lane Books.

Woodson, J. (2016). *Brown girl dreaming*. Puffin Books.

Woodson, J. (2018). *Harbor me*. Puffin Books.

Woodson, J. (2020). *The day you begin*. Nancy Paulsen Books.

Wyeth, S. D. (2002). *Something beautiful*. Dragonfly Books.

Yaccarino, D. (2014). *All the way to America*. Dragonfly Books.

Yamasaki, K. (2019). *Fish for Jimmy*. Holiday House.

Yang, K. (2018). *Front desk*. Scholastic.

Yolen, J. (1996). *Encounter*. Voyager Books.

Youngblood, L. C. (2019). *Love like sky*. Little Brown Books.

Yousafzai, M. (2016). *I am Malala: How one girl stood up for education and changed the world (Young readers edition)*. Little Brown Books.

Zhang, K. (2019). *Amy Wu and the perfect bao*. Simon & Schuster.

Scholarly Works Cited

Adichie, C. (2009). The danger of a single story. TED ideas worth spreading. http://www.ted.com/talks/chimamanda_adichie_the_danger_of_a_single_ story.htm

Ahmed, S. (2018). *Being the change: Lessons and strategies to teach social comprehension*. Heinemann.

Al-Hazza, T. C., & Bucher, K. T. (2008). Building Arab Americans' cultural identity and acceptance with children's literature. *The Reading Teacher, 62*(3), 210–219. https://doi.org/10.1598/RT.62.3.3

Alim, H. S., & Paris, D. (2018). What is culturally sustaining pedagogy and why does it matter? In D. Paris & H. S. Alim (Eds.), *Culturally sustaining pedagogies:*

Teaching and learning for justice in a changing world (pp. 1–23). Teachers College Press.

Atwell, N. (2017). *Lessons that change writers.* Heinemann.

Avery, L. M., & Meyer, D. Z. (2012). Teaching science as science is practiced: Opportunities and limits for enhancing preservice elementary teachers' self-efficacy for science and science teaching. *School Science and Mathematics, 112,* 395–409. https://doi.org/10.1111/j.1949-8594.2012.00159.x

Barrera, R. B., & Quiroa, R. E. (2003). The use of Spanish in Latino children's literature in English: What makes for cultural authenticity? In D. L. Fox and K. G. Short (Eds.), *Stories matter: The complexity of cultural authenticity in children's literature* (pp. 247–265). National Council of Teachers of English.

Bell, M. (2016). Teaching at the intersections. *Teaching Tolerance, 53.* https://www.learningforjustice.org/magazine/summer-2016/teaching-at-the-intersections

Beschorner, B., & Hall, A. (2021). Building inclusivity and empathy through writers' workshop. *The Reading Teacher, 74*(5), 631–634. https://doi.org/10.1002/trtr.1971

Bista, K. (2012). Multicultural literature for children and young adults. *The Educational Forum, 76*(3), 317–325. https://doi.org/10.1080/00131725.2012.682203

Birman, D., & Tran, N. (2015). *The academic engagement of newly arriving Somali Bantu students in a US elementary school.* Migration Policy Institute.

Borsheim-Black, C., Macaluso, M., & Petrone, R. (2014). Critical literature pedagogy. *Journal of Adolescent and Adult Literacy, 58*(2), 123–133. https://doi.org/10.1002/jaal.323

Boyd, F. (2012). The Common Core State Standards and diversity: Unpacking the text exemplars presented in Appendix B. *Reading Today, 30*(3), 10–11.

Boyd, F. B., Causey, L. L., & Galda, L. (2015). Culturally diverse literature: Enriching variety in an era of Common Core State Standards. *The Reading Teacher, 68*(5), 378–387. https://doi.org/10.1002/trtr.1326

Bryan-Gooden, J., Hester, M., & Peoples, L. Q. (2019). *Culturally responsive curriculum scorecard.* Metropolitan Center for Research on Equity and the Transformation of Schools, New York University.

Boushey, G., & Moser, J. (2006). *The daily five.* Stenhouse Publishers.

Bui, X., Quirk, C., Almazan, S., & Valenti, M. (2010). *Inclusive education research and practice.* Maryland Coalition for Inclusive Education.

Burke, A., & Collier, D. R. (2017). "I was kind of teaching myself": Teachers' conversations about social justice and teaching for change. *Teacher Development, 21*(2), 269–287. http://doi.org/10.1080/13664530.2016.1235607

Cai, M. (2003). Can we fly across cultural gaps on the wings of imagination? Ethnicity, experience, and cultural authenticity. In D. L. Fox & K. G. Short (Eds.), *Stories matter: The complexity of cultural authenticity in children's literature.* National Council of Teachers of English.

Calkins, L. (2001). *The art of teaching reading.* Longman.

Carger, C. L. (2004). Art and literacy with bilingual children. *Language Arts, 81*(4), 283–292.

Carter, P. L., & Welner, K. G. (2013). *Closing the opportunity gap: What America must do to give every child an even chance.* Oxford.

Center for Education Policy Analysis. (2019). *Racial and ethnic achievement gaps.* https://cepa.stanford.edu/educational-opportunity-monitoring-project/achieve-ment-gaps/race/

Ching, S. H. D. (2005). Multicultural children's literature as an instrument of power. *Language Arts, 83*(2), 128–136.

Christ, T., Chiu, M. M., Rider, S., Kitson, D., Hanser, K., McConnell, E., Dipzinski, R., & Mayernik, H. (2018). Cultural relevance and informal reading inventory performance: African-American primary and middle school students. *Literacy Research and Instruction, 57*(2), 117–134. https://doi.org/10.1080/19388071.2018.1424274

Christ, T., & Cho, H. (2021). Sharing power in read-alouds with emergent bilingual students. *The Reading Teacher, 75*(3), 269–278. https://doi.org/10.1002/trtr.2021

Ciardiello, A. V. (2004). Democracy's young heroes: An instructional model of critical literacy practices. *The Reading Teacher, 58*(2), 138–147. https://doi.org/10.1598/RT.58.2.2

Cloud, N., Genessee, F., & Hamayan, E. (2009). *Literacy instruction for English language learners: A teachers' guide to research-based practices.* Heinemann.

Cochran-Smith, M., & Fries, K. (2005). Researching teacher education in changing times: Paradigms and politics. In M. Cochran-Smith & K. Zeichner (Eds.), *Studying teacher education: The report of the AERA panel on research and teacher education* (pp. 37–68). Lawrence Erlbaum.

Coleman, D., & Pimentel, S. (2012). Revised publishers' criteria for the Common Core State Standards in English language arts and literacy, Grades 3–12. http://www.corestandards.org/assets/Publishers_Criteria_for_3-12.pdf

Collier, V. P., & Thomas, W. P. (2007). Predicting second language academic success in English using the Prism Model. In J. Cummins & C. Davison (Eds.), *International handbook of English language teaching, Part 1* (pp. 333–348). Springer.

Colwell, J. (2019). Selecting texts for disciplinary literacy instruction. *The Reading Teacher, 72*(5), 631–637. https://doi.org/10.1002/trtr.1762

Comber, B. (2016). *Literacy, place, and pedagogies of possibility.* Routledge.

Comber, B., & Simpson, A. (2001). *Negotiating critical literacies in classrooms.* Lawrence Erlbaum.

Cooperative Children's Book Center. (2020). *The numbers are in: 2019 CCBC diversity statistics.* http://ccblogc.blogspot.com/2020/06/the-numbers-are-in-2019-ccbc-diversity.html

Cope, B., & Kalantzis, M. (1997). White noise: The attack on political correctness and the struggle for the western Canon. *Interchange, 28*(4), 283–329. https://doi.org/10.1023/A:1007483416121

Crenshaw, K. (1991). Mapping the margins: Intersectionality, identity politics, and violence against women of color. *Stanford Law Review, 43*(6), 1241–1299. https://doi.org/10.2307/1229039

Cruz, B., & Thornton, S. J. (2013). *Teaching social studies to English language learners.* Routledge.

Cutler, L., & Graham, S. (2008). Primary grade writing instruction: A national survey. *Journal of Educational Psychology, 100*(4), 907–919. https://doi.org/10.1037/a0012656

Daniels, H. (2002). *Literature circles: Voice and choice in book clubs and reading groups*. Stenhouse.

Dávila, D., Noguerón, S., & Vásquez-Dominguez, M. (2017). The Latinx family: Learning y la literatura at the library. *The Bilingual Review, 33*(5), 91–106.

Demko, M. (2010). Teachers become zombies: The ugly side of scripted reading curriculum. *Language Arts, 17*(3), 62–64.

DeNicolo, C. P., & Franquiz, M. E. (2006). "Do I have to say it?": Critical encounters with multicultural children's literature. *Language Arts, 84*(2), 157–170.

Dresser, R. (2012). The impact of scripted literacy instruction on teachers and students. *Issues in Teacher Education, 21*(1), 71–87.

Dunn, D. S., & Burcaw, S. (2013). Disability identity: Exploring narrative accounts of disability. *Rehabilitation Psychology, 58*(2), 148–157. https://doi.org/10.1037/a0031691

Ebarvia, T., Germán, L., Parker, K. N., & Torres, J. (2020). #DisruptTexts: An introduction. *English Journal, 110*(1), 100–102.

Ebe, A. E. (2010). Culturally relevant texts and reading assessment for English language learners. *Reading Horizons, 50*(3), 193–210. http://scholarworks.wmich.edu/reading_horizons/vol50/iss3/5

Ebe, A. E. (2012). Supporting the reading development of middle school English language learners through culturally relevant texts. *Reading & Writing Quarterly, 28*(2), 179–198. https://doi.org/10.1080/10573569.2012.651078

Edmondson, J. (2004). *Understanding and applying critical policy study: Reading educators advocating for change*. International Reading Association.

Erbach, M. (2008). The art of the picture book.*The Newbery and Caldecott Awards*. American Library Association.

Fain, J. G. (2008). "Um, they weren't thinking about their thinking": Children's talk about issues of oppression. *Multicultural Perspectives, 10*(4), 201–208. https://doi.org/10.1080/15210960802526102

Feger, M. V. (2006). I want to read: How culturally relevant texts increase student engagement in reading. *Multicultural Education, 13*, 18–19.

Fisher, D., Flood, J., Lapp, D., & Frey, N. (2004). Interactive read-alouds: Is there a common set of implementation practices? *The Reading Teacher, 58*(1), 8–17. https://doi.org/10.1598/RT.58.1.1

Fisher, D., Frey, N., & Akhavan, N. (2019). *This is balanced literacy, grades K-6*. Corwin.

Fletcher, R., & Portalupi, J. (2001). *Writing workshop: The essential guide*. Heinemann.

Flores, N. (2019). From academic language to language architecture: Challenging raciolinguistic ideologies in research and practice. *Theory into Practice, 59*(1), 22–31. https://doi.org/10.1080/00405841.2019.1665411

Flores, T. T. (2018). Cultivando la voz mujer: Latina adolescent girls and their mothers rewriting their pasts and imagining their futures. *Literacy Research: Theory, Method, and Practice, 67*(1), 211–227. https://doi.org/10.1177/2381336918786733

Florio-Ruane, S. (2001). *Teacher education and the cultural imagination: Autobiography, conversation, and narrative*. Lawrence Erlbaum.

Fountas, I., & Pinnell, G. S. (2012). Guided reading: The romance and the reality. *The Reading Teacher, 66*(4), 268–284. https://doi.org/10.1002/TRTR.01123

Fountas, I., & Pinnell, G. S. (2018). *The reading mini-lessons book*. Heinemann.

Fox, K. R. (2007). Using author-illustrator studies in children's literature to explore social justice issues. *The Social Studies, 97*(6), 251–256.

Freeman, D. E., & Freeman, Y. S. (2007). *English language learners: The essential guide*. Scholastic.

Freeman, Y. S., & Freeman, D. E. (2004). Connecting students to culturally relevant texts. *Talking Points, 15*(2), 7–11.

Freire, P., & Macedo, D. P. (1987). *Literacy: Reading the word & the world*. Routledge & Kegan Paul.

Fry, S. W. (2009). Exploring social studies through multicultural literature: Legend of the St. Ann's Flood. *The Social Studies, 100*(2), 85–92. https://doi.org/10.3200/tsss.100.2.85-92

Gainer, J. (2013). 21st-century mentor texts developing critical literacies in the information age. *Journal of Adolescent & Adult Literacy, 57*(1), 16–19. https://doi.org/10.1002/JAAL.210

Gallagher, K. (2011). *Write like this: Teaching real-world writing through modeling & mentor texts*. Stenhouse.

Gambrell, L. B. (2011). Seven rules of engagement: What's most important to know about motivation to read. *The Reading Teacher, 65*(3), 172–178. https://doi.org/10.1002/TRTR.01024

García, O. (2009). *Bilingual education in the 21st century: A global perspective*. Wiley/Blackwell.

García, O., Ibarra Johnson, S., & Seltzer, K. (2017). *The translanguaging classroom: Leveraging student bilingualism for learning*. Caslon.

Gay, G. (2018). *Culturally responsive teaching: Theory, research, and practice* (3rd edition). Teachers College Press.

Giroir, S., Grimaldo, L. R., Vaughn, S., & Roberts, G. (2015). Interactive read-alouds for English learners in the elementary grades. *The Reading Teacher, 68*(8), 639–648. https://doi.org/10.1002/trtr.1354

Glazier, J., & Seo, J. A. (2005). Multicultural literature and discussion as mirror and window? *Journal of Adolescent & Adult Literacy, 48*(8), 686–700. https://doi.org/10.1598/JAAL.48.8.6

Gomez-Najarro, J. (2020). Children's intersecting identities matter: Beyond rabbits and princesses in the Common Core book exemplars. *Children's Literature in Education, 51*(2), 392–410. https://doi.org/10.1007/s10583-019-09390-9

Gopalakrishnan, A. G. (2011). *Multicultural children's literature: A critical issues approach*. Sage.

Grace, C. M. (2004). Exploring the African American oral tradition: Instructional implications for literacy learning. *Language Arts, 81*(6), 481–490.

Guthrie, J. T., Hoa, A. L. W., Wigfield, A., Tonks, S. M., Humenick, N. M., & Littles, E. (2007). Reading motivation and reading comprehension growth in the later elementary years. *Contemporary Educational Psychology, 32*(3), 282–313. https://doi.org/10.1016/j.cedpsych.2006.05.004

Guthrie, J., & Wigfield, A. (1999). How motivation fits into a science of reading. *Scientific Studies of Reading, 3*(3), 199–205. https://doi.org/10.1207/s1532799xssr0303_1

Gutierrez, K. D., & Rogoff, B. (2003). Cultural ways of learning. *Educational Researcher, 32*, 19–25. https://doi.org/10.3102/0013189X032005019

Hadaway, N. (2007). Building bridges of understanding. In N. Hadaway & M. McKenna (Eds.), *Breaking boundaries with global literature* (pp. 1–6). International Reading Association.

Hadley, K. M., & Dorward, J. (2011). Investigating the relationship among elementary teacher mathematics anxiety, mathematical instructional practices, and student mathematics achievement. *Journal of Curriculum & Instruction, 5*(2), 27–44. https://doi.org/10.3776/joci.2011.v5n2p27-44

Hall, L. A., & Piazza, S. V. (2008). Critically reading texts: What students do and how teachers can help. *The Reading Teacher, 62*(1), 32–41. https://doi.org/10.1598/RT.62.1.4

Harste, J. C. (2000). *Supporting critical conversations in classrooms.* In K. M. Pierce (Ed.), *Adventuring with books: A booklist for pre-K-grade 6* (12th ed., pp. 507–554). National Council of Teachers of English.

Harste, J. C., Breau, A., Leland, C., Lewison, M., Ociepka, A., & Vasquez, V. (2000). Supporting critical conversations in classrooms. In K. M. Pierce (Ed.), *Adventuring with books* (12th ed., pp. 507–554). National Council of Teachers of English.

Hartman, J. A., & Hartman, D. K. (1994). *Arranging multi-text reading experiences that expand the reader's role* (Tech. Report No. 604). University of Illinois, Center for the Study of Reading.

Hartman, P., & Machado, E. (2019). Language, race, and critical conversations in a primary-grade writers' workshop. *The Reading Teacher, 73*(3), 313–323. https://doi.org/10.1002/trtr.1845

Hayik, R. (2016). What does this story say about females? Challenging gender-biased texts in the English-language classroom. *Journal of Adolescent & Adult Literacy, 59*(4), 409–419. https://doi.org/10.1002/jaal.468

Heineke, A. J. (2014). Dialoging about English learners: Preparing teachers through culturally relevant literature circles. *Action in Teacher Education, 36*(2), 117–140. https://doi.org/10.1080/01626620.2014.898600

Heineke, A. J., & McTighe, J. (2018). *Using Understanding by Design in the culturally and linguistically diverse classroom.* Association for Supervision and Curriculum Development.

Heritage, M., Walqui, A., & Linquanti, R. (2015). *English language learners and the new standards: Developing language, content knowledge, and analytical practices in the classroom.* Harvard Educational Press.

Herman, J. L., Flores, A. R., Brown, T. N. T., Wilson, B. D. M., & Conron, K. J. (2017). *Age of individuals who identify as transgender in the United States.* Williams Institute.

Herrera, S. G. (2016). *Biography-driven culturally responsive teaching* (2nd edition). Teachers College Press.

Hornberger, N. H. (2004). The continua of biliteracy and the bilingual educator: Educational linguistics in practice. *International Journal of Bilingual Education and Bilingualism, 7*(2–3), 155–171.

Hoyt, L. (2016). *Interactive read alouds.* Heinemann.

Huyck, D., & Dahlen, S. P. (2019). *Diversity in children's books 2018.* https://readingspark.wordpress.com/2019/06/19/picture-this-diversity-in-childrens-books-2018-infographic

Iliev, N., & D'Angelo, F. (2014). Teaching mathematics through multicultural literature. *Teaching Children Mathematics, 20,* 452–457.

Illustrative Mathematics. (2016). *The Djinni's offer*. https://tasks.illustrativemathe matics.org/content-standards/6/EE/A/1/tasks/532

Janks, H. (2018). Texts, identities, and ethics: Critical literacy in a post-truth world. *Journal of Adolescent & Adult Literacy, 62*(1), 95–99. doi:10.1002/jaal.761

Jenkins, C. B. (2006). "Did I tell you that you are the BEST writer in the world?": Author studies in the elementary classroom. *Journal of Children's Literature, 32*(1), 64–78.

Jewett, P. (2007). Reading knee deep. *Reading Psychology, 28*(2), 149–162. https://doi.org/10.1080/02702710601186365

Jiménez, L. M. (2021). Mirrors and windows with texts and readers: Intersectional social justice at work in the classroom. *Language Arts, 98*(3), 156–161.

Jiménez, R., & Gámez, A. (1996). Literature-based cognitive strategy instruction for middle school Latina/o students. *Journal of Adolescent & Adult Literacy, 40*(2), 84–91.

Jocius, R., & Shealy, S. (2017). Critical book clubs: Reimagining literature reading and response. *The Reading Teacher, 71*(2), 691–702. https://doi.org/10.1002/trtr.1655

Johnson, N. J., Koss, M. D., & Martinez, M. (2018). Through the sliding glass door: #EmpowerTheReader. *The Reading Teacher, 71*(5), 569–577. https://doi.org/10.1002/trtr.1659

Kim, S. J., Wee, S., & Lee, Y. M. (2016). Teaching kindergartners racial diversity through multicultural literature: A case study in a kindergarten classroom in Korea. *Early Education and Development, 27*(3), 402–420. https://doi.org/10.1080/10409289.2015.1069110

Kincade, K. M., & Pruitt, N. E. (1996). Using multicultural literature as an ally to elementary social studies texts. *Reading Research and Instruction, 36*(1), 18–32.

Knobel, M. (2007). Foreword. In L. P. Stevens & T. W. Bean, *Critical literacy: Context, research, and practice in the K-12 classroom*. Sage.

Kosciw, J. G., Clark, C. M., Truong, N. L., & Zongrone, A. D. (2019). *The 2019 national school climate survey: The experiences of lesbian, gay, bisexual, transgender, and queer youth in our nation's schools*. GLSEN.

Ladson-Billings, G. (1995). But that's just good teaching! The case for culturally relevant pedagogy. *Theory into Practice, 34*(3), 159–165. https://doi.org/10.1080/00405849509543675

Ladson-Billings, G. (2014). The (r)evolution will not be standardized: Teacher education, hip-hop pedagogy, and culturally relevant pedagogy 2.0. In D. Paris & H. S. Alim (Eds.), *Culturally sustaining pedagogies: Teaching and learning for justice in a changing world* (pp. 141–156). Teachers College Press.

Ladson-Billings, G. (2018). Culturally relevant pedagogy 2.0: a.k.a. the remix. *Harvard Educational Review, 84*(1), 74–86. https://doi.org/10.17763/haer.84.1.p2rj131485484751

Lapp, D., Fisher, D., & Frey, N. (2013). Pathways to the canon. *Voices from the Middle, 21*, 7–9.

Larrick, N. (1965). The all-white world of children's books. *Saturday Review, 48 (September 11):* 63–65, 84–85.

Lasky, K. (2003). To Stingo with love: An author's perspective on writing outside one's culture. In D. L. Fox & K. G. Short (Eds.), *Stories matter: The complexity of cultural authenticity in children's literature* (pp. 84–92). National Council of Teachers of English.

Laughter, J. C., & Adams, A. D. (2012). Culturally relevant science teaching in middle school. *Urban Education, 47*(6), 1106–1134. https://doi.org/10.1177/0042085912454443

Lee, A. Y., & Handsfield, L. J. (2018). Code-meshing and writing instruction in multilingual classrooms. *The Reading Teacher, 72*(2), 159–168. https://doi.org/10.1002/trtr.1688

Lee & Low Books. (2017). *Classroom library questionnaire.* https://www.leeandlow.com/uploads/loaded_document/408/Classroom-Library-Questionnaire_FINAL.pdf

Leland, C., Lewison, M., & Harste, J. (2018). *Teaching children's literature: It's critical!* Routledge.

Leonard, J., Moore, C. M., & Brooks, W. (2014). Multicultural children's literature as a context for teaching mathematics for cultural relevance in urban schools. *Urban Review, 46*, 325–348. https://doi.org/10.1007/s11256-013-0264-3

Lewison, M., Flint, A. S., & Van Sluys, K. (2002). Taking on critical literacy: The journey of newcomers and novices. *Language Arts, 79*(5), 382–392.

Lewison, M., Leland, C., & Harste, J. C. (2008). *Creating critical classrooms: K-8 reading and writing with an edge.* Lawrence Erlbaum.

Loewen, J. W. (2018). *What really happened? How to avoid the tyranny of textbooks and get students excited about doing history.* Teachers College Press.

López-Robertson, J. (2017). Diciendo cuentos/telling stories: Learning from and about the community cultural wealth of Latina mamás through Latino children's literature. *Language Arts, 95*(1), 7–16.

López-Robertson, J., & Haney, M. J. (2017). Their eyes sparkled: Building classroom community through multicultural literature. *Journal of Children's Literature, 43*(1), 48–54.

Lucas, T. & Villegas, A. M. (2013). Preparing linguistically responsive teachers: Laying the foundation in preservice teacher education. *Theory into Practice, 52*(2), 98–109. https://doi.org/10.1080/00405841.2013.770327

Luke, A. (2013). Regrounding critical literacy: Representation, facts and reality. In M. R. Hawkins (Ed.), *Framing languages and literacies: Socially situated views and perspectives* (pp. 136–148). Routledge.

Luke, A., & Freebody, P. (1997). Shaping the social practices of reading. In S. Muspratt, A. Luke, & P. Freebody (Eds.), *Constructing critical literacies: Teaching and learning textual practice* (pp. 185–225). Hampton Press.

Marchetti, A., & O'Dell, R. (2015). *Writing with mentors: How to reach every writer in the room using current, engaging mentor texts.* Heinemann.

Marshall, E. (2004). Stripping for the wolf: Rethinking representations of gender in children's literature. *Reading Research Quarterly, 39*(3), 256–270. https://doi.org/10.1598/RRQ.39.3.1

Martínez-Álvarez, P., & Ghiso, M. P. (2017). On languaging and communities: Latino/a emergent bilinguals' expansive learning and critical inquiries into global childhoods. *International Journal of Bilingual Education and Bilingualism, 20*(6), 667–687. https://doi.org/10.1080/13670050.2015.1068270

Martínez-Roldán, C. M., & Heineke, A. J. (2011). Latino literature mediating teacher learning. *Journal of Latinos and Education, 10*(3), 245–260. https://doi.org/10.1080/15348431.2011.581111

Martínez-Roldán, C., & López-Robertson, J. M. (1999). Initiating literature circles in a first-grade bilingual classroom. *The Reading Teacher, 53*(4), 270–281.

May, L. A. (2011). Animating talk and texts: Culturally relevant teacher read-alouds of informational texts. *Journal of Literacy Research, 43*(1), 3–38. https://doi.org/10.1177/1086296X10397869

McCarthey, S. J., & Moje, E. B. (2002). Identity matters. *Reading Research Quarterly, 37*(2), 228–238. https://doi.org/10.1598/RRQ.37.2.6

McCarty, D. M. (2007). Using multicultural National Council for the Social Studies notable books in the elementary classroom. *The Social Studies, 98*(2), 49–53. https://doi.org/10.3200/TSSS.98.2.49-53

McCullough, R. G. (2013). The relationship between reader response and prior knowledge on African American students' reading comprehension performance using multicultural literature. *Reading Psychology, 34*(5), 397–435. https://doi.org/10.1080/02702711.2011.643531

McDermott, R., & Varenne, H. (1995). Culture as disability. *Anthropology & Education, 26*(3), 324–348. https://doi.org/10.1525/aeq.1995.26.3.05x0936z

McLaughlin, M., & DeVoogd, G. (2018). Trade books that represent critical literacy. In D. Lapp & D. Fisher (Eds.), *Handbook of research on teaching the English language arts* (4th ed., Ch. 4 online resources). Routledge.

McLaughlin, M., & DeVoogd, G. (2019). Critical expressionism: Expanding reader response in critical literacy. *The Reading Teacher, 73*(5), 587–595. https://doi.org/10.1002/trtr.1878

Medina, C. L. (2004). Drama wor(l)ds: Explorations of Latina/o realistic fiction. *Language Arts, 81*(4), 272–282.

Medina, C. L., & Martínez-Roldán, C. (2011). Culturally relevant literature pedagogies: Latino students reading in the borderlands. In J. C. Naidoo (Ed.), *Celebrating cuentos: Promoting Latino children's literature and literacy in classrooms and libraries* (pp. 259–272). ABC-CLIO.

Meller, W. B., Richardson, D., & Hatch, J. A. (2009). Using read-alouds with critical literacy literature in K-3 classrooms. *Young Children, 64*(6), 76–78.

Méndez-Newman, B. (2012). Mentor texts and funds of knowledge: Situating writing within our students' worlds. *Voices from the Middle, 20*(1), 25–30.

Mills, H., & Jennings, L. (2011). Talking about talk: Reclaiming the value and power of literature circles. *The Reading Teacher, 64*(8), 590–598. https://doi.org/10.1598/RT.64.8.4

Milner, H. R. (2013). Scripted and narrowed curriculum reform in urban schools. *Urban Education, 48*(2), 162–170. https://doi.org/10.1177/0042085913478022

Moje, E. B. (2007). Developing socially just subject-matter instruction: A review of the literature on disciplinary literacy teaching. *Review of Research in Education, 31*(1), 1–44. https://doi.org/10.3102/0091732X07300046001

Moll, L. C., Amanti, C., Neff, D., & González, N. (1992). Funds of knowledge for teaching: Using qualitative approach to connect homes and classrooms. *Theory into Practice, 31*(2), 132–141. https://doi.org/10.1080/00405849209543534

Moll, L. C., & González, N. (1997). Teachers as social scientists: Learning about culture from household research. In P. Hall (Ed.), *Race, ethnicity, and multiculturalism* (Vol. 1, pp. 89–114). Garland.

Moreillon, J. (2003). The candle and the mirror: One author's journey as an outsider. In D. L. Fox & K. G. Short (Eds.), *Stories matter: The complexity of cultural authenticity in children's literature* (pp. 61–77). National Council of Teachers of English.

Morrell, E. (2009). Critical research and the future of literacy education. *Journal of adolescent and adult literacy, 53*(2), 96–104. https://doi.org/10.1598/JAAL.53.2.1

Moss, B. (2013). The Common Core text exemplars—A worthy new canon or not? *Language Arts, 21*(1), 48–52.

Muhammad, G. (2020). *Cultivating genius: An equity framework for culturally and historically responsive literacy.* Scholastic.

Nagy, W. E., & Anderson, R. C. (1995). *Metalinguistic awareness and literacy acquisition in different languages.* University of Illinois.

Nathenson-Mejia, S., & Escamilla, K. (2003). Connecting with Latino children: Bridging cultural gaps with children literature. *Bilingual Research Journal, 27*(1), 101–116. https://doi.org/10.1080/15235882.2003.10162593

National Center for Education Statistics. (2021). *Students with disabilities.* https://nces.ed.gov/programs/coe/indicator_cgg.asp

National Center for Education Statistics. (2019a). *Status and trends in the education of racial and ethnic groups.* https://nces.ed.gov/pubs2019/2019038.pdf

National Center for Education Statistics. (2019b). *Characteristics of public school teachers by race/ethnicity.* https://nces.ed.gov/programs/raceindicators/spotlight_a.asp

National Council for the Social Studies. (2013). *The college, career, and civic life (C3) framework for social studies state standards: Guidance for enhancing the rigor of K-12 civics, economics, geography, and history.* Author.

National Center for the Social Studies. (2021). *Notable social studies trade books for young people.* https://www.cbcbooks.org/wp-content/uploads/2021/06/Notable2021.pdf

National Governors Association Center for Best Practices & Council of Chief State School Officers. (2010a). *Common Core state standards for English language arts and literacy in history/social studies, science, and technical subjects. Appendix B: Text exemplars and sample performance tasks.* Author.

National Governors Association Center for Best Practices & Council of Chief State School Officers. (2010b). *Common Core state standards: English language arts.* Author.

National Governors Association Center for Best Practices & Council of Chief State School Officers. (2010c). *Common Core state standards: Mathematics.* Author.

NGSS Lead States. (2013). *Next Generation Science Standards: For states, by states.* National Academies Press.

Nel, P. (2014). Was the cat in the hat Black? Exploring Dr. Seuss's racial imagination. *Children's Literature, 42,* 71–98. https://doi.org/10.1353/chl.2014.0019

Newstreet, C., Sarker, A., & Shearer, R. (2018). Teaching empathy: Exploring multiple perspectives to address Islamophobia through children's literature. *The Reading Teacher, 72*(5), 559–568. https://doi.org/10.1002/trtr.1764

Nikolajeva, M. (2013). Picturebooks and emotional literacy. *The Reading Teacher, 67*(4), 249–254. https://doi.org/10.1002/trtr.1229

Opitz, M. F. (1998). Text sets: One way to flex your grouping—in first grade too! *The Reading Teacher, 51*(7), 622.

Page, M. (2017). From awareness to action: Teacher attitude and implementation of LGBT-inclusive curriculum in the English language arts classroom. *SAGE Open.* https://doi.org/10.1177/2158244017739949

Pampati, S., Andzejewski, J., Sheremenko, G., Johns, M., Lesesne, C. A., & Rasberry, C. N. (2020). School climate among transgender high school students: An exploration of school connectedness, perceived safety, bullying, and absenteeism. *Journal of School Nursing 36*(4), 1–11. https://doi.org/10.1177/1059840518818259

Papola, A. L. (2013). Critical literacy, Common Core, and "close reading." *Colorado Reading Journal. 24,* 46–50. https://ecommons.luc.edu/cgi/viewcontent.cgi?article=1078&context=education_facpubs

Papola-Ellis, A. (2014). Teaching under policy cascades: Common Core and literacy instruction. *Journal of Language and Literacy Education, 10*(1), 166–187.

Papola-Ellis, A., & Heineke, A. J. (2019). Interrupting teachers' assumptions about English learners through literature discussion. *Action in Teacher Education, 42*(3), 234–252. https://doi.org/10.1080/01626620.2019.1649743

Pardo, L., Highfield, K., & Florio-Ruane, S. (2011). *Standing for literacy: Teaching in the context of change.* Hampton Press.

Paris, D. (2012). Culturally sustaining pedagogy: A need for change in stance, terminology, and practice. *Educational Researcher, 41*(3), 93–97. https://doi.org/10.3102/0013189X12441244

Paulsen, E. J., & Freeman, A. E. (2003). *Insight from the eyes: The science of effective reading instruction.* Heinemann.

Pennell, A. E., Wollak, B., & Koppenhaver, D. A. (2017). Respectful representations of disability in picture books. *The Reading Teacher, 71*(4), 411–419. https://doi.org/10.1002/trtr.1632

Perez, B. (2004). Creating a classroom community for literacy. In B. Perez (Ed.), *Sociocultural context of language and literacy* (2nd ed., pp. 309–338). Lawrence Erlbaum.

Perry, T. B., & Stallworth, B. J. (2013). 21st century students demand a balanced, more inclusive canon. *Voices from the Middle, 21*(1), 15–18.

Peterson, B., Gunn, A. M., Brice, A., & Alley, K. (2015). Exploring names and identity through multicultural literature in K-8 classrooms. *Multicultural Perspectives, 17*(1), 39–45. https://doi.org/10.1080/15210960.2015.994434

Pilonieta, P., & Hancock, S. D. (2012). Negotiating first graders' reading stance: The relationship between their efferent and aesthetic connections and their reading comprehension. *Current Issues in Education, 15*(2), 1–9.

Project Zero. (2019). *Resources.* Harvard Graduate School of Education. http://www.pz.harvard.edu/search/resources

Raphael, T. E., & McMahon, S. I. (1994). Book club: An alternative framework for reading instruction. *The Reading Teacher, 48*(2), 102–116.

Reimer, V. P. (2019). Hidden children: Using children's literature to develop understanding and empathy toward children of incarcerated parents. *Language & Literacy, 21*(1), 98–121. https://doi.org/10.20360/langandlit29369

Reutzel, R. D., Jones, C. D., Clark, S. K., & Kumar, T. (2016). The informational text structure survey (ITS2): An exploration of primary grade teachers' sensitivity to text structure in young children's informational texts. *The Journal of Educational Research, 109*(1), 81-98. https://doi.org/10.1080/00220671.2014.918927

Rockefeller, E. I. (2009). Selection, inclusion, evaluation, and defense of transgender-inclusive fiction for young adults: A resource guide. *Journal of LGBT Youth, 6*(2–3), 288–309. https://doi.org/10.1080/19361650902962641

Rogoff, B. (2003). *The cultural nature of human development.* Oxford University Press.

Rountree, W. (2008). *Just us girls: The contemporary African American young adult novel.* Peter Lang.

Rowan, L. (2001). *Write me in: Inclusive texts in the primary classroom.* Primary English Teaching Association.

Ryan, C. L., & Hermann-Wilmarth, J. M. (2018). *Reading the rainbow: LGBTQ-inclusive literacy instruction in the elementary classroom.* Teachers College Press.

Ryan, C. L., & Hermann-Wilmart, J. M. (2019). Putting your read-alouds to work for LGBTQ-inclusive, critically literate classrooms. *Language Arts, 96*(5), 312–317.

Saint-Hilaire, L. A. (2014). Multicultural literature for elementary science classrooms. *Ohio Journal of English Language Arts, 54*(1), 27–37.

Schrodt, K., Fain, J. G., & Hasty, M. (2015). Exploring culturally relevant texts with kindergartners and their families. *The Reading Teacher, 68*(8), 589–598. https://doi.org/10.1002/trtr.1363

Serafini, F. (2001). *The reading workshop: Creating space for readers.* Heinemann.

Shannon, P. (1990). *The struggle to continue: Progressive reading instruction in the United States.* Heinemann.

Short, D. L., & Fox, K. G. (2003). The complexity of cultural authenticity in children's literature: Why the debates really matter. In D. L. Fox & K. G. Short (Eds.), *Stories matter: The complexity of cultural authenticity in children's literature* (pp. 3–24). National Council of Teachers of English.

Short, D. L., Harste, J., & Burke, C. (1996). *Creating classrooms for authors and inquirers* (2nd edition). Heinemann.

Sims Bishop, R. (1990). Mirrors, windows, and sliding glass doors. *Perspectives, 1*(3), ix–xi.

Sims Bishop, R. (1997). Selecting literature for a multicultural curriculum. In V. J. Harris (Ed.), *Using multiethnic literature in the K-8 classroom* (pp. 1–19). Christopher-Gordon.

Sims Bishop, R. (2003). Reframing the debate about cultural authenticity. In D. Fox & K. G. Short (Eds.), *Stories matter: The complexity of cultural authenticity in children's literature* (pp. 25–37). National Council of Teachers of English.

Souto-Manning, M. (2009). Negotiating culturally responsive pedagogy through multicultural children's literature: Towards critical democratic literacy practices in a first-grade classroom. *Journal of Early Childhood Literacy, 9*, 50–74. https://doi.org/10.1177/1468798408101105

St. Amour, M. J. (2003). Connecting children's stories to children's literature: Meeting diversity needs. *Early Childhood Education Journal, 31*, 47–51. https://doi.org/10.1023/A:1025136802668

Stevens, L. P., & Bean, T. W. (2007). *Critical literacy: Context, research, and practice in the K-12 classroom.* Sage.

Stevenson, H. C. (2014). *Promoting racial literacy in schools: Differences that make a difference.* Teachers College Press.

Stillman, J., & Anderson, L. (2011). To follow, reject, or flip the script: Managing instructional tension in an era of high-stakes accountability. *Language Arts*, 89(1), 22–37.

Strauss, V. (2014, August 21). For first time, minority students expected to be majority in U.S. public schools this fall. *The Washington Post*. https://www .washingtonpost.com/news/answer-sheet/wp/2014/08/21/for-first-time-minor ity-students-expected-to-be-majority-in-u-s-public-schools-this-fall/

Strickland, J. (2001). Multicultural literature in rural schools: A social studies unit that promotes cultural awareness. *Southern Social Studies*, 27(1), 20–37.

Suárez-Orozco, C., Abo-Zena, M. M., & Marks, A. (2015). *Transitions: The development of children of immigrants*. New York University Press.

Suárez-Orozco, C., Suárez-Orozco, M., & Todorova, I. (2007). *Learning a new land: Immigrant students in American schools*. Harvard.

Tatum, A. W. (2000). Breaking down barriers that disenfranchise African American adolescent readers in low-level tracks. *Journal of Adolescent & Adult Literacy*, 44(1), 52–64.

Tschida, C. M., & Buchanan, L. (2015). Tackling controversial topics: Developing thematic text sets for elementary social studies. *Social Studies Research & Practice*, 10(3), 40–56.

Tschida, C. M., & Buchanan, L. (2017). What makes a family? Sharing multiple perspectives through an inclusive text set. *Social Studies and the Young Learner*, 30(2), 3–7.

Tschida, C., Ryan, C. L., & Ticknor, A. (2014). Building on windows and mirrors: Encouraging the disruption of "single stories" through children's literature. *Journal of Children's Literature*, 40(1), 28–39.

Vasquez, V. M. (2015). Podcasting as transformative work. *Theory into Practice*, 54(2), 147–153. https://doi.org/10.1080/00405841.2015.1010848

Vasquez, V. M. (2017). *Critical literacy across the K-6 curriculum*. Routledge.

Vasquez, V. M., Janks, H., & Comber, B. (2019). Critical literacy as a way of being and doing. *Language Arts*, 96(5), 300–311.

Verden, C. E. (2012). Reading culturally relevant literature aloud to urban youths with behavioral challenges. *Journal of Adolescent and Adult Literacy*, 55(7), 619–628. https://doi.org/10.1002/JAAL.00073

Verden, C. E., & Hickman, P. (2009). "Teacher, it's just like what happens at my house." *Teaching Exceptional Children Plus*, 5(6), 1–20.

Villegas, A. M., & Lucas, T. (2007). The culturally responsive teacher. *Educational Leadership*, 64(6), 28–33.

Wiggins, G. P., & McTighe, J. (2005). *Understanding by Design*. Association for Supervision and Curriculum Development.

Wiggins, G. P., & McTighe, J. (2011). *The Understanding by Design guide to creating high quality units*. Association for Supervision and Curriculum Development.

Wood, S., & Jocius, R. (2013). Combating "I hate this stupid book!": Black males and critical literacy. *The Reading Teacher*, 66(8), 661–669. https://doi.org/10 .1002/trtr.1177

Zacarian, D., Alvarez-Ortiz, L., & Haynes, J. (2017). *Teaching to strengths: Supporting students living with trauma, violence, and chronic stress*. Association for Supervision and Curriculum Development.

Index

About the Authors

Amy J. Heineke is a professor of education at Loyola University Chicago. She facilitates the professional learning of current and future teachers of multilingual learners from preschool to high school. Dr. Heineke began her career in education as a primary teacher in Phoenix, Arizona, which continues to shape her research and practice with educators across the United States and Latin America. Her work seeks to disrupt assimilation and monolingualism in schools by prioritizing pluralism and multilingualism in policy and practice. Dr. Heineke lives outside of Chicago with her husband, daughter, and Labrador retriever.

Aimee Papola-Ellis is an associate professor of education at Loyola University Chicago. She teaches courses in the areas of literacy education and children's literature. Her research interests center on the use of inclusive texts, critical literacy, and literacy instruction in diverse classrooms. Prior to coming to Loyola, Dr. Papola-Ellis spent 12 years in public schools across the United States, as a classroom teacher, reading specialist, and literacy coach. She lives in a Chicago suburb with her husband, son, and two Shiba Inus.